Basics of
C++ Programming

BASICS OF C++ PROGRAMMING

By

NISHANT KUNDALIA

RAMESH BANGIA
B.Sc. Dip. Comp. Sc. (IIT D)
Formerly: Incharge Computer Centre, Hindustan Copper Limited, New Delhi
Ex. Managing Editor: Software Today

FIREWALL MEDIA

(An Imprint of Laxmi Publications Pvt. Ltd.)
An ISO 9001:2008 Company

BENGALURU • CHENNAI • COCHIN • GUWAHATI • HYDERABAD
JALANDHAR • KOLKATA • LUCKNOW • MUMBAI • RANCHI • NEW DELHI
BOSTON (USA) • ACCRA (GHANA) • NAIROBI (KENYA)

BASICS OF C++ PROGRAMMING

Printed and bound in India

Typeset at : Goswami Associates, Delhi.

First Edition : 2002, *Second Edition* : 2004, *Third Edition* : 2009, *Reprint* : 2016

ISBN : 978-93-80298-00-9

Published in India by

FIREWALL MEDIA

(An Imprint of Laxmi Publications Pvt. Ltd.)

An ISO 9001:2008 Company

113, GOLDEN HOUSE, DARYAGANJ, NEW DELHI-110002, INDIA

Telephone : 91-11-4353 2500, 4353 2501

Fax : 91-11-2325 2572, 4353 2528

www.laxmipublications.com info@laxmipublications.com

Branches

© Bengaluru	080-26 75 69 30
© Chennai	044-24 34 47 26
© Cochin	0484-237 70 04, 405 13 03
© Guwahati	0361-254 36 69, 251 38 81
© Hyderabad	040-27 55 53 83, 27 55 53 93
© Jalandhar	0181-222 12 72
© Kolkata	033-22 27 43 84
© Lucknow	0522-220 99 16
© Mumbai	022-24 91 54 15, 24 92 78 69
© Ranchi	0651-220 44 64

C—10368/015/06

PREFACE

The book deals with programming language C++. The presentation of the subject matter is very systematic and language of text is quite lucid. The matter of book is quite simple to understand. It is specially useful to students who sometimes do not get adequate coaching. One can self-understand the subject only by reading this book. The fundamentals are explained thoroughly in a simple lucid language. A number of figures have been added in each chapter to make subject matter self speaking to a great extent.

Each chapter has been saturated with worked examples, graded properly to enable the students to understand and attempt different type of questions in examination and any other projects undertaken.

Unsolved examples have been added at end of each chapter to make the book complete unit in all respects.

— Author

ABOUT THE AUTHOR

Nishant Kundalia is a Professional Programmer and was a visiting faculty as well as permanent faculty in many computer institutes. At present he is a senior faculty and a course coordinator in a computer institute. He is also developing software projects independently in C, C++, Java.

CONTENTS

1
Introduction

1.1 Introduction

This book teaches you, how to program in C++. C++ is a language which supports 'object-oriented programming'.

Now the question that arises is 'Why do we need object-oriented programming ?' The answer is explained in this chapter and is compared with the procedural approach of a language like C, Pascal etc. If you find this discussion, somewhat abstract, there is no need to worry as we will focus on each topic later in this book.

First we take the view of procedural languages like C, Pascal, Fortran etc. Here each statement given tells the computer to do something *e.g.*, get a input of two numbers, add it, then divide by 6 and finally display the output.

A program in a procedural language like this is just a list of instructions. This type of procedural concept is 'OK' for small programs. But when a programmer faces 'large-size' programs, then applying this concept can put programmers to trouble, especially when the job of debugging comes into picture. It is also inconvenient when the programmer wants to use the part of code in other programs. So there are several drawbacks of (structured) procedural programming :

1. Hard to maintain when program is lengthy.
2. Inconvenient to use partial code.
3. It takes very long time to debug the programs.
4. Hard to rectify the errors.

So due to these drawbacks we take a move to object-oriented programming concept which is shortly called as 'OOP' concept.

1.2 Object-Oriented Approach

What is an object ?

(*i*) The fundamental idea of 'OOPS' concept is object. A object is a single unit which is formed of the data and function. Here the function operates on the data. The function inside the object is called the 'member function' of the object. Its syntax is : `object . member`.

Here slightly, its confusing. So we take a object of C++ with analogy of real-life object. Here we take real life object as a car. Now the car is called a object. The steering and the accelerator are called as data of object. The performance meaning the (data) steering works for turning the wheel and (data) accelerator to speed up the car are termed as functions, which is a operation on data.

This is analogous to objects in C++. Also the data is termed as instance variables, and member functions are also termed as methods.

Total OOP Concept

The total concept is made of following things :

(*i*) Objects ; (*ii*) Classes ; (*iii*) Inheritance ; (*iv*) Overloading ; (*v*) Virtual functions ; (*vi*) Polymorphism.

In C++ this forms the total 'OOP' concept. Above we have taken overview of object. The other overviews are :

(*ii*) **Classes.** The classes are much similar like structures in 'C'. In this the definition of functions and data are made. We will discuss in detail later in this book.

(*iii*) **Inheritance.** This concept is used to reuse the same code anywhere in some program or in other programs.

(*iv*) **Overloading.** This concept is used to behave the operators in liking of programmers.

(*v*) **Virtual functions.** This is used to make dummy functions. Sometimes the virtual function is also used in concept of polymorphism.

(*vi*) **Polymorphism.** This concept is used to do different behaviour by the same code. Using the operators or functions in different ways, depending on what they are operated on, is called polymorphism, *e.g.*, when existing '+' or '=', is given the capability to operate on a new data type, it is said to be overloaded. Overloading is a kind of polymorphism.

1.3 C++ and C

C++ is derived from C language. So strictly speaking, it is an extension of C. So almost every correct statement in C is also a correct statement in C++. But the reverse condition is not true. The major difference between 'C' and 'C++' is the 'OOPS' concept. But in fact, the practical differences between C and C++ are larger than you might think. If anyone sees the programs written in C and in C++, they are virtually similar. But, there can be many differences which can erupt during compiling. It is evident that programmers have to implement all the traditional features of C in 'C++'.

If you are now ready to start, then we head on to learn C++.

1.4 Our Aimfloor

Our goal is to help you begin writing OOP programs as easily as possible. However, as we noted, much of C++ is inherited from C, the overall structure of C++ may be OOP.

SUMMARY

OOP is a way of organizing programs. The emphasis is on the way programs are designed. In particular, OOP programs are organized around objects, which contain both data and functions that act on data. A class is a template for number of objects.

C++ is a extension of C. It adds to the capability of C of OOPS. The result is different language.

The general concepts discussed will become more concrete as you learn more detail in C++.

2

Using Turbo C++

So far we have discussed the similarities and advantages of 'C++' over 'C' language. We have also discussed the overview of 'OOPS' concepts, which we will learn in detail in later chapters.

In this chapter we will guide you about how to set up your 'turbo C++' and how to work under 'Integrated Development Environment (IDE)'.

2.1 Setting Up Turbo C++

Turbo C++ provides a highly automated installation procedure. The user has to only answer the prompt questions.

The user has to remember following things while installation :

1. Memory Models

The installation program will ask the user what memory model he or she wants to use from the following : tiny, small, medium, compact, large, huge. Now it depends upon the user what he or she wants to select. For users guidance we give the following chart :

Memory Model	*Code Memory*	*Data Memory*
Tiny	32 K	32 K
Small	64 K	64 K
Medium	More than 64 K	64 K
Compact	64 K	More than 64 K
Large	More than 64 K	More than 64 K
Huge	More than 64 K	More than 64 K

For example, if your program requires more data than will fit in one 64 K segment, but the code is less than a segment, you'll need to use the compact memory model. You'll also need the library routines for this model.

When you install 'Turbo C++' you can specify the memory models you want to use. But, if the user doesn't give any specific memory model, then the routines of all memory models will be installed on the hard-disk of the computer.

2. The Demonstration Tour

The second thing which system asks is to choose whether the user wants to install the demonstration tour. If yes, the user should go to the 'Tour' subdirectory in 'TC' directory and enter 'TCTOUR'. The program explains all the essentials of IDE'S operations automatically.

All the other installation processes are done automatically.

2.2 Using IDE

'IDE' means 'Intetgrated Development Environment'. So, to start Turbo C++, the following steps should be taken :

1. Go to the dos-prompt and type 'C:\>tc'. After typing, the 'C++ IDE' environment will open.

This environment will have the menu bar as :

The steps to use IDE are go to next page, shown below :

File	Edit	Search	Run	Compile	Debug	Project	Options

2. Now click the 'file' menu and open the 'New' window. The window which opens is called an editor window.

Using the Editors

3. **Listing 2.1.**

```
#include<iostream.h>
void main()
    {
        cout<<''Every age has a new language of life'';
    }
```

This program is explained in the next chapter. This is written here just to show you, how program code is written in the editor window.

4. After the program is written, open the file menu and click *'save as'* and enter the file-name so as to save the 'program-code' in the file of your desired name.

5. After saving, compile the program and link with the standard library to make final '.EXE' program, choose any one of the following steps :

(*a*) Open the compile menu and click make exe option.

(*b*) Open the compile menu and click build all option.

(*c*) Press function key *'F9'* and it will automatically make the `'.exe'` file with same name.

Window Help

6. Now if your file is compiled, go to DOS-prompt by going to *'file'* menu and click *'DOS shell'*. So you will come again to DOS environment. Now type `dir;` You will see four files with same name but different extensions. *e.g.*, suppose the name of file of listing 2.1 is `first.cpp;`

Then the files displayed using *dir* command are :

- `first.cpp`
- `first.bak`
- `first.obj`
- `first.exe`

From these four files; the `first.cpp` is a source file in which you had typed a program and saved.

The `first.bak` is a backup file, in which the user can view the source-code in DOS-mode also. This is a provision for recollection of the program back if your `.cpp` file is accidently deleted.

The `first.obj` is an intermediate object file in which the code is written in form of a machine language. It is not readable and can be deleted after the `'.exe'` file is formed.

The `first.exe` is a program file which can be run even when source code is not present or gets deleted.

7. After viewing and knowing the meaning of all the files, now we can run the program in DOS-mode by just typing the name of the program.

Let us type the name `'first'`. After pressing the *'Enter Key'*, we will get the output :

```
'Every age has a new language of life'.
```

Thus, the program is executed.

2.3 Errors

No one is perfect. It may often happen that one gets a syntax error, or one makes a typing mistake. Such errors are discovered by the compiler or by the linker and are displayed at the bottom of the screen. They can also appear during the run-time.

Compiler Errors

Suppose, one forgets a semi-colon ";" at the end of a statement. Then during the compiling process, the compiling window will show an error message : `Error C:\first.cpp:6: statement missing;` in the function `main ( )`.

In the *edit* window, the line with the closing brace is highlighted, and the brace itself will be highlighted in a different colour. This indicates the position where the compiler has found an error.

Linker Errors

Errors can also appear during the linking process. If you have made a typing mistake by typing `maid` instead of `main`. It will give the error as :

```
Linker Error : Undefined symbol main in module co.asm.
```

The linker must find the `main ( )` function to link it to standard libraries. Otherwise, it will show an error.

Run-Time Errors

Comparatively small errors which are not revealed in IDE can appear during the execution of a program. These errors may occur due to mistakes like division of a number by zero, stock-overflow etc.

When all the errors are rectified by the programmers, the compiler window shows 'success' message and `'.exe'` file is formed.

2.4 On-Line Help

This is a help to users and is inbuilt to the 'IDE'. If the user is stuck anywhere inside the 'IDE', he or she can click the *help* menu. Options of many types will appear, but more user-friendly ones are :

- *Contents*
- *Index.*

But the easiest type is, the *'Index'* option. The list will come 'alphabet wise'. The user should press the first letter of the query word. For example, if the user wants to know about function or syntax of *'Cout'* query word then user should press the letter 'C'. All words starting with 'C' will be displayed.

After that the user should go to the required word by mouse or keyboard, highlight and click that word. The details of that keyword or function will be displayed immediately.

In this way user can take help about any reserved keyword or anything related to 'C++' which is terminological.

Keyboard Keys	**Action**
↑	Cursor up one line
↓	Cursor down one line
←	Cursor left one character
→	Cursor right one character
Ctrl+←	Cursor left one word
Ctrl+ →	Cursor right one word
Home	Cursor to first line
End	Cursor to last line
Pg Up	Scroll one screen up
Pg Dn	Scroll one screen down
Enter	Insert line, go to next line
Backspace	Delete character to left of cursor
Del	Delete character under cursor
Ins	Joggle insert/write over

Shortcut Keys	**Action**
Alt+F	To open file menu
F2	To save file
F3	To open file dialog box
Alt+F3	To close window
F5	To make screen full size
F6	To joggle between windows
F8	To debug the code
F9	To compile and link the file
Ctrl+F9	To run the program

Note : *Only 'file' menu shortcut keys are given. The menu shortcut keys can easily be understood by seeing the letter in different colour and joining 'Alt' key to that letter.*

SUMMARY

After reading and understanding this chapter, you will be able to install the system, write the code in the editor window. You will also be able to save, compile and run the program along with the shortcut keys to make your work fast and to save time.

In the next chapter we'll begin our exploration of 'C++' language.

3

C++ Basics

In any language, one should know some fundamentals which can be learned by writing very elementary programs. This chapter introduces the fundamental concepts like input/output (I/O), type-casting, conversion concepts etc.

Most of these topics are not conceptually difficult and are very similar to language 'C'. But the style of writing the programs may differ.

3.1 Basic C++ Program Structure

We repeat the program of Listing 2.1; but we will now look into that program more closely :

Listing 3.1 :

```
First.cpp
#include<iostream.h>
void main()
     {
          cout<<''Every age has a new language of life'';
     }
```

Despite its small size, this program demonstrates a great deal about 'C++' program. Let us study it in detail :

1. Preprocessor Directive

The first line of `first.cpp` program is :

```
#include<iostream.h>
```

It might look like a program statement, but it is not. It is also not part of a function and it does not end with a semicolon (;). Instead it starts with a number sign (#). So it is called a preprocessor directive. Recall that the program statements are instructions to the computer while a preprocessor is an instruction to the compiler. The compiler deals with preprocessor before beginning the compiling process.

`# include Directive.`

The preprocessor # `include` tells the compiler to insert the header file `<iostream.h>` into your source file `''first.cpp''` and then compile the entire code of `<isotream.h>` with `''first.cpp''` to make the application `''first.exe''`.

Similarly any header file can be included above the source-code.

2. The second line of the program is :

```
void main( )
```

The `'void'` is reserved keyword of C++; which assures that the main function does not pass parameters to any other function since the brackets[( )] are empty and also does not receive any argument from any other function which is indicated by `'void'`.

The *main()* function is a complete function and it is required in 'C++' code to compile it into an application (`.exe file`). If there is no function called *main()* in your program, the linker will signal an error.

3. The third line is :

```
{
```

This is called an opening brace of the program code in which a number of statements of a program can be written.

4. The fourth line is :

```
cout<<''Every age has a new language of life'';
```

This program statement is fundamental unit in C++. Here, since it is your first program, it has only one statement. The statement always ends with a semi-colon. The matter or content which you want to print on screen should always come in double quotes (" "); since it is a string constant.

5. The fifth line is :

```
}
```

This is called a closing brace which marks the end of the code.

Now we have known the common approach of writing a program in C++.

3.2 Variables

Variables are the most fundamental part of any language. They are a symbolic name that can be assigned with a variety of values. They are stored at a particular place in the memory of computer. So when a variable is given a value; it is actually stored in a memory space occupied by the variable.

The general variable types which are used are :

Basic C++ Variable Types

Keyword	*Numerical range*		*Digits of precision*	*Bytes of Memory*
	Low	*High*		
`char`	−128	127	n/a	1
`int`	−32,768	32,767	n/a	2
`long`	−2,147,483,648	2,147,483,647	n/a	4
`float`	3.4×10^{-38}	3.4×10^{38}	7	4
`double`	1.7×10^{-308}	1.7×10^{308}	15	8
`long double`	3.4×10^{-4932}	1.1×10^{4932}	19	10

Explanation of a table of 'C++ Variable Types'

(*a*) The *keyword* term defines the reserved keyword in 'C++'. Thus, the `'char'` is a reserved keyword for character variable. `'int'` is a reserved keyword for the integer variable. `'float'` is a reserved keyword for 'floating-point' variable and similar is the case with others.

(*b*) The term *Numerical range* indicates the number of characters in `'Ascii'` value from lowest to highest range in `'char'` variable and the length of digits from lowest to highest in range of all other variables that a particular variable can take.

(*c*) Bytes of memory indicates how much space of memory is consumed by a particular variable of a particular type. *i.e.*, it indicates storage space.

Defining Variables

Here we will discuss how to define variables of different data types and their operations.

Listing 3.2 :

```
/*intvars.cpp.
demonstrates integer variables*/
#include<iostream.h>
void main()
  {
     int a, b;                          //define two variables a & b.
     a = 20;                            //assign value to a.
     b = a + 30;                        //assign value to b.
     cout<<''The value of b is'';       //output text
     cout<<b;                           //output value of b.
  }
```

Type this program and compile it. You will get the desired output which is :

The value of *b* is 50.

Explanation of testing 3.2.

Comments are of two types *viz., multiline* and *single line*. "/* */" is a multiline comment, which is used to comment the lines written on more than one line. While the (''//'') single line comment is used to describe the code statements.

e.g., //define two variables *a* and *b*.

The `''#include''` and `''void main( )''` statements are described previously, so we skip these lines.

The line : `int a, b;`

This line defines the two variables '*a*' and '*b*' of datatype integer. The keyword in 'C' and 'C++' of datatype integer is `'int'`. The keyword `'int'` signals the type of variable. The statement is terminated by ';'. This definition sets aside 2 bytes of memory for each variable : *a* and *b*.

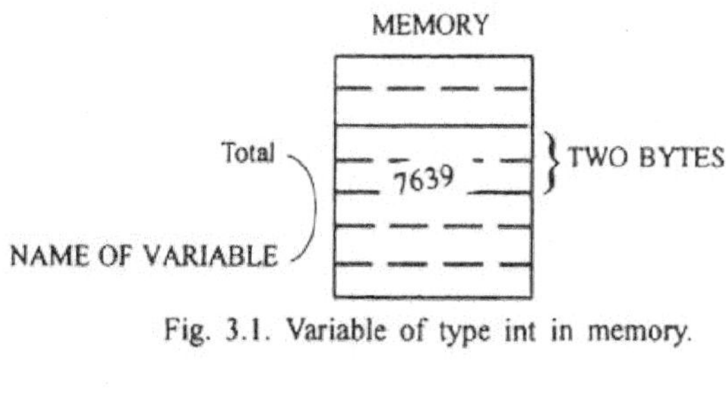

Fig. 3.1. Variable of type int in memory.

The line : `a = 20; b = a + 30;`

This line assigns the value of 20 to integer variable *a*. So the value of 20 is stored in variable '*a*' which consumes 2 bytes. Similarly, *b* variable stores the value of 50, which consumes 2 bytes.

The equal sign '=', as you might have guessed, assigns the value of right variable to the variable on the left with the sign '='.

Integer Constants and Operators

The number 20 is an integer constant. Constants do not change during the course of program.

Also, in the next line, the '+' sign adds the value in '*a*' variable and constant integer 30, and the final result is stored in variable *b*.

3.3 Input and Output

In C++, the programmer can output the statement using the keyword 'cout'.

The syntax of 'cout' statement is,

```
cout<<statements
```

For example,

```
cout<< ''Every language has its own features'';
```

In the above example, we have used the keyword 'cout'. Then, the inserter '<<' operator is used and the statement which is to be printed out is written thereafter in double quotation marks.

The insertion operator '<<' directs the contents of the variable to the object on its left.

Similarly, C++ programmers can also take the input from the user and store in variable using the keyword 'cin'.

The syntax of 'cin' statement is,

```
cin>>statements<variable name>
```

The example is,

```
cin>>temp;
```

In the above example, the keyword 'cin' is used. Then the extraction operator '>>' is used, which takes the value from stream object on its left and places it in variable on its right.

Listing 3.3 :

```
//demonstrates input and output.
#include<iostream.h>
void main()
    {
        int temp;
        cout<<''Enter temperature in fahrenheit:'';
        cin>>temp;
        int celcius=(temp-32)*5/9;
        cout<<''Temperature in celcius:<<celcius<<'\n';
    }
```

3.4 Arithmetic Operators

There are four normal arithmetic operators for C and C++, namely :

Name	*Operators*
Addition	+
Subtraction	–
Multiplication	*
Division	/

There is a fifth arithmetic operator that works only with the integer variables, called as a remainder operator (%).

Here, we take a program that covers all the arithmetic operators.

Listing 3.4 :

```
//demonstrates arithmetic operators.
#include<iostream.h>
void main()
    {
        int no1, no2, no3;
        cout<<''Enter two numbers\n'';
        cin>>no1;
        cin>>no2;
        no3=no1+no2;
        cout<<''The addition is''<<no3<<endl;
        no3=no1-no2; no3=0;
        cout<<''The subtraction is''<<no3<<endl;
        no3=no1*no2;
        cout<<''The multiplication is''<<no3<<endl;
        no3=0;
        no3=no1/no2;
        cout<<''The quotient is''<<no3<<endl;
        no3=0;
        no3=no1%no2;
        cout<<''The remainder is''<<no3<<endl;
    }
```

3.5 Assignment Operators

C++ offers several options to assign the value to the variable using the arithmetic assignment operator. The assignment operator is commonly used in most languages including C++.

The example is,

```
total = total + item;
```

In this statement, the value of item is added to the existing value. But, the problem is that `'total'` operand appears twice.

In order to overcome this problem, C++ uses a condensed approach of arithmetic assignment operator, which combines an arithmetic operator and an assignment operator and eliminates the repeated operand.

Here's a statement that has exactly the same effect as the above :

```
total + = item;
```

Listing 3.5 :

```
//demonstrates assignment operators.
#include<iostream.h>
void main()
   {
      int a=30;
      a+=10;            //same as : a=a+10;
      cout<<a;
      a-=7;
      cout<<a;
      a*=2;
      cout<<a;
      a/=3;
      cout<<a;
      a%=3;
      cout<<a<<endl;
   }
```

The above program demonstrates all arithmetic operators.

3.6 Increment Operators

These are more specialized operators in which you can add 1 to an existing variable.
Let us take an example to increment count with a statement.

```
count = count + 1;
```

Alternatively, this statement can also be written using arithmetic assignment operator as :

```
count + = 1;
```

But, there's an even more condensed approach to write it :

```
++count;
```

This '++' operator is called an increment operator and it adds 1 to its argument.

Decrement Operator

Similarly, you can subtract 1 from an argument using '– –'. This is called a decrement operator.

e.g., `count - -;`

Prefix and Postfix

The increment operators can be used in two ways : As a 'prefix' and 'postfix'.
In 'prefix', the operator precedes the variable.

e.g., `total = ++ count;`

Here the '++' operator is prefixed. Therefore, first the 'count' variable increments its value and then assigns the value to the variable 'total'.

In 'postfix', the operator follows the variable.

e.g., `total = count ++.`

Here, the '++' operator is postfixed. So the 'count' variable assigns its value to the variable 'total' and then increments its value. Similarly, all operators can be postfixed and prefixed.

3.7 Type Conversions

C++, like C treats expression involving several different data-types and expressions.

Listing 3.6 :

```
//demonstrates conversions.
#include<iostream.h>
void main()
    {
        int no=10;
        float ans=25.36;
        double ans=no*ans;
        cout<<''The answer is''<<ans<<endl;
    }
```

In this program, the variable `'no'` of type `'int'` is multiplied by a variable `'ans'` of type `'float'` to yield a result of type `'double'`.

This program compiles without error because the result is automatically converted to the type `'double'`.

This feature is termed as 'Automatic Conversion'. When two operands of different types are encountered in same expression, the lower-type variable is converted to the type of higher-type variable.

In our program, the `'int'` value of `'no'` is converted to the type `'float'` and stored in a temporary variable before being multiplied by `'float'` variable `'ans'`. The result is then converted to `'double'` so that it can be assigned to `'double'` variable `'ans'`.

These conversions take place invisibly and C++ does it automatically, as desired.

Casts

In C++, the term *cast* applies to data conversions specified by programmer, as opposed to the automatic conversions of data that we described earlier. The question that arises then is, what are *casts* for ?

Sometimes a programmer needs to convert a value from one type to another in a situation where compiler can not do it automatically. In such a case, we might be able to solve the problem by using a 'cast'.

Here's an example :

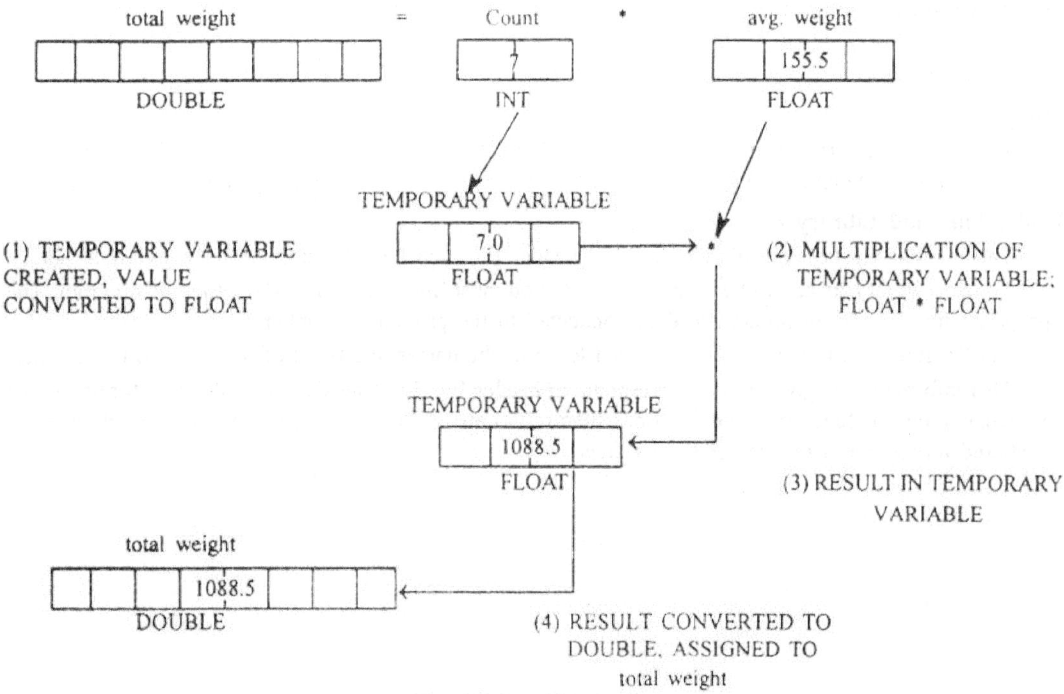

Fig. 3.2. Data Conversion

Listing 3.7 :

```
//cast.cpp
#include<iostream.h>
#define var 25000
void main()
  {
     int Var;
     var=(var*10);
     cout <<''The value is<<var<<endl;
     var=(long(var)*10);
     cout<<''The value is<<var<<endl;
  }
```

Preprocessor Directives

The preprocessor directive typed as '#' is used for two purposes :

(*i*) To include header file

(*ii*) To define a macro.

(*i*) **Header Files.** The header files are included in order to compile your program.

For example, in the above example, the header file `'iostream.h'` is included because the prototypes of function `'cout'` are defined in that header file.

The angle brackets are used so that the compiler finds these header files directly in the standard directory.

The function of these preprocessor directives is to compile the code inside the header file before compiling the program.

There are two ways to include the header files :

```
#include<isotream.h>
#include''myfile.h''
```

Where `'myfile.h'` is our created header file.

Library Files

We mentioned earlier that a file containing library functions and objects will usually be linked to your program to create an executable file using an linker. These files are stored by an extension `'.lib'`.

Header Files and Library Files

The relationship between library files and header files can be confusing, so let's review it again.

To use a library function like `'sqrt ( )'`, you must link file `'CS.Lib'` to your program. The appropriate functions from library are then connected to the program by linker.

But the functions in your source file need to know the names and types of functions in library files.

This information is given in the corresponding header file. Each header file contains information for a particular group of functions. The functions themselves are in `'CS.Lib'`, but information about them is scattered throughout a number of header files.

This relationship between header and library files is shown in the figure below :

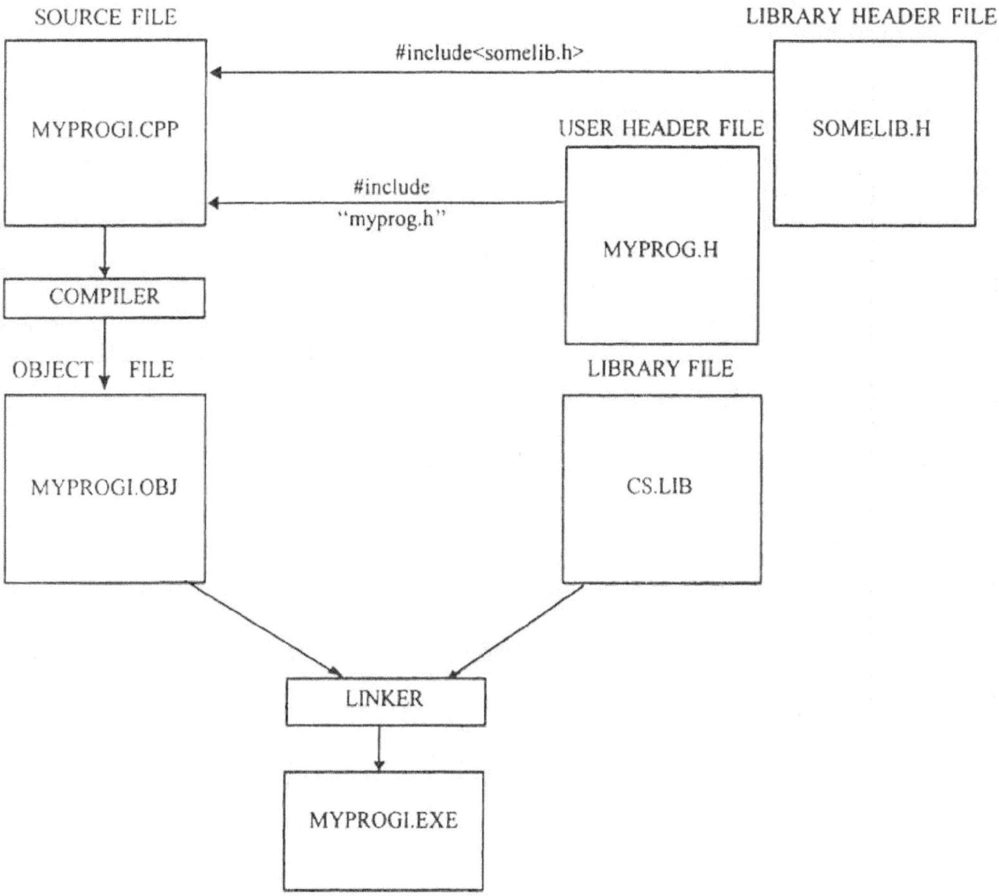

Fig. 3.3. Header and Library Files

(*ii*) The second use of preprocessor directive is to define a macro. The statement in previous program,

```
#define var 25000
```

means that the macro `'var'` is defined to the value 25000. Thus, whenever this macro is used in the program, it is replaced with the value 25000.

The advantage is that, suppose you want to change the value from 25000 to 28000 in `'#define'` statement then, it is automatically changed in every part of program.

But, the drawback is that, it occupies more memory because it is precompiled as it is a preprocessor.

SUMMARY

In this chapter we've learned about the building blocks of C++ programs. The function named 'main()' is essential to execute the program.

A function is a group of statements which instructs the computer to perform something which is written. Every statement ends with a semicolon.

The output in C++ is handled by the object 'cout' and insertion operator '<<'. Similarly input in C++ is handled by the object 'cin' and extractor operator '>>'.

There are six major built in datatypes : 'char', 'ent', 'long int', 'float', 'double' and 'long double'.

A variable is converted from one type to another by method of 'casting'.

There are increment operators '+ +' and decrement operator '– –'.

The preprocessor directives '#include' and '#define' consists of instructions given to compiler rather than to computer. The '#include' directive tells compiler to insert another file into present source file which is linked by the linker. The '#define' directive tells to substitute one thing for another.

EXERCISES

1. Write a program in which you input two numbers and give the result in
   (*i*) multiplication
   (*ii*) division
   (*iii*) addition
   (*iv*) subtraction.
2. Write a program in which you input a number and then the output should that number, the number less than 1 of original number and more of 1 than of original number.
3. Write a program that generates following using single cout statement :

2000	500
2001	5500
2002	55005

4

Loops and Decisions

In normal day-to-day programming, all the programs cannot be executed in strict order from beginning to end.

Most of the programs decide to respond according to the decisions taken by the program which is instructed by the programmer in the form of conditional statements.

Suppose a specific code of program has to be executed for a number of times depending upon certain conditions, which are evaluated either as true or false and then execute the corresponding code as instructed by the programmer. Here, much of the manual work is lessened due to repetitive structures.

4.1 Relational Operators

A relational operator is used to compare two values.

This program will illustrate the use of some relational operators.

Listing 4.1 :

```
//relate.cpp
#include<iostream.h>
void main()
    {
        int n;
        cout<<''Enter a numbers :'';
        cin>>n;
        cout<<''n<10  is''<<(n<10)<<endl;
        cout<<''n>10  is''<<(n>10)<<endl;
        cout<<''n= =10  is''<<(10= =10)<<endl;
    }
```

This program performs three types of comparisons, of 'less than', 'greater than' or of 'equal to' relational operator.

Explanation of Listing 4.1

The first expression is true if variable 'n' is less than 10.

The second expression is true if 'n' is greater than 10.

The third expression is true if 'n' is equal to 10.

Now suppose, the user enters the number '15'.

Then the output will be :

```
Enter a number : 15
n < 10 is 0
n > 10 is 1
n = = 10 is 0
```

From the above output it is clear that if the relational condition is true then the compiler outputs the result value as 1, otherwise, the result value is 0.

Here, since the expression 'n > 10' is true, it outputs result value as '1' while others as '0'.

Here's a complete list of C++ relational operators :

Operator	*Meaning*
>	Greater than
<	Less than
==	Equal to
!=	Not equal to
>=	Greater than or equal to
<=	Less than or equal to

Here is the other listing of code which gives the illustration of other three relational operators.

Listing 4.2 :

```
//demonstrates relate1.cpp
#include<iostream.h>
void main()
    {
        int n1, n2;                    //variable declaration.
        n1=40;                         //assignment statement
        n2=20;                         //assignment statement
        cout<<''n1!=n2 is''<<(n1!=n2)<<endl;
        cout<<''n1>=42 is''<<(n1>=42)<<endl;
        cout<<''n2<=n1 is''<<(n2<=n1)<<endl;
    }
```

Output

```
n1 != n2 is 1        //'1' means expression is true.
n1 >= 42 is 0        //'0' means expression is false.
n2 <= n1 is 1        //'1' means expression is true.
```

The 'endl' manipulator is used in the program for the cursor to go to the next line after the display of 'cout' statement.

4.2 Conditional Statement

A conditional statement allows the program to take the selective processing of a statement according to the given conditions.

There are two forms of conditional statements :

(*i*) if-statement.

(*ii*) if-else statement.

(*i*) if-statement

The if-statement is used to specify conditional execution of a statement or group of statements enclosed in braces.

The general format of if-statement :

```
if (expression)
    {
        statements...;
        .........
    }
```

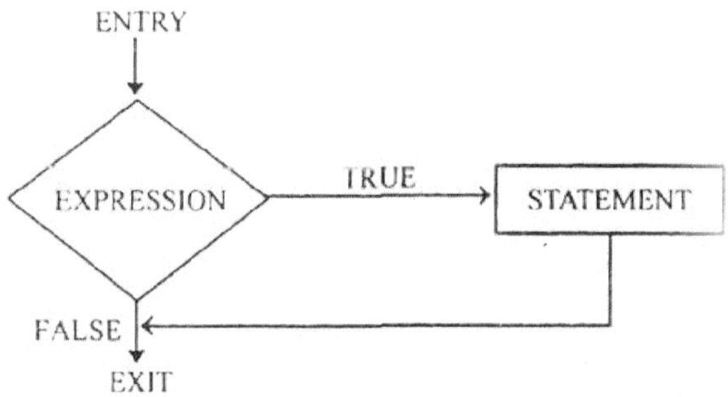

Fig. 4.1

Listing 4.3 :

```
//demonstrates if condition
#include<iostream.h>
void main()
    {
        int a, b, large;
        cout<<''Enter a, b''<<endl;
        cin>>a;
        cin>>b>>endl;
        large=a;
        if(b>a){large=b};
        cout<<''The large is''<<large<<endl;
    }
```

Explanation of Listing 4.3

Here we will discuss only the if-condition, since all other statements were discussed in previous chapter.

The if-condition is given in statement as follows :

```
if (b>a)
```

It means that, if integer variable b is greater than integer variable a then only the next statement,

```
large = b;
```

will be executed, otherwise the control from statement,

```
large = b;
```

will be passed directly to 'cout' statement.

(*ii*) **if-else statement**

The if-statement allows conditional execution of a group of statements. But, there are various situations when two groups of statements are given and it is expected for the program code to select one of the two groups of statements if condition is true; else to execute the other group of statements.

The general format of if-else statement :

```
if (expression=true)
   {
       statements-1;
   }
else
   {
       statements-2;
   }
```

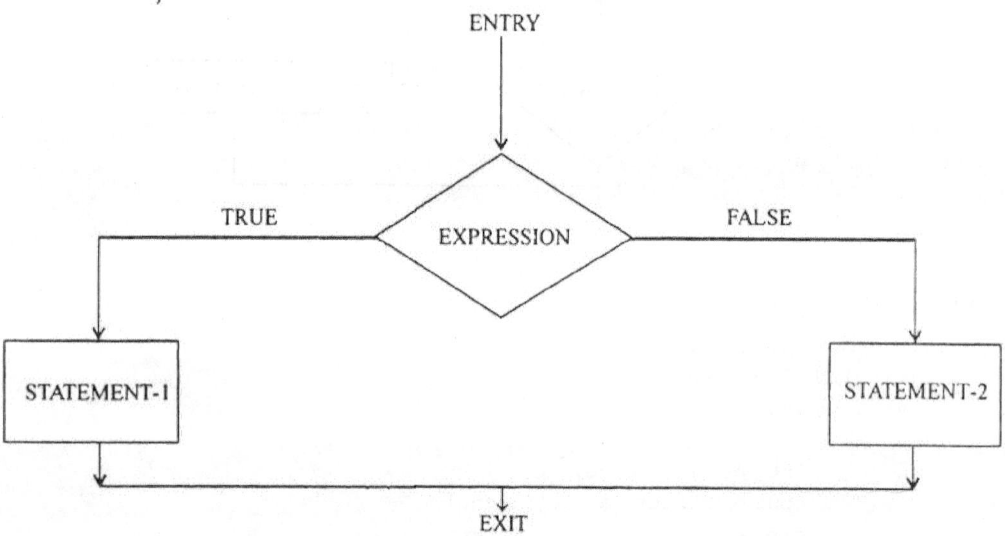

Fig. 4.2

Listing 4.4 :

```
//demonstrates if-else condition
#include<iostream.h>
void main()
{
int a, b, large;
cout<<''Enter a, b''<<endl;
cin>>a;
cin>>b; cin>>endl;
if(a>b)
```

```
    {
        large=a;                //statement1
    }
else
    {
        large=6;                //statement2
    }
    cout<<''The  large  is''<<large<<endl;
}
```

Explanation of Listing 4.4

Here, we will discuss only the code in the if-else block.

When an if-else statement is encountered, if the value of expression is non-zero (true), then the statement inside the if-block is executed. The statement in the else-block is skipped and the program execution continues after the statement inside the else-block.

But, if the condition of if expression is evaluated as false, then the statement inside the if-block is skipped and the statement inside the else-block is executed. The program restores its execution from the next statement.

Here, in our listing 4.4; if the value stored in variable `a` is greater than the value stored in variable `b`, then the statement inside the if-block :

```
large = a;
```

is executed. Otherwise, the statement inside the else-block :

```
large = b;
```

is executed.

Finally the output can be seen by `cout` statement.

Nested Conditions

In professional programs, many a times, situation arises, where one expression is nested inside the other expression.

The general format is :

```
if (expression=true)
    {
        statements-1;
    }
else {
if (expression=true)
    {
        statements-2;}
    }
else
    {
        statements-3;
    }
```

We can know from this general format, that if condition of first if-statement is true, then statements-1 set is executed; if the condition is false, then the condition of if-statement inside the else-block is evaluated.

If that expression is evaluated as true, then the statements-2 set is executed, otherwise directly the statements-3 set is executed.

In this way, one can execute and nest any number of conditions, one inside the another.

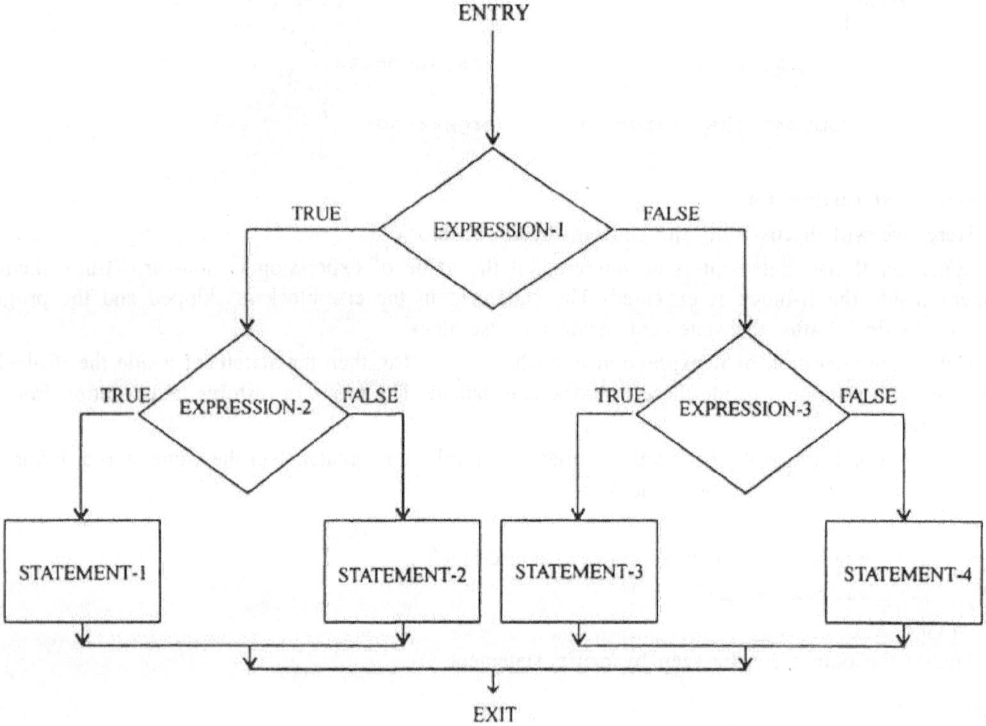

Fig. 4.3

Listing 4.5 :

```
//demonstrates if-else nested loops
#include<iostream.h>
void main()
{
int a, b, c, d;
int max = 0;        //define and assign the value
cout<<''Enter a, b, c, d''<<endl;
cin>>a;
cin>>b;
cin>>c;
cin>>d>>endl;
if (a>b)
{
    cout<<''a is greater than b'';
      b=a;
    }
```

```
else {
if (b>a)
{
    cout<<''b is greater than a'';
    a=b;
    }
    else
    {
    if (c>a)
    {
        cout<<''c is greater than a'';
        a=c;
        }
        else
        {
        if (a>c)
        {
            cout<<''a is greater than c'';
            c=a;
            }
            else
            {
            if (d>a)
            {
                cout<<''d is greater than a'';
                a=d;
                }
                else
                {
                    cout<<''a is greater than d'';
                    d=a;
                }
            }
        }
    }
}
```

This program is almost self-explanatory. So it is not described in detail.

But, it shows that one can nest the condition upto any depth, in this way.

4.3 Switch Statement

In nested if-else statements, you might have seen that it becomes somewhat confusing and tedious, to use if a decision tree is very large.

It is thus better to use another control structure called `'switch'` structure. This is used when all decisions depend on the value of some variable.

The general format is :

```
switch(var)
    {
        case selection 1:
          statements; break;
        case selection 2:
          statements; break;
              :
        default selection:
          statements;
    }
```

The `switch` is reserved keyword. Variable `var` which is followed by keyword `switch` is evaluated and its value is successively compared with `case selections`. If a `case selection` value matches the value of variable `var`, then the statement associated with that `case selection` is executed. After completing its execution; the `break` statement is encountered.

Break statement

When the break statement of the form

```
break;
```

is encountered, the execution of the loop or conditional statements is interrupted and the program transfers control to the exit point of the loop or conditional statements. The program control then starts from the statements which comes after the completion of the loop or conditional statements.

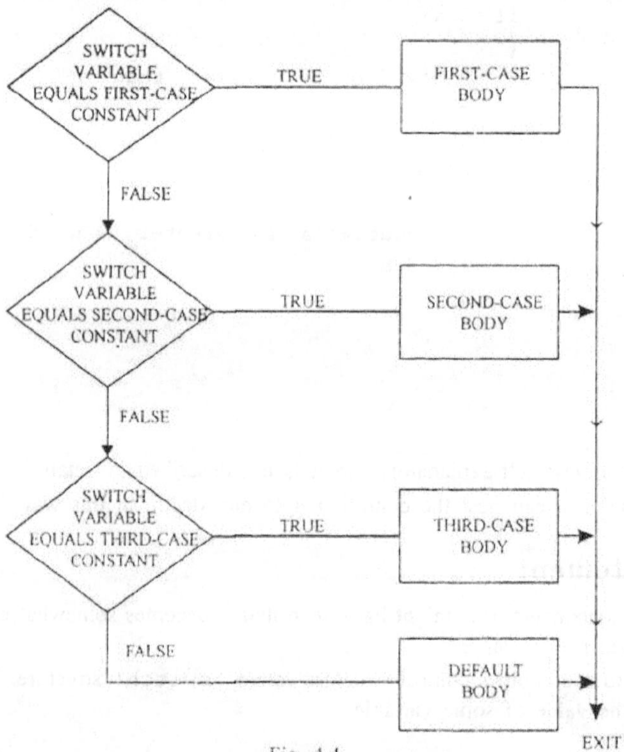

Fig. 4.4

Listing 4.6 :

```
//demonstrates  switch  conditional  method
#include<iostream.h>
void  main()
{
    char  op;
    float  op1,  op2;
    cout<<''Enter  operand''<<endl;
    cin>>op;
    cout<<''Enter  operand 1''<<endl;
    cin>>op1;
    cout<<''Enter  operand 2''<<endl;
    cin>>op2;
    switch(op)
    {
        case  '+';
        cout<<''operand 1+operand 2''<<endl;
        break;
        case  '-';
        cout<<''operand 1-operand 2''<<endl;
        break;
        case  '*';
        cout<<''operand 1*operand 2''<<endl;
        break;
        case  '/';
        cout<<''operand 1/operand 2''<<endl;
        break;
        default;
        cout<<''invalid  expression''<<endl;
    }
}
```

Note that no two case values should be the same in `switch` statement. However, more than one case value can be associated with a set of statements by listing multiple case values before that particular set. It is not necessary to terminate each `case` with `break` statement.

The *default* statement is used because if none of the `case` values match the value of `switch` variable, the *default* statement is executed.

4.4 Conditional Operator

The conditional operator, unlike all other operators, is not unary or binary. It is a ternary operator and takes three arguments.

It has general format :

```
expression-1  ?  expression-2  :  expression-3.
```

Here (?) question mark and colon (:) are the two symbols that denote this operator. A conditional expression is evaluated by first evaluating expression-1. If the resultant value is non-zero *i.e.*, true, then expression-2 is evaluated and the value of expression-2 becomes the result of the conditional expression. Otherwise, expression-3 is evaluated and its value becomes the result.

Thus, the conditional operator is similar to if-else statement as follows :

if (expression-1)
then (expression-2)
else (expression-3)

We have completed the conditional statements and now we will proceed towards the repetitive structures.

We call these repetitive structures as loops.

4.5 Loops

There are three types of loops in C++ :

(*i*) while-loop
(*ii*) do-while-loop
(*iii*) for loop.

Let us discuss each loop in detail.

(*i*) **while-loop**

The while loop is a pretest loop.

Its general format is :

```
loop  initialization
while(expression)
{
    statements...
}
```

The `loop initialization` defines the entry point of the structure. In the `while` statement, expression provides loop continuation condition to iterate the statements upto certain number of times.

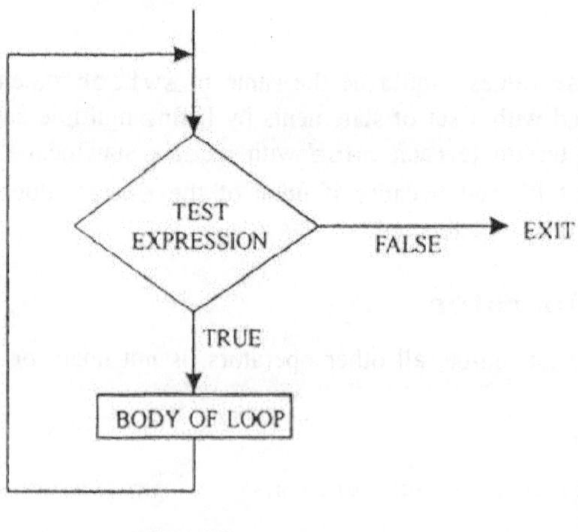

Fig. 4.5

When the reserved keyword `while` is encountered, `expression` is evaluated. If the `expression` evaluated is true, the `statements` are executed. As soon as the condition which is evaluated after each iteration becomes false, the program control terminates the loop; and immediately transfers the control to the statement outside the loop.

Listing 4.7 :

```
//demonstrates the while-loop
#include<iostream.h>
void main()
{
    int ch, count;
    count=0;
    ch=getchar();
    while(ch!=EOF)              //while statement
    {
        putchar(ch);
        count++;                //Iteritive statement
        ch=getchar();
    }
    cout<<''Total characters echoed=''<<count;
}
```

Explanation of Listing 4.7

We begin by initializing zero to a counter `count` in which we store the count of characters to be echoed. We have used `getchar ()` function outside the while-loop to read the first character and store it in control variable `ch`.

When the keyword `while` is encountered, the control variable `ch` is evaluated. Here it is checked, whether `ch` is equal to 'end-of-file'. If the result is true, then it terminates the loop and control goes to `cout` statement.

Otherwise, it will continue to iterate until the condition becomes false; and the total number of characters echoed are output in `cout` statement.

(*ii*) do-while loop

The do-while is a post-test loop, whose general format is :

```
loop initialization
do
    {
        statements-1;
    }
while(expression);
        statements-2;
```

It is similar to 'while'-loop but with one difference. As soon as `do` keyword is encountered, it executes the `statements-1` set of statements and then the `while-expression` is evaluated.

If the `while-condition` is true, then the whole `do-while` loop is repeated as long as the condition becomes false.

When the condition becomes false, it exits the do-while loop and the control transfers to statements-2.

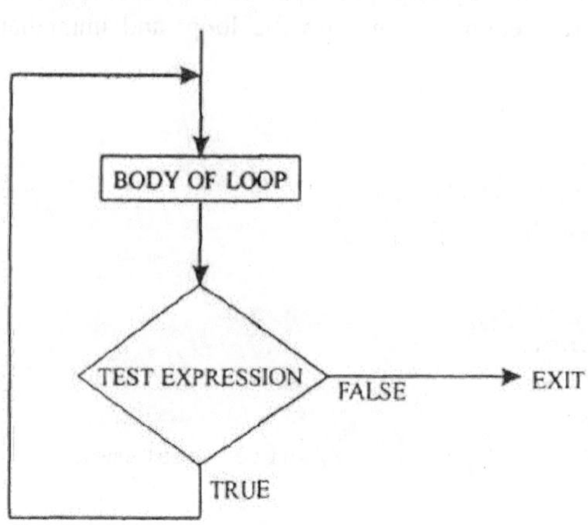

Fig. 4.6

Listing 4.8 :

```
//demonstrates do-while loop
#include<iostream.h>
void main()
{
    int no, digit, sum;
    digit=sum=0;
    cout<<''Enter the number''<<endl;
    cin>>no;
    do
    {
        sum+=no.%10;
        no/=10;
        digit++;
    }
    while(no>0);
    cout<<''number of digits=''<<digit<<''/n'';
    cout<<''sum is''<<sum<<endl;
}
```

Explanation of Listing 4.8

Here, we determine the number of digits and its sum. The two quantities will be stored in variables digit and sum respectively.

Then the keyword do is encountered of do-while loop. In each iteration of the loop, first the right-most digit of the number no. is extracted and is added to sum; and this digit is truncated from the number. The test that the number has not become zero provides the loop continuation condition. Thus, the no. is loop control variable in this structure. Note that the loop would be executed as many times as number of digits in no. variable.

Once the condition becomes false, the control is transferred to `cout` statement.

Here, we used some professional 'C++' short forms as :

```
(1) sum + = no. % 10; similar to
    sum = sum + (no. % 10);
(2) no / = 10; similar to
    no = no / 10;
```

(*iii*) for loop

The for loop is a powerful and flexible repetitive structure.

The general format is :

```
for (initialization, condition, counter)
    {
        statements-1...
    }
        statements-2
```

The `initialization` defines the entry point of the loop and is used to initialize the variable at the start of the loop. The `condition` states the loop continuation condition. The loop iterates as long as condition is true and terminates as soon as condition becomes false. `Counter` keeps track of the number of iterations and increments each time unless the condition becomes false.

The `for`-loop is normally used for situations where the number of repetitions are fixed.

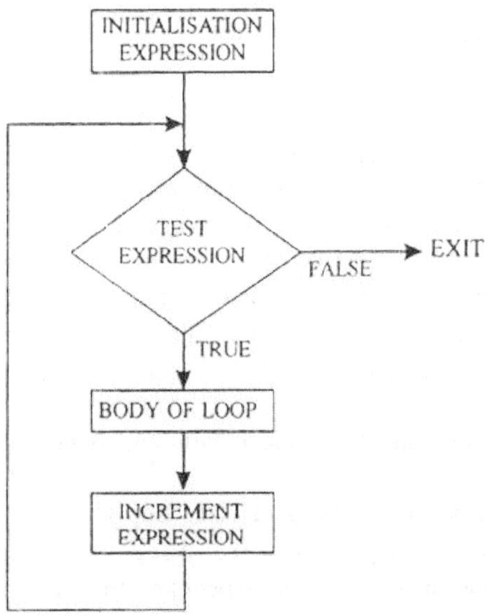

Fig. 4.7

Listing 4.9 :

```
//demonstrates for-loop in nested form
#include<iostream.h>
```

```
void main()
{
    int prin, rate, years, i, j, k, int;
    cout<<''Enter principal amount\n'';
    cin>>prin;
    cout<<''Enter rate\n'';
    cin>>rate;
    cout<<''Enter number of years\n'';
    cin>>years;
    for(i=1;i<=prin;i+=1000)
    {
        for(j=1;j<=rate;j+=rate)
        {
            for(k=1;k<=years;k++)
            {
                int=prin*(rate/100)*years;
                cout<<''principal=''<<prin<<''rate=''
                        <<rate<<''years=''<<years
                        <<''interest=''<<int<<endl;
            }
        } //exit of years loop
    } //exit of rate loop
} //exit of principal loop
```

Explanation of Listing 4.9

This program involves three `for` loops : inner, middle and outer. The inner loop is nested in the middle loop, which is again nested in the outer `for`-loop.

When the first `for`-loop is encountered, the counter `i` is initialised to *one* and then the condition is evaluated. If the condition is true, the counter is incremented and execution of its loop body begins.

The control then enters the middle loop and same procedure as of the outer loop is followed.

After that, the control enters the inner loop following the same procedure.

Then, if the evaluation of the condition of inner loop is true, it iterates the number of times "space" as in our case is no. of years.

After the completion of inner loop, the middle and outer loops again get iterated as long as condition becomes false.

Thus, in nested loops, no. of iterations of inner loop are :

```
inner loop = middle loop * outer loop.
```

Since, we have completed all forms of repetitive structures, now we will move on to logical operators.

4.6 Logical Operators

So far we saw two families of operators *i.e.*, arithmetic operators +, –, *, / and % and relational operators <, >, < =, > =, = = and ! =.

Now, let us learn about the third family of operators called logical operators. These operators allow you to combine boolean (true/false) values along with the existing operators.

There are three logical operators :

(*i*) **Logical Operator 'and' (&&).** Here, the test expression will be true, if both the values of the condition is true.

Here is an example of logical operator 'and' (&&).

Listing 4.10 :

```
//demonstrates logical And operator
#include<iostream.h>
#include<process.h>                    //for exit()
#include<conis.h>                      //for getche()
void main()
{
    char dir='a';
    int x=10, y=10;
    while(dir!='r')
    {
        cout<<''/n your location is''<<x<<'','<<y;
        cout<<''Enter direction (n, s, e, w):'';
        dir=getche();                  //get direction
        switch(dir)
        {
            case 'n':y--; break;
            case 's':y++; break;
            case 'e':x++; break;
            case 'w':x--; break;
        }
        if (x= =7&&y= =11)
        {
            cout<<''in treasure found/n'';
            exit(o)
        }
    }
}
```

Explanation of Listing 4.10

Here, only the part of logical operator 'and' is explained. The condition given is

`if (x= =7&&y= =11)`

which means that if both conditions, x is equal to 7 and y is equal to 11 are true then only `if` condition is satisfied and executed.

(*ii*) **Logical Operator 'OR' (||).** Here, any separate program-listing is not required. One can modify the condition of 'if' in listing 4.10 from '&&' operator to '||' operator.

The condition becomes true in OR (||) operator if any one of the two values is true; and the expression will be evaluated as true.

(*iii*) **Logical operator 'NOT' (|).** This is a unary operator and takes only one operand.

It negates the value of expression. It means, if the condition evaluated is true, it makes it false and vice-versa.

Precedence Summary

Here, we list the operators according to the level of precedence, *i.e.*, the operators which are higher on the list have higher precedence and lower on list have lower precedence.

Operator Type	*Operators*
Unary	!, + +, – –, –
Arithmetic :	
Multiplicative	*, /, %
Additive	+, –
Relational :	
inequality	<, >, < =, > =
equality	= =, ! =
Logical :	
and	&&
or	||
Conditional :	? :
Assignment	=, + =, – =, * =, / =, % =

Continue Statement

The `continue` statement is another loop interruption statement. But unlike 'break', it doesn't terminate the loop. It only interrupts the particular iteration. The `continue` statement is of the form,

```
continue;
```

When a `continue` statement is encountered within any loop body, all remaining statements in the loop following a `continue` statement are skipped and loop continuation condition is evaluated next.

Let us see an example, so that we can understand `continue` statement more easily.

```
for (i = 1; i <= n; i ++)
    {
        if (i%10= =0)  continue;
        sum=sum+i;
    }
```

Following the execution of `continue` statement, the assignment statement which adds `i` to sum,

```
sum = sum + i
```

is skipped, but reinitialization expression that increments `i` is still executed.

Goto Statement

The `goto` statement is mentioned only for the sake of your knowledge; since it is considered poor to use it in practice while programming.

Insert a label in your code at the desired destination for `goto`. The label is always terminated by a colon. The keyword `goto`, followed by this label name, takes you to label.

e.g.,
```
goto system;
        //statements
         System:
        //control will begin here following control
```

SUMMARY

In this chapter, we have learnt about 'relational operators'; its application and usefulness in conditional statements.

We also learned about various types of loops : 'while', 'do-while' and 'for loops'.

The 'for' loop is most often used when you know in advance, the number of times you want to execute the loop.

The 'do-while' loop is often used when you want to program 'data-validation' code since it is executed at least once.

The 'while' loop can be used at any time according to logic of programmer. The loop body can have one statement or group of statements.

Then we studied about 'switch' statement, which is a simplified form of nested 'if-else' conditions about various logical operators and learnt the 'precedence' table.

Now we will move forward to learn the 'structures'.

EXERCISES

1. Your meterologist friend has asked you to write a temperature conversion program. The program should read the measured temperature and output the display in both the 'Celsius' and 'Fahrenheit' scale.
2. Write a program that reads the real coefficients a, b and c (a ≠ 0) or quadratic equation $ax^2 + bx + c = 0$ and computes its real roots.

   $$\text{Formula : } \left(-b \pm \sqrt{b^2 - 4ac}\right)\Big/2a$$

   The roots are real when the discriminant $b^2 - 4ac \geq 0$. If $b^2 - 4ac = 0$, the two real roots are equal, each being $-b/2a$.
3. Create the equivalent of a four function calculator. The program should request the user to enter a number, an operator, another number. Then carry out specified arithmetical operation : adding, subtracting, multiplying or dividing two numbers.

   You had to use 'switch' statement to select operation and finally it should display result.

   After display of result, the user is prompted for yes (y) or no (n). If yes (y) then the program should re-execute, if no (n) then the user should exit the program.
4. Write a program that determines what fraction of a given text consists of vowels, using a while loop.
5. Write a program that reads an integer N and computes N! using a loop of 'do-while' and 'for' loop.
6. Write a program to calculate acceleration, velocity and height of test rockets as per the following formula :

$$\text{Acceleration} = 4.25 - 0.015t^2 + \frac{6.07t^{2.75}}{9995} \ \text{ft/sec}^2$$

$$\text{Velocity} = 4.25t - \frac{0.015t^3}{3} + \frac{6.07t^{3.75}}{3.75 * 9995} \ \text{ft/sec}$$

$$\text{Height} = 90 + \frac{4.25t^2}{2} - \frac{0.015t^4}{12} + \frac{6.07t^{4.75}}{4.75}$$

Where t is time elapsed in seconds.

5

Structures

We have seen the inbuilt variables like `int`, `char` and `float`. These type of variables represent one item of information at a time.

C++ has a way to construct user-defined datatype called as 'structure'. The 'structure' consists of a group of datatypes.

5.1 Structures

A 'structure' is a collection of simple variables. The variables in a structure can be of different types *i.e.*, one can be 'int', other can be 'float' and so on.

The data items in a structure are called as 'members' of structure. An understanding of a 'structure' is very essential since it forms the building block for understanding 'classes and objects'.

A Simple Structure

Let us start with a structure that contains three variables : two integers and a floating-point number. This structure consists of a company part with particular model number and the cost associated with it.

This program specifies the structure called `part`.

Listing 5.1 :

```
//#a program that demonstrates structures
#include<iostream.h>
struct part                        //specify a structure
    {
        int model;
        int part;
        float cost;
    };
    void main()
    {
        part p1;                   //define a structure variable
```

```
        p1.model=6244;          /*gives value to
        p1.part=575;            structure members*/
        p1.cost=8.54;
        cout<<''\n  Model''<<p1.model;
        cout<<''\n  Part''<<p1.part;
        cout<<''\n  Cost''<<p1.cost;
    }
```

Explanation of Listing 5.1

Here is the explanation of the program listed above.

Syntax of Structure

The keyword `struct` introduces the specifier. It is a reserved keyword of C and C++.

Next comes the 'tag-name' `part`. The structure members : `model` of type `int`, `part` of type integer and `cost` of type float are declared inside the braces. Then comes the semicolon (;) after the close of braces which indicates the termination of the declaration of structure.

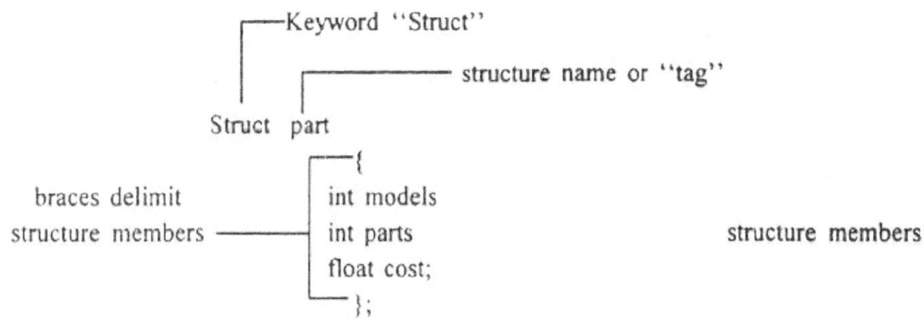

Fig. 5.1

SYNTAX OF STRUCTURE SPECIFIER

Defining a Structure Variable

The first statement in main () is

```
part p1;
```

which defines a variable 'p1' of data-type `part`. The part is a 'structure', so this definition reserves some space in the memory. But you will ask, how much memory, will it reserve ?

The answer is it occupies that much space of memory that is equal to the sum of individual members of a structure.

So in our case, the total memory reserved for `struct part` is 2 bytes of model which is integer data-type; +2 bytes of part, +4 bytes of cost which is float data-type.

So, structure part = 2 + 2 + 4

= 8 bytes.

The total memory reserved by variable p1 is 8 bytes.

If you look at the definition, it closely resembles the inbuilt data-type like integer.

This similarity is not accidental, but C++ provides the syntax in such a way that 'user-defined' data-type like 'structure' closely resembles the 'inbuilt data-type' like 'integer'.

Note. In 'C', while declaring a structure variable you had to use 'struct' keyword in structure definition.

So part p1 becomes

struct part p1 in C.

But, in C++, the keyword is not necessary.

5.2 Accessing Structure Members

Once a structure variable is defined, its members can be accessed using a dot (.) operator.

Here, in our example we have;

```
p1.model  =  6244;
```

The structure member is written in three parts : first, the name of structure variable p1, (remember, not the name of structure *i.e.*, tagname); second the dot operator (.) and finally the member name (model). This means 'model' is a member of 'p1'.

This completes the explanation of structures. Now, we can move on and see how to implement the structures as a complex entity.

You can use nested structures for that, *i.e.*, structure within a structure.

5.3 Nested Structures (Structures within Structures)

You can nest one structure within another structure and it can extend to any depth.

Here we consider an example of nested structure.

Listing 5.2 :

```
//demonstrates nested structures
#include<iostream.h>
struct distance
    {
        int feet;
        float inches;
    };
    struct room                         //nested structure distance
    {                                   //inside a structure
        distance length;                //room
        distance width;
    };
    void main()
    {
        room d;                         //define a room
        d.length.feet=13;
        d.length.inches=20.0;           //assign values to
        d.width.feet=5;                 //room
        d.width.inches=6.25;
        float l=d.length.feet+d.length.inches/12;
        cout<<''\n the length is:''<<l;
```

Explanation of Listing 5.2

This program defines a single variable `d` of type `room`. The structure `room` is nested inside the other structure `distance`. To access any member variable inside the structure `distance`, we have to use the dot operator twice. So, here in our program, we have

```
d.length.feet=13;
```

In this statement, we are accessing a member variable `feet` inside a structure `distance` via member variable `length` which is again, inside a structure `room`.

Then the length is calculated and displayed. So this statement means that the `feet` member of `length` member of variable `d` of type `room` is taken.

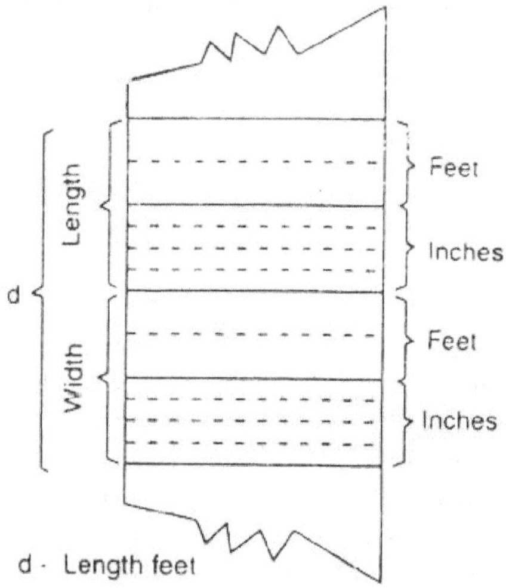

Fig. 5.2

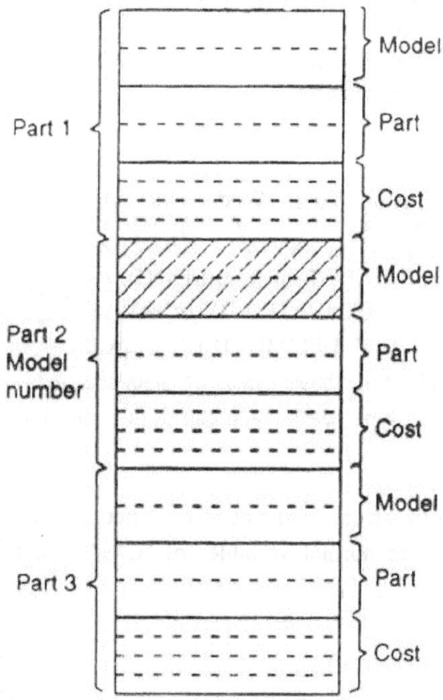

Fig. 5.3

5.4 The Data Operator

Enumerated Data-Types

As we've seen, the user can make their own data-types by using 'structures'. There is another approach to define our own data-type which is the 'enumerated data-type'.

This feature is less crucial than 'structures' since good object-oriented programs can be written in 'C++' even without the knowledge of 'enumerated data-types'. Since it exists in all programming languages, it is included here for knowledge-sake. It entirely depends on programmers, to use it or not in professional practice.

Enumerated types work when you know in advance, a finite list of values that a data-type can take on.

Listing 5.3 :

```
//demonstrates enum types
#include<iostream.h>
enum days {Sun, Mon, Tue, Wed, Thu, Fri, Sat};
void main()
    {
            days d1, d2;              //define variables
            d1=Mon;                   //values given to
            d2=Sun;                   //variables
        int difference=d2-d1;
        cout<<''Days between=''<<difference<<endl;
        if(d1<d2)                     //can do comparisons
        cout<<''Day1 comes before Day2\n'';
    }
```

Explanation of Listing 5.3

Here, on enum specifier defines the set of all names which will be permissible values of the type. The permissible values are called the 'members'.

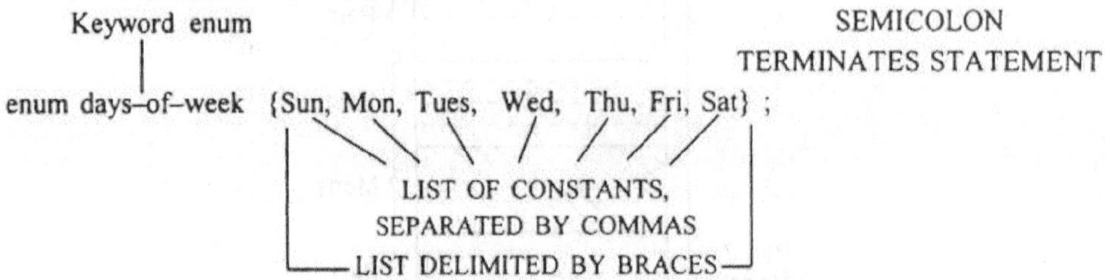

Fig. 5.4. Shows syntax of enum specifier.

Once you've specified the data-type 'days', you can define variables of that data-type. In our example, we defined it as :

```
days d1, d2;
```

In C++, the reserved keyword enum need not to be typed while defining the variables.

These variables can be used as normal variables of 'C++'. But the values that are not listed in specifier cannot be used.

For example,

```
d1 = sweet;
```

is illegal since sweet is not specified in the list.

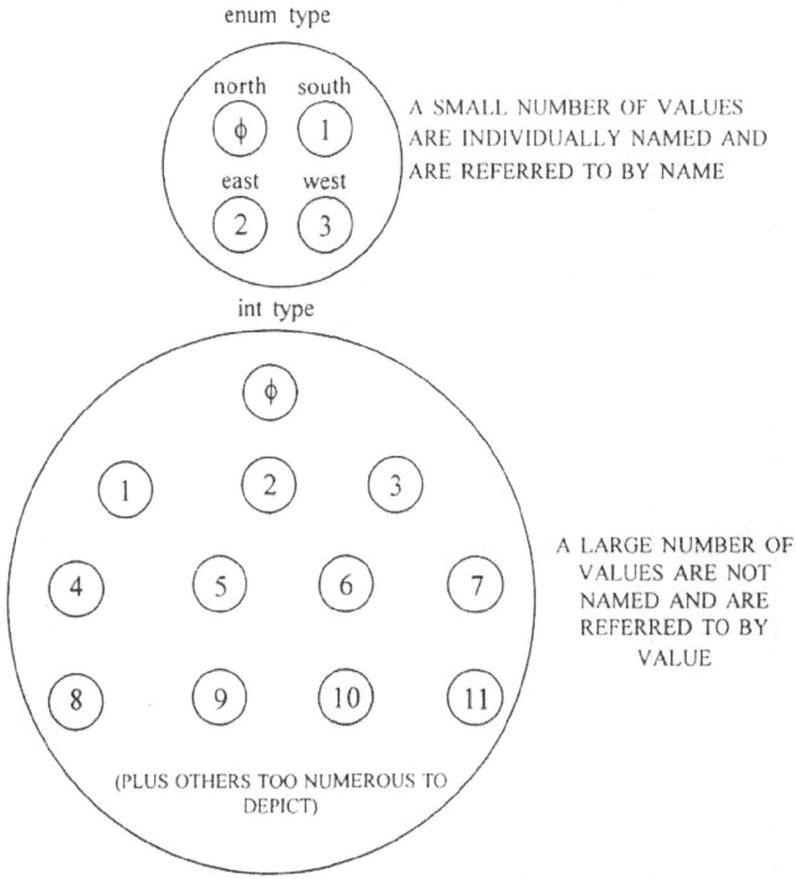

Fig. 5.5. Use of int's and enum's

SUMMARY

We have covered here the structures and enumerated data-type since they are important components of C++, and their syntax is same as classes.

Structures are typically used to define the user-defined data-types. It denotes the collection of data of different data-types; which are packaged to form a single user-defined data-type. So it is a complex form of datatype. A structure definition allocates the definite memory block for a certain amount of storage.

Structures should not be confused with the enumerated datatypes since they are programmer-defined type which is limited to a fixed list of values. Internally, the compiler treats enumerated variables as integers.

EXERCISES

1. Create a structure called 'Volume' that uses three variables of type 'Distance' to model the volume of a room. Initialize a variable of type 'Volume' to specific dimensions and calculate the volume. Convert each dimension from 'Distance' variable to 'float' type variable to calculate volume.
2. Define a structure to represent time in hours (0—23), minutes (0—59) and seconds (0—59) and then write a function that accepts as an argument a time represented by this structure and updates it by 1 second.
3. Define a structure for employee record :
   (*a*) name
   (*b*) date of birth
   (*c*) maritial status :
      (*i*) married ⇒ name of spouse
      (*ii*) widowed ⇒ date of marriage
      (*iii*) divorced ⇒ date of divorce
      (*iv*) single
   (*d*) children
   (*e*) annual salary.

   Write a program to display the structure as per record number.

6

Functions

A function groups a number of program statements into a unit and gives it a name. This unit can be called and involved from any part of the main( ) program.

The *functions* are used to increase the modularity of the programs and packages. By use of functions, the size of the individual program reduces and the function code, when used repeatedly in the main( ) program code, executes as many times as it is declared. But it is stored in only one place in the memory.

6.1 Functions

We demonstrate here the first simple example of functions, so that you can understand the concept of function more easily from the example.

Listing 6.1 :

```
//demonstrates simple function
#include<iostream.h>
void line();                          //function declaration
void main()
   {
      line();                         //call to function
      cout<<''Data type Meaning''<<endl;
      line();                         //call to function
      cout<<''char character''<<endl;
      <<''int integer''<<endl;
      <<''float floating-point''<<endl;
      line( );                        //call to function
   }
   //function definition of line()
   void line()
```

```
{
    for (int  i=0;  i<45;  i++)
    cout<<'-';
    cout<<endl;
}
```

Explanation of Listing 6.1

The above program consists of two functions: `main( )` and `line( )`. Since we have already seen the use of the `main( )` previously; without which the `.exe` file of 'C++' source code cannot be formed. Other than `main( )`, our own defined function is `line( )`. The components necessary to add a function are : function declaration, calls to function and function definition.

Function Declaration

The statement we encountered in `main( )` program is :

```
void line( );
```

As we can't use the variable before declaring it, similarly, we cannot use the function also before declaring it.

The declaration indicates the compiler that at some later point the declared function will be used. The keyword 'void' in function indicates that the function has no return value, and empty paranthesis indicate that it takes no arguments. Since the function declaration which is also called as 'prototype' is considered as a statement; it is terminated with semicolon.

Calling a Function

After declaring a function, we call it from the main( ) when required. This is known as invoking of a function.

```
line( );
```

Thus, we always need to invoke a function as the function name followed by parantheses. This syntax is very similar to function declaration except that the return type is not used.

Execution of the call statement sends the program control to the named function, executes that function and control returns to the statement following the function call.

Function Declaration Definition

Finally, we come to the function itself, which is referred to as 'function definition'. This definition refers to actual code of function :

```
line();
void  line()
{
    for (i=0;  i<45;  i++)
    cout<<'-';
    cout<<endl;
{
```

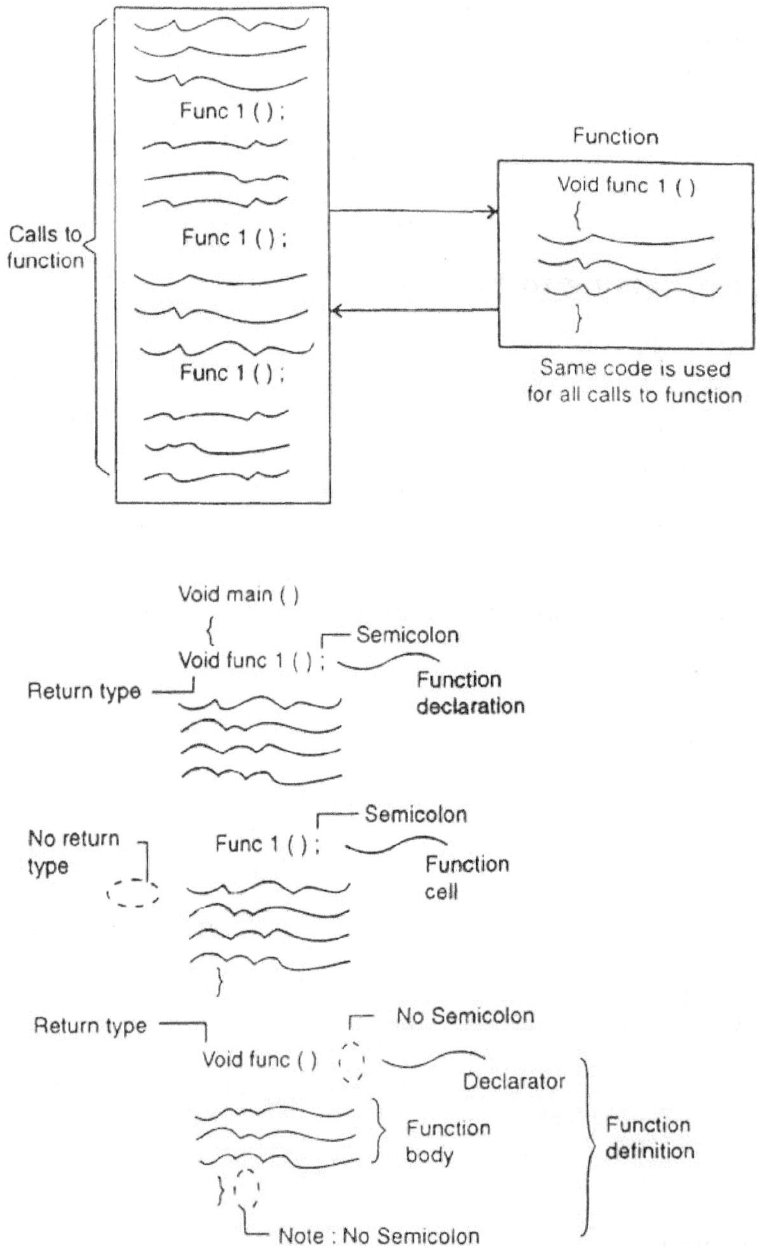

Fig. 6.1

The definition consists of a line :

```
void line();
```

It is called the declarator which is not terminated by semicolon (;) : The control after executing the declarator statements enters the function body and executes it. When the control encounters the closing brace—it returns to the calling program.

This completes the explanation of the listed program.

Eliminating the Declaration

One can eliminate the function declaration if the function definition appears in the listing before the first call to function.

So the user should write the code of function before the main( ) function code.

6.2 Arguments Passing to Functions

An argument is a piece of data passed from a program to function in order to operate with different values.

One can pass three different types of things to the functions :

(*i*) Passing Constants
(*ii*) Passing Variables
(*iii*) Passing by Value.

Passing Constants

In last example we have seen that, in `line( )` function, it always prints 45 '-' dashes everytime when it is called. Instead we can make a function that prints any passed 'character' any number of times.

Listing 6.2 :

```
//demonstrates function arguments
#include<iostream.h>
void repchar(char, int)                  //function prototype
void main()
   {
      repchar('*',50);                   //call to function
      cout<<''Data Printed''<<endl;
      repchar('-',40);                   //call to function
   }
   //repchar function
   void repchar(char ch, int n)          //function declarator
      {
         for (int i=0; i<n; i++)         //function body
         cout<<ch;
         cout<<endl;
      }
```

Explanation of Listing 6.2

In the above listing, the new function called `repchar (char, int)` has two data-types in paranthesis; integer and character.

When the function is invoked, the two items of data-types *'character' 'char'* and *'integer' 'int'* are passed to function *'repchar'*.

When repchar is invoked first time;

```
repchar ('*', 50);
```

The character '*' and integer '50' are passed from main( ) program to *'repchar'* function. These constants are captured in the variables which are in the paranthesis of *'repchar'* function (in our function; variables are 'ch' and 'n'). Then the function is executed and returns to the calling program.

The same procedure is repeated when the function is called again in main( );

```
repchar ('—', 40);
```

When the function is called, its parameters are automatically initialized to the value passed by the calling program.

Passing Variables

In the above example, the arguments which were passed were constants : '*', 50 and so on.

Instead of constants, we can also pass the variables. Passing the variables is flexible, because every time the user can input new values to be stored in variables and function behaves accordingly when invoked.

Listing 6.3 :

```
//demonstrates variable arguments
#include<iostream.h>
void repchar(char, int)                 //prototype of function
void main()
    {
        char ch;
        int n;
        cout<<''Enter character:''>;
        cin>>ch;
        cout<<''Enter number of times to repeat it:'';
        cin>>n;
        repchar(ch,n);
    }
    //repchar function
    void repchar(char ch, int n)
        {
            for (int i=0; i<n; i++)
            cout<<ch;
            cout<<endl;
        }
```

Explanation of Listing 6.3

Here, the working of program code and function code is same as in previous example except that the data-types of variables are used as arguments to be passed. In our example, the arguments passed are 'ch' and 'n'.

Passing by Value

In listing 6.3, the particular values possessed by ch and n will pass to the function as soon as the function call is executed. As the constants are passed, the function creates new variables to hold the values of these variable arguments. The function gives these new variables the names and data-types of parameters specified in the function prototype, as in our case : 'ch' of type 'char' and 'n' of type 'int'. It initializes these parameters to the values passed.

Passing arguments in this way, where the function creates copies of arguments passed to it, is called 'passing by value'.

Returning Values from Functions

When a function completes its execution, it returns a single value to calling program. That return value usually is an answer to the problem solved by the function.

Listing 6.4 :

```
//demonstrates return values
#include<iostream.h>
float convert (float);
void main()
    {
        float gms;
        cout<<''/n enter your weight in grams:'';
        cin>>gm;
        cout<<''Your weight in kgs is''<<convert(gm);
    }
    //function convert
      float convert (float g)
        {
            return 1000xg;
        }
```

Explanation of Listing 6.4

The return statement. An argument representing a weight in 'grams' is passed to the function `convert`. It stores it in parameter 'g'. It calculates the corresponding weight in 'kilograms' and returns to the calling program using a 'return' statement.

6.3 Reference Arguments

We've seen examples of function arguments passed by value. When arguments are passed by value, the called function creates a new variable of some type as the argument and copies the argument value into it. So original value is not transferred but only a copy of it is created in the calling program.

Passing arguments by 'reference' uses a different mechanism. Instead of value being passed to the function, a reference to the original variable is passed to the calling program. The primary advantage of this is, the function can access the original variables of the calling program.

Listing 6.5 :

```
//demonstrates reference arguments
#include<iostream.h>
void main()
    {
```

```
        void intfrac(float, float &, float &);  //prototype
        float number, int part, fract; //variables
        do
        {
            cout<<''\n Enter a real number:'';
            cin>>number;
            intfrac(number, intpart, fract);
            cout<<''Integer:''<<int part<<'',fraction:<<fract;
        }   while(number!=0);              //exit on 0
    }
    //intfrac function
    void intfrac(float n, float & inta, float & frac)
        {
            intp=float(log(n));
            frac=n-inta;
        }
```

Explanation of Listing 6.5

In the program listed above, the *'reference'* arguments are indicated by ampersand (&) following the data-type of argument :

```
float & inta;
```

The '&' indicates that *'inta'* is an alias or another name for whatever variable passed as an argument (in our case, variable is intpart). In other words, one can use name *'inta'* in the *'intfrac'* function, while he is actually referring to *'intpart'* in *'main()'*.

From the function call alone, it cannot be said whether an argument will be passed by reference or by value.

In our example, the variables *'intpart'* and *'fract'* are passed by *'reference'* while variable number is passed by *'value'*.

6.4 Default Arguments

Can you call a function without specifying all its arguments ? (Remember, in void function also, 'void' argument has to be passed.)

The answer is 'no'. It will work on any function. If you want it to work, you should provide the 'default values' in the 'function prototype' so that the function considers the 'default values' as 'arguments' when no 'argument' is supplied externally. Let's take an example and understand it practically. We again take same example of listing 6.2, but with a different approach.

Listing 6.6 :

```
//demonstrates default arguments
#include<iostream.h>
void repchar(char='*', int=45);          //prototype
                                         //with default arguments
void main()
    {
```

```
    repchar();                     //prints 45 asteriks
    repchar(?);                    //prints 45 question marks
    repchar('+',20)                //prints 20 plus signs
}
//function repchar
void repchar(char c, int n)
    {
        for (int i=0; i<n; i++)
        cout<<c<<endl;
    }
```

Explanation of Listing 6.6

In the program listed above, first time the function from 'main( )' is called with no arguments, second time with one argument and third time with two arguments.

Then why do first two calls work ?

They work because the called function provides the default arguments, which will be used if calling program doesn't supply them.

The default arguments are specified in the prototype to 'upchar( )' :

```
void repchar (char='*', int=45);
```

The default argument follows an equal sign, which is placed directly after type name.

If one argument is missing when the function is called, it is assumed to be the lost argument. The 'repchar( )' function assigns the value of single argument to 'ch' variable and uses default value 45 to 'n' variable.

If both the arguments are missing, then the default value '*' is assigned to 'ch' variable and default value '45' is assigned to 'n' variable.

These are useful in cases, where the programmer wants to increase capability of a function by adding another argument after a program is written.

6.5 Storage Classes

The 'storage class' of a 'variable' determines the part of the program that can access that variable and it can stay in existence.

There are three storage classes :

1. Automatic
2. External
3. Static.

1. Automatic Variables

Variables defined inside a function body or in a main( ) body (since main( ) is a function) are termed as 'automatic' variables. However, since this a default type of declaring a variable, there is seldom any need to use the 'auto' keyword.

```
void func1() {
int var1=10;        //automatic variables
float var2=10.5;
}
```

An 'automatic' variable is not created until the function in which it is defined, is called. So the variables var1, var2 do not exist until the function func1 is executed. That is, there is no place in memory where their values are stored, *i.e.*, they are undefined.

When control is transferred to the function func1 ( ), storage space for variables var1 and var2 are allocated in the memory and this is called 'automatic' creation of variables on execution of the function.

On exit of the function func1 ( ), the created variables are 'automatically' destroyed. Since the construction and destruction of variables are done automatically, they are termed as 'automatic' variables.

The scope of these variables, also termed as visibility, is inside the function only. So the programmer can use the variables of 'same names' in two different functions.

Automatic variables are also called 'local' variables, since they are visible only 'locally' inside the function.

2. External Variables

Automatic variables are defined inside the function while 'external variables' are defined outside the function. They are also called 'global variables'.

Here we take a program in which all 3 functions can access the external variables.

Listing 6.7 :

```
//demonstrates external variables
#include<iostream.h>
#include<conio.h>                      //for getch()
    char ch='z';                       //external variable ch
    void getachar();                   //function prototype
    void putachar();
    void main()
    {
        while(ch!='\n')
            {
                getachar()
                putachar()
            }
    }
    void getachar()
        {
            ch=getch();
        }
    void putachar()
        {
            cout<<ch;
        }
```

Explanation of Listing 6.7

In the program listed above, the significant thing is that the variable ch is not defined in any of functions. Instead, it is defined as a global variable (above main( )). It is an external variable and any function that follows the definition of ch in program can access it. So in this case the visibility of variable ch is in all the functions (in entire source file).

Thus, external variables exist for the entire program *i.e.*, the memory space is set aside for them since the program begins and it exists till the program ends.

The external variables are destroyed only after the termination of the entire program.

Static Variables

A static automatic variable has a visibility of 'local' variable but scope of 'external' variable. Thus it is visible only inside a function in which it is defined, but it remains in existence for entire program.

It is defined by using a keyword `static` before defining a variable.

e.g., static float count = 0;

It is used when function has to remember a value which is not being executed, *i.e.*, between calls to the function.

6.6 Recursion

'Recursion' is a process whereby a function operates on itself. Functions may be defined recursively; *i.e.*, a function may directly or indirectly call itself in course of its execution.

If a call to a function occurs inside a function itself, the recursion call is said to be 'direct'.

If a call to a function occurs by another function, which in turn makes a call to the first one, the recursion call to be 'indirect' is said.

Listing 6.8 :

In this listing, we are not giving entire program of C++ but only a function is given which loops recursively. So you can use this function anywhere in your main( ) program.

This remains an exercise to the readers.

```
int  factorial(int  n)
     {
        if (n= =0)
           return  1;                   /*termination  of
        else                            program*/
        return  n*factorial(n-1);   *recursive*/
     }
```

In this program factorial function is used as a 'direct recursion'.

SUMMARY

Functions provide a way to structured programming. It helps to reduce the individual program size. It enhances the modularity of the programs.

Functions arguments can be passed by value or by reference.

Functions can return only one value at a time. Arguments and return types can be either single data-types or structures or any user defined data-types.c

Functions can be used recursively and with default arguments so that it may not include all the arguments.

Variables possess a characteristic of a storage class which defines the scope and life of the variable inside a function.

In the last chapter we had seen the 'structures' and in this chapter we have seen the 'functions'. Now we can gather the knowledge of these two to understand next chapter—'objects and classes'.

EXERCISES

1. Write a program to calculate partial sums of harmonic series :

$$1 + \frac{1}{2} + \frac{1}{3} + \ldots + \frac{1}{n}.$$

The result should be in rational form *i.e.*, in $\frac{\text{numerator}}{\text{denominator}}$.

2. Define a function to calculate

$(x^2 + y^2 + z^2)^{1/2}$ and use it to calculate

$$\alpha = \frac{1}{\left(u^2 + v^2 + w^2\right)^{1/2}}, \qquad \beta = (3u^2)^{1/2}\,(12v^2)^{1/2}\,(27w^2)^{1/2}$$

$(u^2 + v^2 + w^2)^{1/2}$

3. Write a recursive function to print an integer as a string.
4. Write a program to find mean $\bar{x}$ and standard deviation σ using a formula :

$$\bar{x} = \frac{\sum_{i=1}^{n} x_i}{n}, \qquad \sigma^2 = \frac{n\sum_{i=1}^{n} x_i^2 - \left[\sum_{i=1}^{n} x_i\right]^2}{n(n-1)}$$

5. Write a following recursive function for following sawtooth.

7

Classes and Objects

Now we have reached the topic that you are waiting for : classes and objects. We have already learnt about structures; it provides a way to group data variables and functions to organize program action and provide modularity to the program code.

Now we will combine the ideas of 'structures' and 'functions' and implement it in 'classes' and 'objects'. We will start the chapter with simple class examples moving on to complicated ones.

This is an OOP concept and at the end of chapter we'll discuss its benefits.

7.1 Classes

A class is similar to the structure definition. The specifier starts with a `class` keyword, followed by the class name. Like a structure, it is delimited by braces ({}) and terminated by a semicolon (;).

So first, we define a class and implement it, with help of a small program.

Listing 7.1 :

```
//demonstrates class
#include<iostream.h>
class small                              //specify a class
    {
        private:
        int data;                        //class data
        public:
        void setdata(ent d)              //member function
            {                            //setdata
                data=d;
            }
        void show()
            {
                cout<<''in data is:''<<data<<endl;
            }
```

```
};
void main()
    {
        small s1, s2;            //define two objects s1, s2
        s1.setdata(100);         //of class named small
        s2.setdata(150);
        s1.show();               //call member function
        s2.show();
    }
```

Explanation of Listing 7.1

Here, in above program, the specifier starts with a keyword *'class'* followed by class name *'small'* and is terminated by semicolon. In this way the class is defined.

But in definition we come across two unfamiliar keywords *'private'* and *'public'*. Let us discuss them in detail.

7.2 Private and Public

The main aim of applying 'OOP' concept is data-hiding. These terms mean the conceding of data within a class, so that it cannot be accessed mistakenly by the functions outside the class. So the primary mechanism for hiding the data is to put in a class and make it 'private' since 'private' data or functions can only be accessed within the class.

In our example, the 'data' of type integer is made private. The 'data' can be accessed from inside the class only and cannot be directly accessed even from main( ) function or any outside function.

On the other hand, the functions 'setdata' and 'show' are made public so that they are accessible even from outside the class. These functions are called 'member functions' or 'methods' of the class.

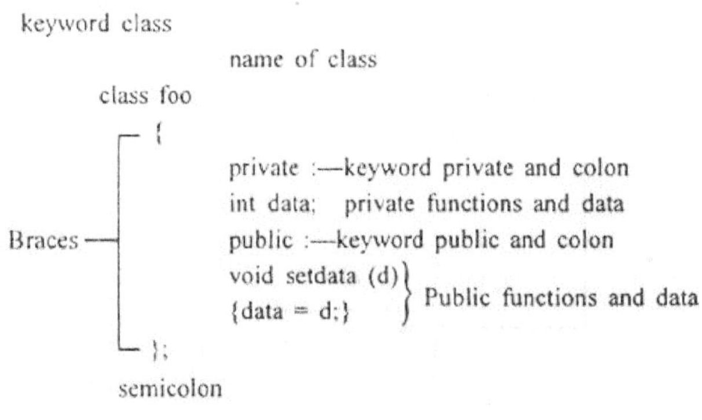

Fig. 7.1. Syntax of a Class Specifier

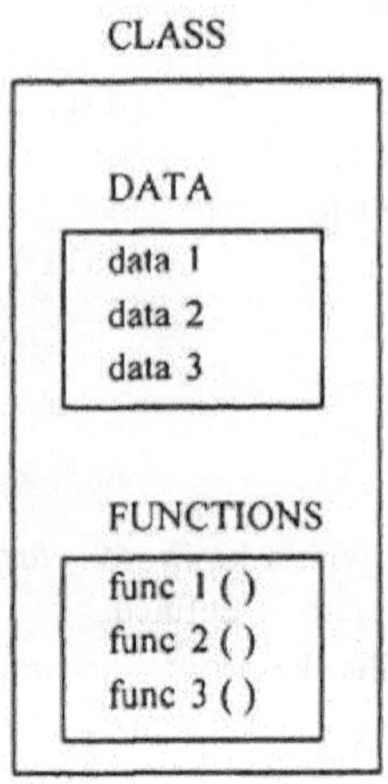

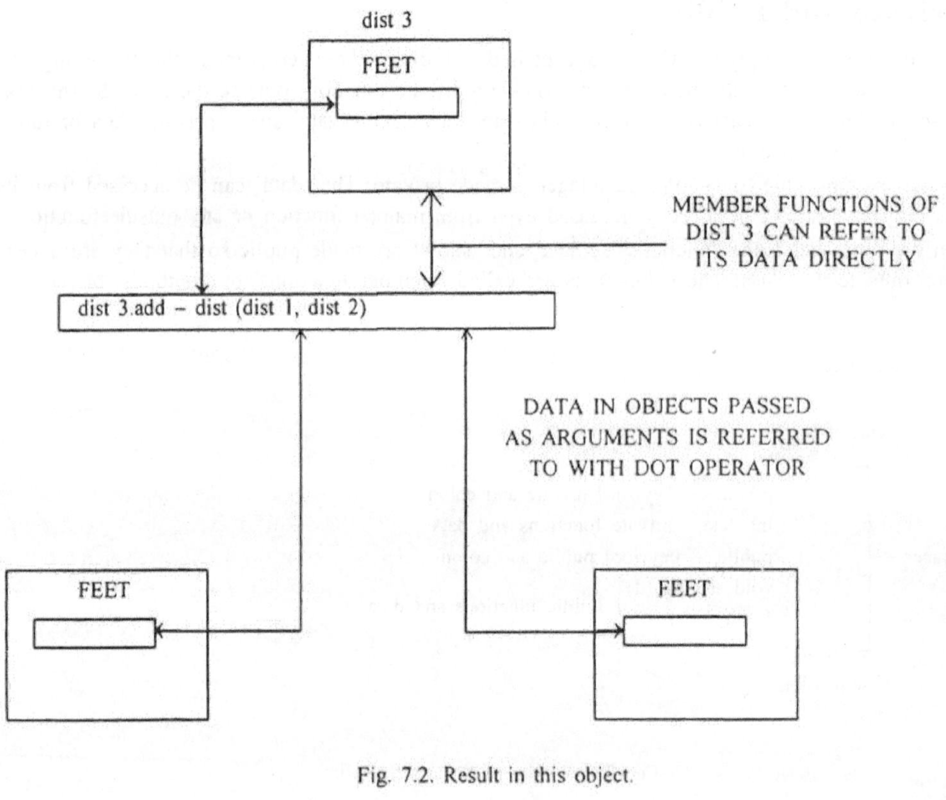

Fig. 7.2. Result in this object.

7.3 Usages of Class : Objects

Since we know that we can now make user-defined data-types by using structures and classes, we can define the variables to that class (user-defined data-type). These variables are called 'objects'.

In our program, the statement

```
small s1, s2;
```

defines two objects `s1, s2` of class (data-type) `small`. So remember that specification of class itself does not create any object. It is the definition that actually creates objects that can be used in a program.

Thus, defining an object is very similar to defining a variable of any data-type; space is set aside in memory after declaration of the object.

Calling Member Functions

The next two statements in *main()* call the member function *setdata()* :

```
s1.setdata (100);
s2.setdata (150);
```

If you see these member functions, you will notice that the function `setdata` is associated to the object `s2` with a dot operator. This dot operator is called as *'class'* member *'access'* operator.

Remember, the call of function without attaching it to a object has no meaning.

```
setdata (100); //meaningless
```

This is because a member function is always called to act on a specific object, not on class in general. Member functions of a class can be accessed only by an object of that class.

You can also see that, the value '100' in braces is passed as an argument to 'data' variable of type integer.

Recall that, the 'data' variable cannot be accessed directly. It can be accessed indirectly as shown in the steps given below :

(1) The value '100' of member function 'setdata' of object s1 is passed to variable 'd' of type integer of member function 'setdata' inside a class 'small'.

(2) Then that value in parameter 'd' is assigned to the 'data' variable of type integer.

(3) That value in 'data' variable is printed with help of 'show' member function.

This completes the listing of 7.1.

7.4 Constructors and Destructors

What is a constructor ?

A special member function which is automatically initialized is called a *constructor* and it is executed automatically whenever an object is created.

Let us take one example to understand it.

Listing 7.2 :

```
//demonstrates constructor and destructor
#include<iostream.h>
class time
    {
        Private:
        int hrs, mins, secs;
```

```
        public:
        time()                                  //no-arg  constructor
            {
                hrs=mins=secs=0;
            }
        time(int h,  int m,  int s)             //3-arg  constructor
            {
                hrs=h;
                mins=m;
                secs=s;
            }
        void  display()
            {
                cout<<hrs<<'':''<<mins<<'':''<<secs;
            }
            time()
            {                                   //destructor  (with  some)
            }                                   //name  but  with  title
    }
        void  main()
            {
                time  t3;
                time  t4(6,25,59);              //creates  and  initialize
                cout<<''/n  the  time  is:''<<t3.display();
                cout<<''/n  the  time  is:''<<t4.display();
            }
```

Explanation of Listing 7.2

In the above example we have created two-types of constructors :

(*i*) With no argument.

(*ii*) With three arguments.

Remember, the name of constructor and name of class should be same.

First, when the object `t3` of type `time` is created, the functional constructor with no arguments is invoked since we did not `supply` any arguments while defining a object `t3`.

Another time, when object `t4` is created, the constructor with three arguments is invoked and initialized with the arguments passed from main( ) function.

After completing the execution of the program, another function known as *'destructor'* is called automatically.

The *destructor* function has a same name as of constructor function but with a 'tilde' character. This is called to destroy the object and hence, all the values associated with it.

Destructors do not have any return value and they do not take any arguments.

Use of Objects as Functions

Here we will see how to use objects as the arguments in a function.

Listing 7.3 :

```
//demonstrates objects as function arguments
#include<iostream.h>
Class Dist
    {
        private:
          int feet;
        public:
          Dist()
            {                                   //constructor (no-args)
        feet=0;
            }
        Dist(int ft)                            //constructor (1-arg)
            {
        feet=ft;
            }
        void getdist()
            {
                cout<<''\n Enter feet:'';
                cin>>feet;
            }
        void showdist()
            {
                cout<<feet;
            }
        Dist add (Dist);                        //add function
    };
        Dist Dist::add(Dist d2)
            {
                Dist t;
                t.feet+=feet+d2.feet;
                retur t;
            }
        void main()
            {
                Dist d1, d3;                    //define two lengths
                Dist d2(20);
                d1.getdist();
                d3=d1.add(d2)                   //d3=d1+d2
        cout<<''In d1='';d1.showdist();
        cout<<''In d2='';d2.showdist();
        cout<<''In d3='';d3.showdist();
    }
```

Explanation of Listing 7.3

So far we've seen member functions that were defined inside the class specifier. But if you want you can also declare the function prototype inside the class as :

```
Dist add (dist);
```

This tells the compiler that the function is a member of a class but defined outside the class.

The external declaration of a class can be defined by naming the function preceded by (::) scope resolution operator and the class name.

In our example :

```
Dist Dist :: add (Dist d2)
```

This means that the function add is declared of type `Dist` with a return type `Dist` and is joined by (: :) scope resolution operator.

Thus, add is a member function of `Dist` class. Here d2 of type `Dist` is passed as an argument. Here, how the 'object' 'd2' is passed as function argument. It is added to object d1, of which 'add' is a member function and result is assigned to object 'd3'.

The result is stored in 't' variable which is then returned by function using the statement.

```
return t;
```

This completes the explanation of the listing.

Storage Pattern

By viewing and understanding the previous examples, you might have guessed that each object created from class might have a separate copy of that class's data and function. This is good as first approximation, since it emphasizes that the objects are complete, self-contained entities.

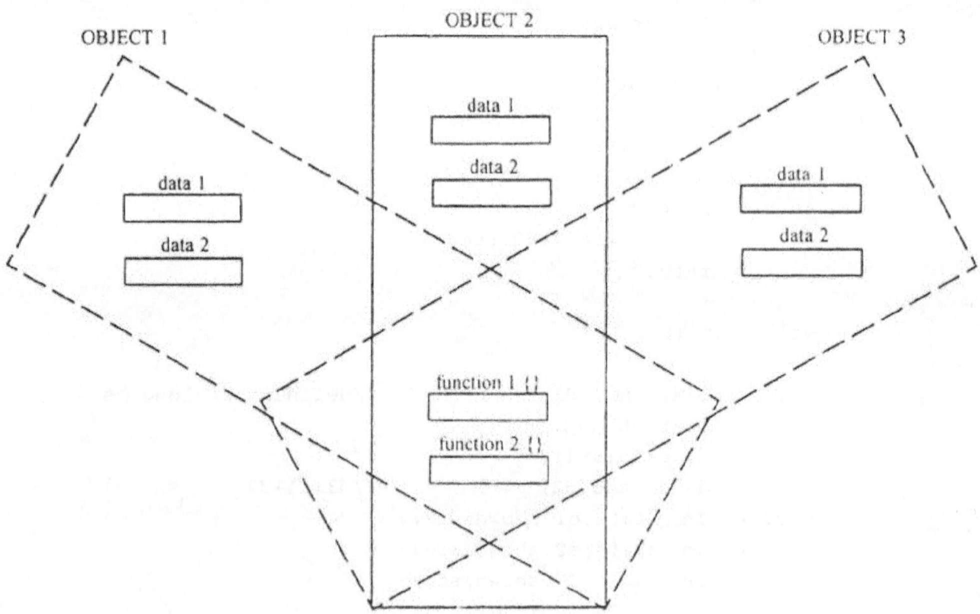

Fig. 7.3. Objects, Data, Functions and Memory.

But, this mental image is not true. The member functions are created and placed in a memory only once-when they are defined inside a class. They are not duplicated by every creation of new object but shared by all the objects.

Since data items hold different values, there is a separate instance of each data item in each object.

This is how it is stored in the memory.

Benefits of 'OOP' Concept

The benefits of object oriented programming is that it provides the connection of modelling a simulation of a software object with a real-world object.

You can break the program into smaller modules and it can be used in any part of project as and when necessary.

It also provides the facility of raising the object again without coding it for another time. This prevents the code redundancy and thus saves the time.

SUMMARY

A class is a specification for number of objects which consists of both data and functions that operate on data. There are three types of class specifiers :

(*i*) Private : provides access only by member functions of that class.

(*ii*) Public : provides access by any function in program.

(*iii*) Protected : provides access only by inherited functions.

Constructors and destructors are used inside the class. OOP provides close correspondence between real world objects and OOP classes.

EXERCISES

1. Create a class named time and write a program that displays the time in format : 11 : 20 : 25 which is a format of hour : mins : secs.
2. Write a program to develop various shapes where shape is name of a class. Using shape class, write a program to develop square and rectangle as the output.
3. Write a class of box. Using that class, write a program to display boxes of various shapes and sizes.

8

Arrays

8.1 What is an Array ?

In our daily life, it is our common tendency to group similar things into one unit. Similarly, we can group several elements of same data-type in single unit called as *array* in C and C++.

For example, 100 integer numbers are to be stored in one variable, it can be done using a mechanism of *array*.

We shall see the definition and fundamentals of array by taking one example below :

Fundamentals of Array

Listing 8.1 :

```
//demonstrates  array  fundamentals
#include<iostream.h>
void  main()
    {
        int  dob[8];             //array  'dob'  of  8  integers
        for  (int  i=0;  i<8;  i++)
        {                        //get  8  dob
            cout<<''Enter  date  of  birth:'';
            cin>>dob[i];         //access  array  element
        }
        for  (i=0;  i<8;  i++)  //display  8  dob
        cout<<''/n  you  entered  dob:''<<dob[i];
    }
```

Explanation of Listing 8.1

Like another variables in C++, an array also has to be defined before it can be used to store information and like other definitions, an array specifies a variable type and name. But it includes another additional feature : a size.

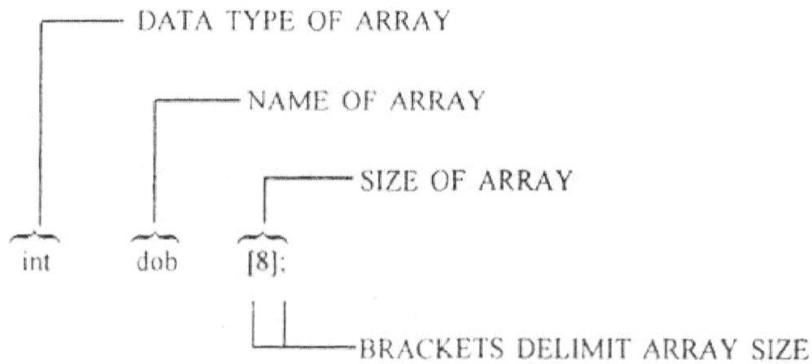

Fig. 8.1. Size of Arrray Definition

The items in an array are called elements which are of same data-type. Here in our example, since 'dob' is of type integer, it accupies two bytes of memory for each item.

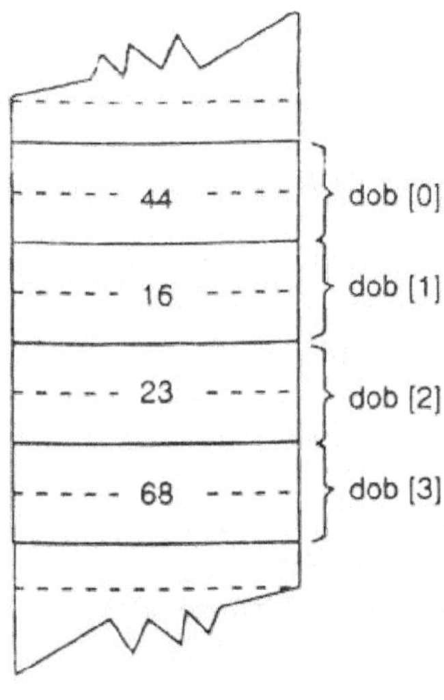

Fig. 8.2

8.2 Accessing Array Elements

In the above example, we are accessing the array elements in a loop. Since we have to input 8 elements one by one, we take a counter and input 8 different elements one by one, everytime by increasing a counter value.

Similarly, it prints all the elements of an array by taking a loop one by one.

Array Initialization

You can give values to each element at the time of defining an array. Suppose if you want to define 12 array elements in array days, then it is as follows :

int days [12] = {31, 28, 31, 30, 31, 30, 31, 31, 30, 31, 30, 31};

You can also define the above definition in a different way :

int days [ ] = {31, 28, 31, 30, 31, 30, 31, 31, 30, 31, 30, 31};

Compiler can figure out by counting the intializing variables.

Multidimensional Arrays

So far, we have seen an array of one dimension, *i.e.*, a single-dimensional array since it specifies only one array position at a time.

An array with two or more dimensions is called a multidimensional array.

Listing 8.2 :

```
//demonstrates multidimensional array
#include<iostream.h>
const int districts=4;                  //array dimensions
const int months=6;
void main()
  {
     int d, m;
     int sales [districts][months]       //2-dimensional
     cout<<endl;                          //array
     for(d=0; d<districts; d++)
     for (m=0; m<months; m++)
        {
           cout<<''Enter sales:''<<d+1;
           cout<<'',month:''<<m+1;
           cin>>sales[d][m]              //put number in array
        }
     for(d=0; d<districts; d++)
        {
           cout<<''\n District''<<d+1;
           for(m=0; m<months; m++)
           cout<<sales[d][m]<<endl;
     } //end for
  } //end main
```

Explanation of Listing 8.2

In the above example, the array is defined with two size specifiers as,

`int sales [districts] [months];`

The statement means that `sales` is array of arrays. There is an array `district` in which each district is again an array of months.

It can be shown as :

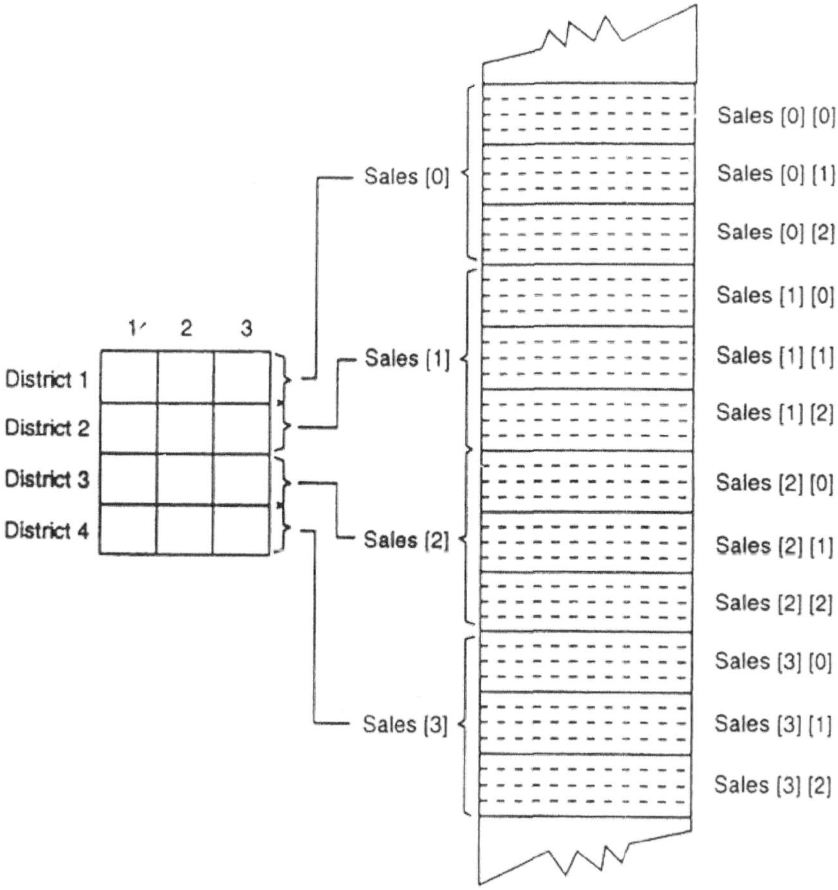

Fig. 8.3

An array of 2-dimensions requires two indexes. So it has to be written only as Sales [d] [m] & cannot be written as Sales [d, m].

Similarly, you can write three dimensional arrays as sales [d] [m] [i] and so on.

Array As Function Arguments

Arrays can be used as other data-types, as arguments to functions. Here is an example of it.

Listing 8.3 :

```
//demonstrates array as arguments
#include<iostream.h>
```

```
const int district=4;                          //array dimensions
const int months=6;
void display(int[districts][months]);          //function prototype
void main()
    {
        int d, m;
        int sales[districts][months];
        cout<<endl;
        for(d=0; d<districts; d++)
        for(m=0; m<months; m++)
            {
                cout<<''Enter sales:''<<d+1;
                cout<<'',month:''<<m+1;
                cin>>sales[d][m]                //put number in array
        }
        display(sales);                         //function call
    }
    // function to display 2-d array passed as argument
void display(int funcsales[districts][months])
    {
        int d, m;
        for(d=0; d<districts; d++)
            {
                cout<<''In District''<<d+1;
                for(m=0; m<months; m++)
                cout<<funcsales[d][m];          //array element
                cout<<endl;
        }
    }
```

Explanation of Listing 8.3

In our program; in a function declaration:

```
void display (int [districts] [months])
```

array arguments are represented by the data-type and size of the array.

When the function is called, only name of array is used as argument.

```
display (sales);
```

The name (`sales`) actually represents the memory address of array.

Using an address for array arguments is similar to using a reference argument. The values of array elements are not duplicated into the function but it works on the original array, although it refers to a different name. No ampersand (&) is used with array name in function declaration.

8.3 Array of Structures

You can also make an array of structure data-type. Here is an example that is self-explanatory.

Listing 8.4 :

```
//Array of structure variables
const int size=4;                    //number of points in array
struct point
   {
      int x;                         //x-coordinate
      int y;                         //y-coordinate
   };
void main()
   {
      int n;                         //counter
      point p[size];                 //array of structures
      for(n=0; n<size; n++)
         {
            cout<<''Enter coordinate of x:'';
            cin>>p.[n].x;
            cout<<''Enter coordinate of y:'';
            cin>>p.[n].y;
         }
      for(n=0; n<size; n++)          //display values
         {
            cout<<''\n x-coordinate:''<<p[n].x;
            cout<<''\n y-coordinate:''<<p[n].y;
         }
   } //end main
```

8.4 Array of Objects

We have seen array of structures. Similarly we can use array on objects called as *array of objects*. The definition of array of objects can be established as :

```
Class distance
   {
      private:
        int feet;
        float inches;
      public
      void getdist()
         {
            cin>>feet;
            cin>>inches;
         }
      void showdist()
         {
            cout<<feet<<''&''<<inches;
         }
   };
```

```
void main()
distance d[100];                          //array of objects distance
```

In the above statement we made an array of 100 'd' objects of class distance.

Strings

So far, we saw arrays of different data-types 'integer', 'objects', 'structures'. But now we will see an array of 'characters'. An array of 'characters' is called a 'string'. As with other data-types, strings can be variables or constants.

We will explain these by taking a example.

Listing 8.5 :

```
//String demonstration
#include<iostream.h>
const int max=80;                           //max characters in string
void main()
   {
      char name[max];                       //string variable 'name'
      cout<<''/n Enter name:'';
      cin>>name;                            //input string
      cout<<''Name is:<<name;               //output string
   }
```

Explanation of Listing 8.5

In the above program, the string variable 'name' looks like (and is) the definition of array of type 'char'.

```
char name [max];
```

We input a string in a variable name by using an insertion operator (>>). Each character occupies one byte of memory and it is always terminated by character constant NULL ('\0') which is character of ASCII value 0.

It is shown as in figure below :

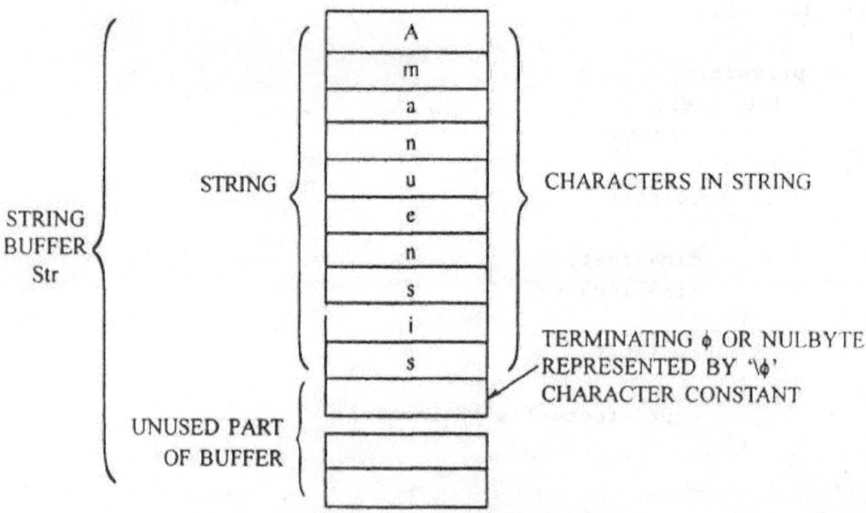

Fig. 8.4. String Stored in String Variable.

Avoiding Buffer Overflow

In the above program, there is no problem until user inputs a name which is 80 characters long.

But what happens if a user inputs a name of more than 80 characters ?

Since there is no inbuilt mechanism in C++ to keep a program from inserting array elements outside a array. So ultimately, it will crash the system. In order to prevent this, we have provided 'safety-code inside the program itself.' Here is the code :

Listing 8.6 :

```
//avoids buffer overflow
#include<iostream.h>
#<include<iomanip.h>                      //for setw
const int max=30;
void main()
   {
       char name[max];                    //string variable name
       cout<<''\n Enter name:'';
       cin>>setw(max)>>name;
       cout<<''Name is:''<<name;
   }
```

Explanation of Listing 8.5

In the above program, the header file `'iomanip.h'` is used to include the 'setw' function.

The 'setw' manipulator specifies the maximum number of characters the input buffer can accept. If the user types more characters than also, the '>>' operator won't insert them into array.

Actually one character less than number of characters specified in 'max' is inserted since last room of buffer is for NULL character to terminate the string. (In our case only 29 characters are inserted).

String Constants

If one wants, than one can initialize a string to constant value at time of definition.

Listing 8.7 :

```
//demonstrates string constants
#include<iostream.h>
void main()
   {
       char str[]=''Farewell!'';
       char str[I]={'H', 'e', 'l', 'l', 'o'}
       cout<<str<<endl;
       cout<<str1;
   }
```

String Reading

One can program to input the string and output it with multiple lines with the embedded blanks. Here is an example :

Listing 8.8 :

```
//demonstrates multiple line reading
#include<iostream.h>
const int max=80;
void main()
    {
        char para[max];
        cout<<''\n Enter paragraph:\n'';
        cin.get(para, max, '#');          //terminate with
                                          //'#' character
        cout<<''Entered Para is:\n''<<para;
    }
```

Explanation of Listing 8.7

In order to read blank spaces in a string and to input number of lines in a single string variable, we use a `cin.get()` function.

In this syntax, the get() function is a member of 'cin' stream class.

The first argument of `cin::get()` is an array address where the string being input will be placed. The second argument specifies the maximum size of array thus overriding the possibility of buffer overrun.

The third argument ('#') tells the function to read the character. The default character is new line ('\n') character, but if you call function with some other character for this argument, the default will be overridden by specified character.

8.5 Array of Strings

An Array of string is a two dimensional array in which an 'array is a array of characters'.

So it is an 'array of arrays'.

```
//demonstrates array of strings.
#include<iostream.h>
        const int days=7;          //no. of strings in array
        const int max=6;           //max. size of each string
void main()
    {
        char8[days][max]={''Sun'', ''Mon'', ''Tues'' ''Wed'',
            ''Thur'', ''Fri'', ''Sat''};
        for cint i=0; i<days; i++)
        cout<<s[i]<<endl;
    }
```

Here in our program, the first dimension of array, 'days', tells us how many strings are in the array. While the second dimension, 'Max', specifies the maximum length of strings excluding the 'NULL' character.

	0	1	2	3	4	5	6	7	8	9	
0	S	u	n	ϕ							S [1]
1	M	o	n	ϕ							S [2]
2	T	u	e	s	ϕ						S [3]
3	W	e	d	ϕ							S [4]
4	T	h	u	r	ϕ						S [5]
5	F	r	i	ϕ							S [6]
6	S	a	t	ϕ							S [7]

Fig. 8.5. Array of Strings.

Strings As Class Members

We can use the strings or any type of array (*i.e.*, of integers, structures) etc. inside a class as its member.

Listing 8.9 :

```
//demonstrates string as class member
#include<iostream.h>
#<include<string.h>                         //for strcpy()
class part
    {
    private:
        char name[30];                      //name of part
        int no.;                            //ID number of part
        float cost;                         //cost of part
    public:
    void setpart(char pname[], int pn, float pc)
        {
            strcpy(name, pname);
              no=pn;
              cost=pc;
        }
    void showpart()                         //display data
        {
        cout<<''\n Name:''<<name;
        cout<<'',number=''<<no.;
        cout<<'',cost=Rs.''<<cost;
        }
    }
```

```
void main()
    {
        part p1;
        p1.setpart(''handle'', 4573, 419.25);
        cout<<''\n Part is:''; p1.showpart();
    }
```

Explanation of Listing 8.9

In the above program, we have `setpart ( )` member function. In this member function we use `strcpy ( )` string library function to copy the string from argument `pname` to class data member `name`.

Thus this function serves the same purpose with string variables that an assignment statement does with simple variables.

There are other library functions related to 'string' which can be found in online help in 'Turbo C++' help menu along with the syntax and its usage.

SUMMARY

Arrays contain a number of data items of same type. This type can be simple data-type, a structure or class.

The items in an array are called as elements which are accessed by a number called as index. Elements can be initialized to specific values when arrays are defined.

Arrays can be one dimensional and more than one dimensional are called as multidimensional arrays.

The array of characters is called a 'string'. The last character in a string must be null character ('/0'). They are frequently used as class members.

EXERCISES

1. Write an array program to record the age and height of 25 students in a class.
2. Write a program of three dimensional array to classify students by age :
   (*i*) 15-25 years
   (*ii*) 10-15 years
   (*iii*) one of 10 major subjects of study.
3. Write a program to have a following output :

```
            1
        1   2   1
        1   3   3   1
    1   4   4   4   4   1
```

4. Write a program that reads two matrices and determines its product.
5. Write a function of strcat( ).

9
Pointers

9.1 What are 'pointers' for ?

This is the first question which comes in our mind when we hear this word. These are some common uses of pointers :

(1) Accessing array elements

(2) Passing arguments to a function

(3) Obtaining memory from system

(4) Creating data structures such as linked lists.

Pointers are much commonly used in C and C++ than in any other language. Pointers are not compulsory to use since you can write program without using pointers.

Then what are pointers for ?

Actually, use of pointers provides an essential tool for increasing the power of C++. It creates the data structures like linked lists and binary trees. It is also used in virtual functions as 'this' pointer.

It is also used for dynamic memory allocation which is very useful in memory management.

In this chapter we'll introduce pointers gradually, starting with fundamental concepts and working upto pointer applications.

If you already know C, you can probably skim over first half of the chapter, but you will have to read second half of it.

9.2 Pointers and Addresses

The idea behind pointers is simple. The first key concept : Every byte in computer memory has an 'address'. Addresses are just numbers starting from 0 and go up from there—1, 2, 3..... so if you have 1 mB of memory, the highest address is 1,048,575.

When your program is loaded in memory, it occupies certain range of these addresses. It means that, every variable and every function in your program starts at a particular address. (Address number varies from machine to machine).

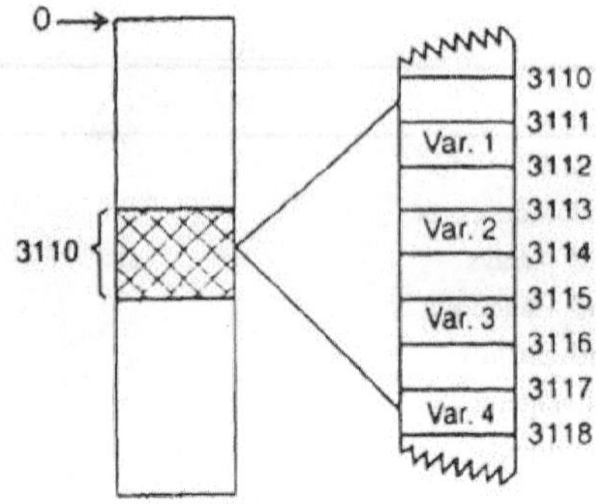

Fig. 9.1

The Address of Operator &

We can find out address occupied by a variable by using 'address of' (&) operator '&'.

Listing 9.1 :

```
//to access address of variables
#include<iostream.h>
void main()
    {
        int a=11;                     //define and initialize
        int b=22;                     //variables
        cout<<endl<<&a;               /*print addresses
        cout<<endl<<&b;               of variables*/
    }
```

Explanation of Listing 9.1

This simple program defines and initializes two integer variables which print out the addresses of these variables.

The actual addresses occupied by the variables in a program depends on the machine, size of the operating systems and if any other program is currently stored in memory.

The '<<' operator interprets the addresses in hexadecimal format & is indicated by the prefix 'OX' before each number.

When you see the output, you will mark that every address from the next differs by two bytes since the variable is of data-type 'integer'. Similarly, if data-type is 'character' than address values differ by one byte only. The address appears in descending order because automatic variables are stored on the stack, which grows downward in memory.

Pointer Variables

Till now, we have seen the variables that store characters, integers, floating-point numbers, double precision numbers and so on. Similarly, you can store addresses.

A variable that holds an address value is called a 'pointer' variable.

Listing 9.2 :

```
//demonstrates pointer variables
#include<iostream.h>
void main()
   {
      int a, b;                   //2 integer variables
      int*ptr;                    //pointer to integer
      ptr=&a;                     //set pointer to address of a
      cout<<endl<<&a;             //print addresses of variable
      cout<<endl<<&b;
      cout<<endl<<ptr;            //print pointer value
      b=11;
      ptr=&b;
      cout<<endl<<*ptr;           //print contents of ptr(11)
      *ptr=40;                    //same as b=40
      a=*ptr;                     //same as a=b
      cout<<a;                    //verify a=40
   }
```

Explanation of Listing 9.2

In the above program, we have defined two integer variables 'a' & 'b'. The program next defines a pointer variable in line.

```
int*ptr;
```

The syntax denotes that variable `ptr` is pointed to data-type integer. The asterisk is a part of variable type (pointer to 'int'), not a part of variable name itself.

There can be pointers pointing to other data-types as follows :

```
char*cptr;              //pointer to character
float*cptr;             //pointer to float
distance*cptr;          //pointer to user defined
                        //distance class
```

When we define a pointer variable, it holds no value unless we initialize it with some value. It may hold a garbage value without initialization.

So, before a pointer is used, a specific address must be placed in it. In our program, `ptr` is first assigned the address of a in line.

```
ptr = &a;
```

Following this, the program prints out the value contained in `ptr` which should be the same address printed for `&a`.

Then we assign value 11 to variable `b`. The address of value in `b` variable is then assigned to pointer variable `ptr` by statement.

```
ptr = &b.
```

So now, the address of `b` variable is stored in the pointer variable `ptr`.

But to print the content of the pointer variable, we use asterisk (`*`) in front of pointer variable in `cout` statement, as we did in

```
cout<<endl<<*ptr;
```

This asterisk is called an indirection operator. It means the 'value of variable pointed to by'. So here output of the above statement is value stored in `ptr` variable which is same in integer variable `b`.

Similarly pointer variables are used as other common variables for assignment in last part of program.

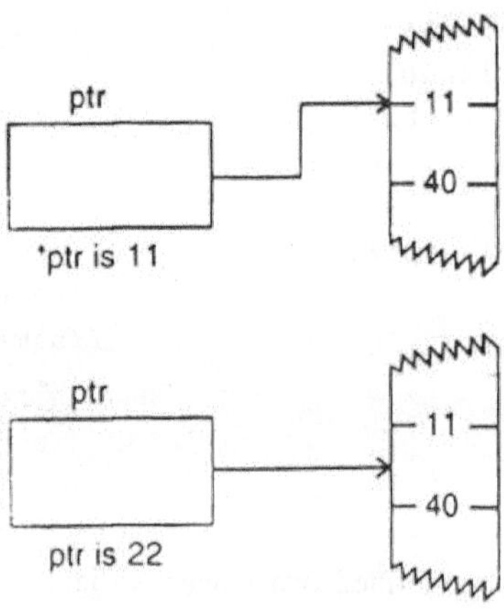

Fig. 9.2

Pointer to 'Void'

We have seen that, the pointer which stores address must be the same type as the pointer. It means that, you can't assign the address of a 'float' variable to a pointer to 'int' data-type.

There is a general-purpose pointer that can point to any data-type known as pointer to 'void': and it is defined as

```
void*ptr        //ptr can point to any datatype
```

We take an example to look at this concept.

Listing 9.3 :

```
//demonstration of void pointer
#include<iostream.h>
void main()
   {
      int iv;                        //integer variable
      flout fv;                      //float variable
      int*pv;                        //pointer to int
```

```
        float*fv1;                      //pointer to float
        void*pvoid;                     //pointer to void
        pv=&iv;
    //  pv=&fv;                         //error, float*to int*
        fv1=&fv;
    //  fv1=&iv;                        //error, int*to float*
        pvoid=&iv;                      //ok
        pvoid=&fv;                      //ok.
```

So, you can see that, you can assign the address of `iv` to `pv` because they are both integer types but you can't assign the address of float variable `fv` to pointer variable `pv` because the second is type `int*`. However `pvoid` can be given any pointer value, because it is a pointer to `void`.

9.3 Pointers and Arrays

First, we take one example of array which is much of same type as in last chapter.

Listing 9.4 :

```
//demonstration of array
#include<iostream.h>
void main()
    {
        int a[5]={10, 20, 30, 40, 50};       //array
        for (int i=0; i<5; i++)
        cout<<endl<<a[i];                   //print value
    }
```

The `cout` statement prints each element one-by-one. If i = 3, then a[3] prints the fourth array element *i.e.*, '40'. Since array addresses start from 'zeroth element'.

Now we will see that, the above program can also be written with help of 'pointers'.

Listing 9.4 (*a*) :

```
//demonstration of array with pointer
//notation
#include<iostream.h>
void main()
    {
        int a[5]={10, 20, 30, 40, 50};       //array
        for(int i=0; i<5; i++)
        cout<<endl<<*(a+i)                  //print value
    }
```

Explanation of Listing 9.4 (*a*)

The output of both the programs listing 9.4 and 9.4 (*a*) are same since the expression '*(a + i)' has the same effect as 'a [i]' in listing 9.4.

But how do we interpret the expression *(a + i) ?

To understand this expression we consider the position where i= 2. So our expression becomes *(a + 2). It represents the third element in the array and prints its content *i.e.*, 30 in our case.

Remember that, the name of an array is its address. We want the value of third array element, not the address. So to take the value, we use indirection operator '*'.

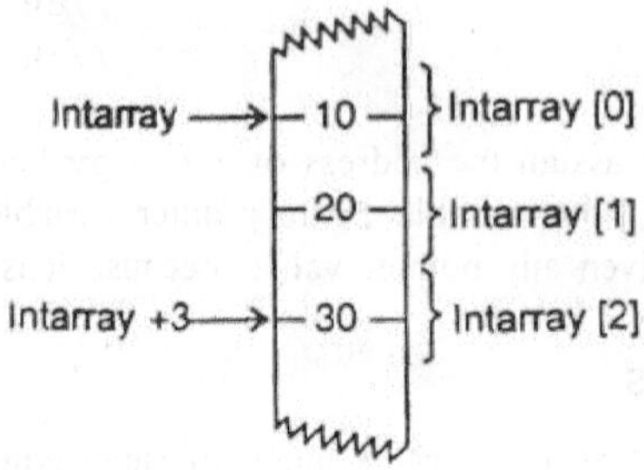

Fig. 9.3

9.4 Pointers and Functions

We have seen three ways to pass the arguments to a function *i.e.*, by value, by reference and by pointers. If the function is intended to modify variables in calling program, we have to pass the arguments either by reference or by pointer.

First we see an example where we pass arguments by reference.

Listing 9.5 :

```
//demonstrates arguments to be passed by reference
#include<iostream.h>
void main()
   {
      void product (float &);          //prototype
      float a=10.0;                    //a has value 10 inches
      cout<<endl<<''a=''<<a<<''inches'';
      product(a);                      //change a to cms.
      cout<<endl<<''a=''<<a<<''cms.'';
   }
   void product(float & b)
      {
         b*=2.54;                      //b is same as a
      }
```

Since you know functions, the above listing is self-explanatory.

We can use a pointer argument instead of reference argument in a function. Let us see the next example which is a modification of the first program.

Listing 9.5 (*a*) :

```
//demonstrates arguments passed by pointer
#include<iostream.h>
void main()
    {
        void product(float*)          //prototype
        float a=10.0;
        cout<<endl<<''a=''<<a<<''inches'';
        product(&a);
        cout<<endl<<''a=''<<a<<''cms'';
    }
    void proudct(float*ptr)
        {
            *ptr*=2.54;               //*ptr is same as a
        }
```

Explanation of Listing 9.5 (*a*)

In the above example we have declared a prototype in which argument is a pointer of data-type 'float'.

Then we come across the statement,

```
product (&a);
```

Here we are not passing the variable itself, as it is in passing by reference. Instead, variable address is passed. Because the 'product( )' function is passed as an address, indirection operator, `'*ptr'` is used to access the value stored in this address.

```
*ptr* = 2.54;
```

Since `ptr` contains an address of variable `a`, anything done to `*ptr` is actually done to variable `a`.

Passing and Sorting Array Elements

To make understand how you can pass the arrays by using pointers and to sort it, we take a bubble-sort example.

Listing 9.6 :

```
//demonstrates bubble-sort method
#include<iostream.h>
void main()
    {
        void bsort(int*, int);            //prototype
        const int N=10;                   //array size
        int a[N]={1, 2, 3, 4, 5, 6, 7, 8, 9, 10};
        bsort(a, N);                      //sort array
        for cint i=0; i<N; i++)           //print sorted
        cout<<a[i]<<'''';                 //array
    }
```

```
void bsort(int*ptr, int n)
    {
        void order(int*, int*)        //prototype
        for(int j=0; j<n-1; j++)      //outer loop
        for(int k=j+1; k<n; k++)      //inner loop
        order(ptr+j, ptr+k);
    }
    void order(int*n1, int*n2)        //orders two numbers
    if(*n1>*n2)                       //if 1st is>2nd no.
        {
          int temp=*n1;
          *n1=*n2;                    //swap them
          *n2=temp;
        }
    }  //end main()
```

Explanation of Listing 9.6

In the above program, the array a of integers in `main( )` is initialized to unsorted values. The address of array and the number of elements are passed to the 'bsort' function. This sorts the array.

`The Bubble sort;`

The `bsort( )` function sorts the array using the method called 'bubble sort'. This is a simple approach to sorting. Here we assume that the sorting of numbers will be in the ascending order.

First element of the array `(a[0])` is compared, in turn with each of the other elements. If it is greater than any of them, the two are swapped. This goes on until all numbers are arranged in ascending order.

The `bsort( )` function consists of two nested loops, each of which controls a pointer. The outer loop uses loop variable j and the expression `ptr + j` moves down the array, starting with the first element (top) of array and stepping down integer by integer until one short of last element (bottom of array). For each position taken by `ptr + j` in outer loop, the expression `ptr + k` in inner loop starts pointing one below `ptr + j` and moves down to bottom of array.

Each time through inner loop, the elements pointed to by `ptr + j` & `ptr + k` are compared, using the order function, and if first is greater than second, they are swapped.

In this way, sorting is achieved.

9.5 Pointers and Strings

Strings are the array of 'characters'. So pointer can be implemented to strings in the same way as to array of 'integers'.

Listing 9.7 :

```
//demonstrates strings using array and pointer notation
#include<iostream.h>
void main()
    {
        char s1[]=''Defined as an array'';
```

```
        char*s2[]=''It  is  a  pointer'';
        cout<<s1<<endl;
        cout<<s2<<endl;
    //  s1++;
        s2++;
        cout<<endl<<s2;
    }
```

Explanation of Listing 9.7

In the above program, s1 is an address—*i.e.*, a pointer constant – while s2 is a pointer variable. So s2 can be changed, while s1 cannot.

When we increment s2 variable, it does not point the first character of string and so its output is from the second character to NULL of the string.

Strings as Functions and Pointers

Listing 9.8 :

```
//demonstrates  strings  as  functions  using  pointers
#include<iostream.h>
void  main()
    {
        void  copy(char*,  char*);     //prototype
        char*s1=''This  is  great'';
        char s2[80];                   //empty  string
        copy(s2,  s1);                 //copy  s1  to  s2
        cout<<endl<<s2;
    }
//function  copy()
void  copy(char*c1,  char*src)
    {
        while(*src)
        *d++=*ssc++;
        *d='\0';
    }
```

Explanation of Listing 9.8

The array addresses of s1 and s2 are passed as an argument when the function copy( ) is called. s2 is passed by value, a copy of it is created in copy( ). This copy is a pointer *src.

A pointer can be changed. So the function increments src. The value at address pointed to by src is taken and placed at the address pointed to by d. Both pointers are then incremented. So next time, the next character will be transferred through the loop. The loop terminates when a null character is found in src; at this point a 'null' is inserted in a variable 'd' and the function returns.

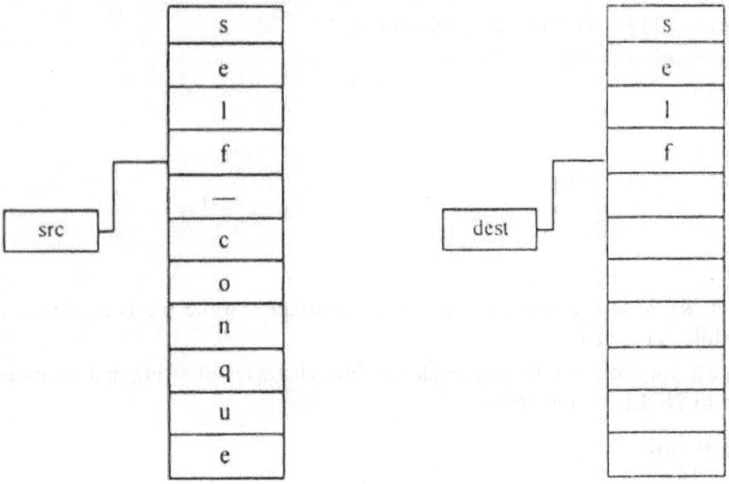

Fig. 9.4. Operation of Copystr

Array of Pointers

In last chapter of arrays, we saw that, in an array of strings, there is one disadvantage. That is, if a subarray in an array holds the string which is small, then the space is wasted. To solve this problem, we can use the pointers.

Listing 9.9 :

```
//an array of pointers to strings
#include<iostream.h>
const int days=7;                          //no. of pointers in array
void main()
    {
        char*s[days]={''Sun'', ''Mon'', ''Tue'', ''Wed'', ''Thur'',
            ''Fri'', ''Sat''};
        for(int i=0; i<days; i++)
            cout<<s[i]<<endl;              //display
    }
```

Explanation of Listing 9.9

When the strings are not a part of array as in the above program, C++ compiles and places them contiguously in memory, so there is no wasted space. So to find strings, there must be an array that holds pointers to them.

A string itself is an array of characters. Therefore, a pointer to string is a pointer to character. Also, an array of pointers to string is an array of pointers to characters. String is always represented by single address: the address of first character in string. It is these addresses that are stored in array.

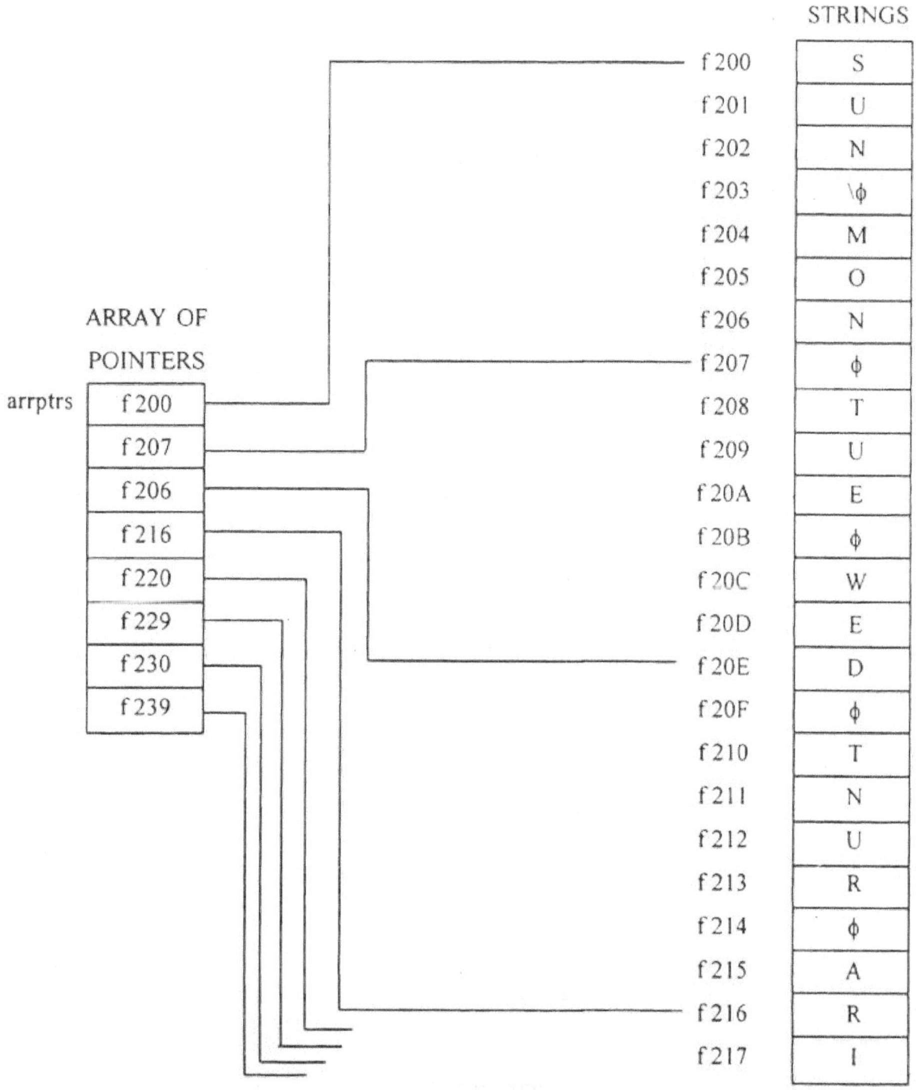

Fig. 9.5. Array of Pointer to Strings.

9.6 Memory Management

We have seen examples where arrays are used for setting aside a block of memory for data storage.

But there is a serious drawback, that one has to specify the size of an array at the time of writing a program. There are many situations where the usage of memory depends on the input of user. So it is impossible to know, how much memory we need until runtime.

This type of allocation of memory which depends on the input of user is called dynamic memory.

The 'new' Operator

The *new* operator obtains memory from the operating system and returns a pointer to its starting point.

Listing 9.10 :

```
//demonstrates 'new' and 'delete' operator in class
#include<iostream.h>
#include<string.h>                           //for strcpy()
#include<ctype.h>                            //for toupper()
class ourstring()
   {
        private:
          char*s;                            //pointer to string
        public:
          ourstring(char*str)                //constructor
            {
                int l=strlen(str);           //length of string
                s=new char(l+1);             //get memory
                strcpy(s, str);              //copy argument
            }
            ~ String()                       //destructor
            {
                delete s;
            }
        void display()
            {
                cout<<s;
            }
        void upper();                        //upper case the string
            }
        void ourstring::upper()
            {
                char*ptr=s;                  //pointer to this string
                while(*ptr)
            {
                *ptr=toupper(*ptr);
                ptr++;
            }
   }
        void main()
            {
                ourstring s1=''This is a string'';
                cout<<''\n s1='';
                s1.display();
                s1.upper();
```

```
            cout<<''\n s1='';
            s1.display();
        }
```

Explanation of Listing 9.10

In the above program the `ourstring` class has only one data item, a pointer to `char`, called `s`. This pointer will point to the string held by the `ourstring` object. There is no array within the object to hold the string. The string is stored somewhere else and only a pointer to it is a member of class.

Then we come across the constructor with one argument. Here, the constructor takes a normal string as an argument and obtains a space in memory with 'new' operator. The `strcpy()` function is used to copy the string into this new space.

When we allocate a memory with the 'new' operator of a object, it is reasonable to deallocate the memory when the object is destroyed. To do this, destructor is used.

The 'delete' operator is used to give back the memory to system when the object is destroyed.

The destructor again gives back to system, the memory obtained when the object was created. Objects like other variables are typically destroyed when function in which they are defined terminates. This destructor ensures that memory occupied by 'ourstring' object is freed and returned to system and not left as unknown occupied space.

Note : C programmers will recognise the 'new' operator role similar to the role of 'malloc( )' function although the syntax is different.

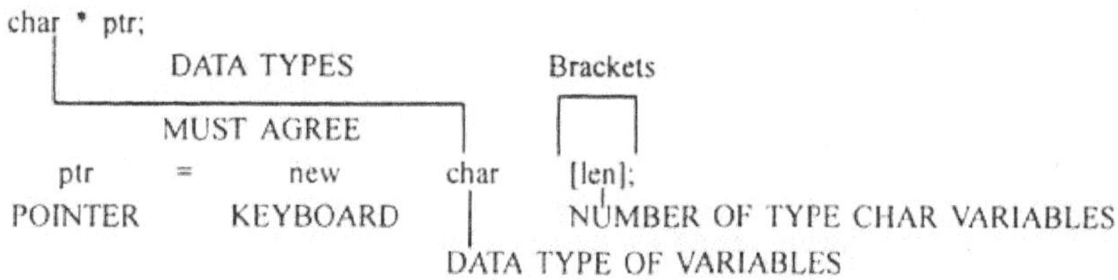

Fig. 9.6. Syntax of 'new' operator.

9.7 Pointers to Objects

Pointers can point to objects like to simple data-types. If we want to create the object at the runtime and it is not known at the time of writing a program, we use 'new' operator to create them.

Here we take an example of it.

Listing 9.11 :

```
//demonstrates pointer to objects
#include<iostream.h>
class distance
    {
        Private:
          int feet;
        Public:
          void get()
            {
```

```
            cout<<''\n Enter feet:'';
            cin>>feet;
        }

     void show()
        {
            cout<<''feet is:''<<feet;
        }
  };
  void main()
        {
            distance d;
            d.get();                    //access members with
            d.show();                   //dot operator
            distance*dptr;              //pointer to distance
            dptr=new distance;
            dptr→get();                 //access members with
            dptr→show();                //→operator
        }
```

Explanation of Listing 9.11

Since you know the creation of objects and access of its members with dot operator, we start directly from statement;

```
distance*dptr;
```

in the above program.

The object pointer `dptr` points to the class named distance.

The next statement creates another object of type `distance` using the new operator and returns a pointer to it called `dptr`.

You might think that, how do we refer to member functions in object pointed to by `dptr`, since dot membership operator will not work here because the dot operator requires the variable on its left to be a variable. But here, 'dptr' is a pointer to a variable. So there is another syntax to access members of class by the object of that class.

The operator used in pointers to access the members is → just as in same way the (.) operator works with objects.

9.8 Linked List

What is a linked list ?

It is another method to store the data dynamically *i.e.*, to store the data directly at the runtime of the program.

It provides a flexible storage system in which use of arrays are eliminated. So there is no need to allocate static memory area at the time of coding.

Instead, space for each data is obtained as needed with 'new' operator and each item is connected or linked to next data item using a pointer.

The individual items need not be located continuously in memory as in arrays but it can be scattered anywhere in memory. Let us take an example to understand the link list.

Listing 9.12 :

```
//demonstrates linked list
#include<iostream.h>
struct link             //one element of list
    {
        int data;
        link*next;                      //pointer to next link
    }
class linklist
    {
        Private:
          link*first;                   //pointer to first link
        Public:
          linklist()                    //constructor
            {
                first=NULL;
            }
        void getitem(intd);             //gets item from user
        void addition();                //add data item
        void display();                 //display all links
    };
        void linklist::getitem(int d)
            {
                cout<<''\n Enter a number'';
                cin>>d;
                link.data=d;
            }
        void linklist::addition()
            {
                link*lI=new link;       //make a new link
                  l1→data;
                  l1→next=first;        //it points to next link
                  first=l1;
            }
        void linklist::display()
            {
                link*current=first;     //set ptr to first link
                while(current!=NULL)
                    {
                        cout<<current→data;//print data
                        current=current→next;   //move to
                    }                           //next link
            }
void main()
    {
```

```
        linklist list I;
        list1.getitem(30);
        list1.addition();
        list1.getitem(40);
        list1.addition();
        list1.display();
    }
```

Explanation of Listing 9.12

In the above example, we have a structure called `link` containing an integer and a pointer to the next link. The list itself stores a pointer to the link at the head of the list.

A LINKED LIST

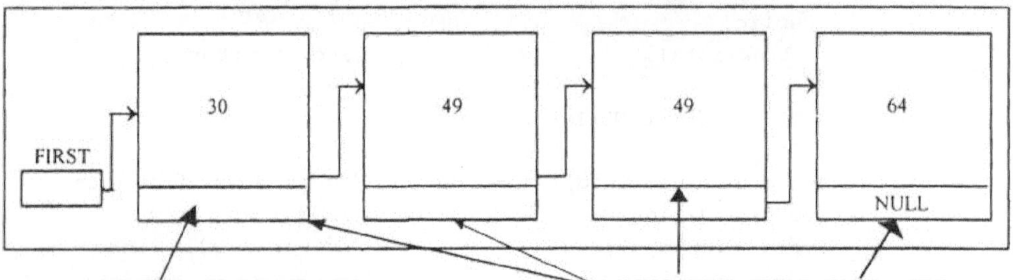

Fig. 9.7

The `linklist` class has only one member data item *i.e.*, pointer to start of the list. When the list is first created, the constructor initializes the pointer 'first' to NULL; which signals that a pointer does not hold a valid address.

Then we have a `getitem` function which gets the data from the user and stores it in the 'data' of integer data-type.

The addition member function adds an item to the linked list. A new link is created and inserted at beginning of the list by the statement;

```
link * l1 = new link;
```

This creates memory for the new 'link' structure with 'new' operator and saves the pointer to it in 'l1' variable.

Then, the `next` pointer points to the address of the pointer named `first` by statement.

```
l1 → next = first;
```

Finally, the `first` variable points to new link :

```
first = l1;
```

This is done to uncouple the connection between 'first' and old first link, insert new link and move old first link to second position.

Once the list is created, we can display the entire list by the statement :

```
cout<<current → data; and
current = current → next.
```

This moves us along from one link to another until value in the `'current'` pointer is not NULL.

This completes the explanation of the above program.

Usage of Linklist

The above program is very simple and is just given to understand the concept of 'linked list'. But more complex situations like making text editors, RDBMS and other things can be successfully handled with the help of linklist.

9.9 Pointers to Pointers—The Concept of 'Double Pointers'

Here we take an example, where array of pointers are used to sort the data in the object.

Listing 9.13 :

```
//demonstrates an array of pointers
#include<iostream.h>
#include<string.h>                        //for strump()
const int days=7;                         //no. of pointers in array
void main()
    {
        void bsort(char**, int);          //prototype
        char*array[days]=
        {''Sunday'', ''Monday'', ''Tuesday'', ''Wednesday'',
         ''Thursday'', ''Friday'', ''Saturday''};
        cout<<''\n Unsorted Data:\n'';
        for(int i=0; i<days, i++)
        cout<<*(array+i)<<endl;
        bsort(array, days);
        cout<<''\n Sorted Data:n'';
        for(i=0; i<days; i++)
        cout<<*(array+i)<<endl;
    }
void bsort(char**p; int a)
    {
        void order(char**, char**);       //prototype
        int i, j;                         //counters for array
        for(i=0; i<a-1; i++)
        for(j=0; j<a; j++)
        order(p+i, p+j);
    }
void order (char**p1, char**p2)
    {
        if(strump(*p1, *p2)>0)
            {
                char*temp=*p1;
                *p1=*p2;                  //swap pointers
                *p2=*temp;
            }
    }  // end main().
```

Explanation of Listing 9.13

In the above program, we have defined an array of pointers of data-type character. Then the main( ) function calls the `bsort ( )` function to sort the data.

You will notice that the first argument of `bsort ( )` function and both the arguments of `order ( )` function have the type `char**0.`

What do the two asterisks mean ?

These arguments are used to pass the address of the array of pointers.

If the array is of type character then address of array would be 'char*' (*i.e.*, a single pointer). Since, we pass the address of array of 'char*', it will be held by the double pointer of that data-type; *i.e.*, char**. It means the 'char**' variable points to 'char*' variable which in turn points to 'char' variable which is the actual data.

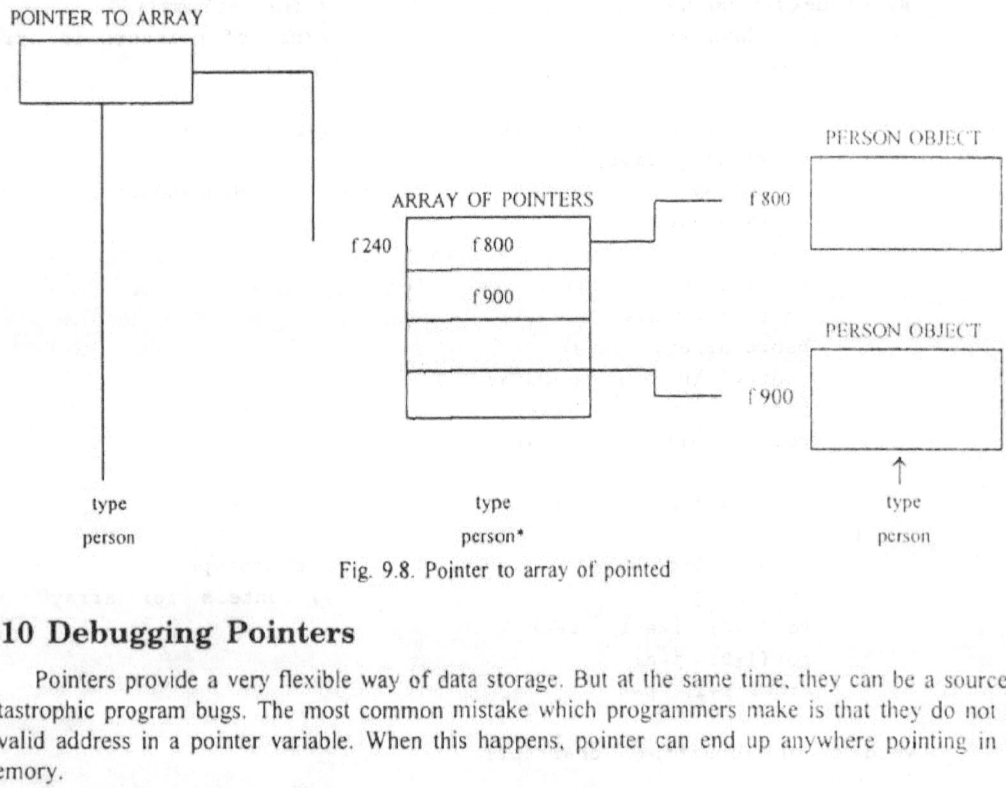

Fig. 9.8. Pointer to array of pointed

9.10 Debugging Pointers

Pointers provide a very flexible way of data storage. But at the same time, they can be a source of catastrophic program bugs. The most common mistake which programmers make is that they do not put a valid address in a pointer variable. When this happens, pointer can end up anywhere pointing in the memory.

If a programmer again inserts a value, it can overwrite the program or operating instructions thus crashing the system.

One should take care that, if a pointer is defined as an external variable then it is automatically initialized to zero. If a program statement attempts to insert a value into address at 0, compiler displays the error message :

```
Null pointer assignment.
```

SUMMARY

Thus we have made a tour to the land of pointers. What we have discussed is just the concept of pointers.

Using this concept, we can exploit the strength of the pointers to the fullest in any field of programming *i.e.*, in system as well as application programming.

The topics we have learnt in this chapter are :

★ The address operator &.

★ Pointer variables and accessing an address.

★ Indirection operator (*).

★ Arrays can be accessed with pointer notations and passing pointers as arguments to functions.

★ New and delete operator.

★ Member access with '→' operator.

★ Double pointers *i.e.*, int**ptr.

EXERCISES

1. Write a program that reads a group of numbers and places them in array of type float. Use pointer notation.
2. Take name as a input from user and print it in ascending order by using bsort( ) and order( ).
3. Using pointers, write a program that sorts a list of integers in the descending order.
4. Write a program using pointers that the string is a palindrome.
5. Write a program that converts a given day of year into date and month.
6. Write a function that replaces the first occurrence of a given substring in a source string by a specified substitution string.
7. Write a program that copies its input to output, except that it removes trailing blanks and tobs from end of lines and prints only one line from each group of adjacent identical lines.
8. Write a function that merges two sorted lists into one.

10

Polymorphism

Polymorphism is one of the most exciting features of object-oriented programming. It can perform different functions and give different meanings to some 'function code' and the operator. So it is also called the operator overloading.

In practice, polymorphism gives the opportunity to redefine C++ language for the programmers. If the programmer is not satisfied by the limited way in which C++ operators work, he can change them to do whatever he wishes by overloading or polymorphise the operators.

In this way, one can create a new definition for operators and can extend C++ to construct a new language.

10.1 The Operator Keyword

How will the C++ operator act on user-defined operand ? To overload C++ operator, we have to use the keyword *operator*. The syntax will be

```
(return type) operator < operator of C++ or user-define operator > ( ).
```

This declarator syntax tells the compiler to call member function whenever 'operator of C++' is encountered, provided the operand is of type of its defined class. This can be understood more clearly by taking an example.

We take an example to overload the increment (++) operator.

Listing 10.1 :

```
//demonstrates overloading of unary operator
#include<iostream.h>
class count
   {
        Private:
          int counter;
        Public:
          count()
             {counter=0;}                //constructor
        int getc();
             {return counter;}
```

```
        void operator++()              //overloaded '++'
            {                          //operator
                counter++;
            }
    };
void main()
    {
        count C1;
        cout<<''\n C1=''<<C1.getc();
        C1++;                          //postfix
        ++C1;                          //prefix
        cout<<''\n C1=''<<C1.getc();
    }
```

Explanation of Listing 10.1

In the above program, we have used the reserved keyword *operator* for overloading the ++ operator.

Since the syntax is given, comparing the general syntax with our program, we come to know that the return type is `void` followed by keyword *operator*, followed by the operator itself `(++)` and finally the argument list enclosed in paranthesis `'()'`. Here the paranthesis are empty since it takes no arguments.

The declarator syntax tells the compiler to call this member function whenever the '++' operator is encountered, provided the operand is of type `'count'`.

The only way for the compiler to distinguish between overloaded operator and inbuilt operator is by looking at the data-type of their arguments.

e.g., If operand is integer as in

```
a++;
```

the compiler will use built in routine to increment an integer.

But if operand is a `'count'`, then compiler will execute user written operator `++( )`. Then we come across a statement.

```
C1++;
```

This statement increments the *'counter'* data in the object of which it is a member function. Since member functions can always access the particular object for which they've been called, this operator requires no arguments.

Return Values

In the previous program, there is one drawback. That is, if we write a statement in ***main()*** as :

```
a = C1++;
```

the compiler will give an error message because we have given a return type `void` in `operator++( )` function.

So to make the above statement valid we have to give the return type as the class name like we did in our example `count`. We implement this in our second version of the above program.

Listing 10.1 (*a*) :

```
//demonstrates operator with return value
#include<iostream.h>
class count
    {
        Private:
          int counter;
        Public:
          count()
             {counter=0;}                //constructor
             count(int C)                //constructor
             {counter=C;}
        int getc
             {
                  return counter;
             }
        count operator++()
             {
                  counter++;
                  return count(counter);
             }
    };
void main()
    {
        count C1, a;
        cout<<''\n C1=''<<C1.getc();
        cout<<''\n a=''<<a.getc();
        C1++;
        a=C1++;
        cout<<''\n C1=''<<C1.getc();
        cout<<''\n a=''<<a++.getc();
    }
```

Explanation of Listing 10.1 (*a*)

In the above program, a single statement

```
return count (counter);
```

makes a temporary `count` object and gives it same value as of this object which returns it to the left hand operand (*i.e.*, left operand to '=' operator). This object has no name but is initialized to value provided by argument `counter`. To do this, we require a constructor which is provided in member function as a statement.

```
count (int C)
    {counter = C;}
```

So the statement,

```
a = C1 ++;
```

returns a value from 'C1++' and assigns to variable `a`.

This is our desired effect of returning the value.

Limitations

There is a limitation in overloading an operator. In our example we have used a prefix `++C1` and postfix notation `C1++`. But in both cases `C1` is incremented before being assigned to a variable. This will not be the case in basic type `(++)` increment operator. The operators like `(.)` dot operator and scope resolution operator `'(::)'` cannot be overloaded.

10.2 Overloading Binary Operators

Binary operators can be overloaded in same manner as unary operators.

Here we take an example of overloading 'equal to' (= =) operator.

We'll use this operator to compare the strings, returning 'true' if strings are same and false otherwise.

Listing 10.2 :

```
//demonstrates '==' overloaded operator
#include<iostream.h>
#include<string.h>                  //for strcmp()
enum boolean {true, false};
class string
   {
      Private:
        char s[100];                //bolds string
      Public:
        string()
          {
          strcpy(s, '''');
          }
      string(char a[])
          {
             strcpy(s, a);
          }
      void display()
          {cout<<s;}
      void gets()                   //read a string
          {
             cin.get(s, 100);
          }
      boolean operator==(string ss)
          {
             return(strcmp(s,ss.s)==0)?true:false;
          }
   };
void main()
   {
      string s1=''overload'';
      string s2;
      cout<<''\n Enter a word'';
      s2.gets();                    //get string from user
      if(s2==s1)
      cout<<''You typed a correct word\n'';
```

```
        else
        cout<<''Invalid  match\n'';
    }
```

Explanation of Listing 10.2

In the above program, the 'operator = = ( )' function uses the standard library function `strcmp ( )` to compare two strings lexicographically. The function returns 0 if strings are equal, a negative number if first is less than second, and positive number if first is greater than second.

Similarly you can overload any binary or unary operators.

10.3 Function Overloading

Till now we have seen the overloading of the operators. Similarly we can also overload the functions; it means to polymorphise a function.

An overloaded function appears to perform different activities depending on the kind of data sent to it. It performs one operation on one kind of data but another operation on a different kind.

It seems mysterious that an overloaded function knows what to do when. Lets clarify it with an example.

Listing 10.3 :

```
//demonstrates  function  overloading
#include<iostream.h>
void  repeat();
void  repeat(char);
void  repeat(char,  int);
void  main()
    {
        repeat();
        repeat('+');
        repeat('-',  45);
    }
//repeat()function
void  repeat()
    {
        for(int  i=0;  i<50;  i++)
        {cout<<'*'
         cout<<endl;}
//repeat(char)function
void  repeat(char  c)
    {
        for(int  i=0;  i<50;  i++)
        cout<<ch<<endl;
    }
//repeat(char,int)function
void  repeat(char  c,  int  n)
```

```
{
    for(int  i=0;  i<n;  i++)
    cout<<ch<<endl;
}
```

Explanation of Listing 10.3

In the above program, there are three functions containing the same name `repeat` having three declarations, three function calls, and three function definitions.

What keeps all functions distinct in spite of the same name is the number of arguments and their data-types.

The compiler will not be confused with the same name since it recognises the function with the number of arguments and not by name.

The program,

```
void  repeat ( );
```

which takes no arguments, describes an entirely different function from the function declaration

```
void  repeat (char);
```

which takes one argument of type `char`, or declaration

```
void  repeat (char,  int);
```

which takes two arguments.

So the function with the same name will behave differently as per the data supplied by the user.

Data Conversion

We can convert the user-defined data-types *i.e.*, objects of basic type *i.e.*, in 'int' to float, 'float' to int etc.

But we can't rely on built-in conversion routine, since compiler doesn't know anything about user-defined data-type.

Here we take an example in which the user-defined `distance` is converted to `meters` and vice-versa.

Listing 10.4 :

```
//demonstrates  data  conversion
#include<iostream.h>
class  distance
    {
        Private:
          int  feet;
        Public:
          distance()                    //constructor
            {
                feet=0;
            }
        distance(float  meters)         //convert  meters  to
            {                           //distance
                float  feet=3.28*meters;
```

```
                feet=int(ffleet);
            }
        distance(int  ft)              //constructor-1  argument
            {
                feet=ft;
            }
        void  get  d()
            {
                cout<<''\n  Enter  feet:'';cin>>feet;
            }
        void  show()
            {
                cout<<''Feet  is:''<<feet;
            }
        operator  float()              //conversion  function
            {                          //converts  distance  to
                float  frac=feet/12;   //meters
                frac+=float(feet);
                return  frac/3.28;
            }
    };
void  main()
    {
        distance  d1=4.85;
        cout<<''\n  d1='';
        d1.show();
        d1=2.00;
        cout<<''\n  d1='';
        d1.show();
        distance  d2(8);
        float  m=float(d2);
        cout<<''\n d2=''<<m<<''meters'';
        m=d1;
        cout<<''\n d1=''<<m<<''meters'';
    }
```

Explanation of Listing 10.4

In `main( )` of the above program, conversions are performed using simple assignment statements.

But, behind the scenes, in `distance` members functions, we are converting a user-defined type to basic type and vice-versa.

From basic to user-defined type, here is the code for this conversion :

```
distance (float  meters)
    {
        float  ffeet=3.28*meters;
        feet=int(ffeet);
    }
```

This function is called when an object of type `distance` is created with a single argument. The function assumes this argument representing `meters` and converts the argument to `feet` and assigns the resulting values to object. Thus the conversion from meters to `distance` is carried out along creation of an object,

```
distance  d1=4.85;  and
d1=2.00;
```

Thus the compiler differentiates between definition and assignment. If no overloaded = operator is available, it will look for constructor to do same job.

User-defined to basic

The trick here is to overload the cast operator in order to convert the user-defined type to basic type.

The code for the conversion is :

```
operator  float()
    {
        float  frac=feet/12;
        fract=float(feet);
        return  frac/3.28;
    }
```

This operator takes the value of `distance` object of which it is a member, converts this value to `float` value representing meters and returns this value.

```
m=float(d2);
```

The above statement converts the `distance` object `d2` into meters.

When the compiler finds that a user-defined type is converted to a basic type, it looks for the conversion function; when overloaded '=' operator is not found.

SUMMARY

In this chapter, we have seen the keyword 'operator'.

We have seen how we can redefine the functions and operators of C++ in our own way.

Then we saw, how we can make the same function behave in many different ways as per given data by user or programmer.

Then we also saw the data conversion from user-defined type to basic type and vice-versa.

EXERCISES

1. Code the unary operator '– –' in an overloaded form.
2. Overloaded the binary operators, '>', '<', '+=', '–='.
3. Modify the 'distance' class to behave having output in 'float' data-type as well as in 'double' data-type.
4. Write a program that substitutes an overloaded '+=' operator for overloaded '+' operator. The operator should allow statement like s1 += s2;

   where 's2' is concatenated to 's1'. It should also allow statements like s3 = s1 += s2.

11

Inheritance

11.1 Introduction

Inheritance is the most powerful feature of 'OOPS' concept. But, what is inheritance ? Inheritance is a process of creating new classes, called as 'derived classes' from an existing class called as 'base class'. The derived class inherits all the capabilities of its base class and also adds the additional capabilities of its own. The base remains unchanged in the process.

The advantage of 'inheritance' property in C++ is that, it permits 'code reusability'. So, once the base class is written and debugged, it need not be touched again since it can be adapted to work in different situations. Reusing the existing code saves time, money and enhances the program's reliability.

11.2 Base and Derived Classes

Suppose we program a 'counter' software to keep track of the number of people entering in a department store. After completing the program, the store owner says that, he want to add another code, that will decrement the counter as the person goes out of store. In order to do this, we have to rewrite the code.

Instead of that, we can use the property of inheritance and the previous code can be reused.

Let's see, how we can do this.

Listing 11.1 :

```
//demonstrates inheritance property
#include<iostream.h>
class count                                //base class
    {
        protected:
        unsigned int counter;
        Public:
            count()
```

```
            {
                counter=0;
            }
        count(int  C)
            {
                counter=C;
            }
        int  getc()
            {
                return  counter;
            }
        count  operator++()
            {
                counter++;
                return  count(counter);
            }
    };
        Class  countdn:public  count
                //derived  class
            {
                Public  :
                count  operator--()
            {
                counter--;
                return  count(counter);
            }
    };
void  main()
    {
        countdn  C1;
        cout<<''\n  C1=''<<C1.getc();
        C1++;  C1++;
        cout<<''\n  C1=''<<C1.getc();
        C1--;
        cout<<''\n  C1=''<<C1.getc();
    }
```

Explanation of Listing 11.1

In the above program, we have defined the `count` class as a base class, which is our normal defined class as usual.

Then we defined a class `countdn` which inherits all the properties and features of base class `count` and is termed as the `derived` class. This class incorporates a new function 'operator– –( )' of its own. The derived class `countdn` also inherits the constructors. The derived class is derived from base class by line,

```
class  countdn  :  public  count.
```

Here, we use a single colon, followed by the keyword *public* and name of base class. When the statement encountered is,

```
countdn C1;
```

The object C1 is created of class `countdn` and initialized to zero by inheriting the constructor of base class. The object C1 also inherits the 'operator+ +( )' and 'getc( )' from base class.

Wait a minute. When we defined the base class, we used the access specifier as 'protected' instead of 'private'.

This we did in order to allow the access of 'member functions' by derived class from the base class *i.e.*, to allow the inheritance.

This is not possible if access is 'private'. But in 'protected' access also, member functions can be accessed from its own class but not from functions outside these classes such as 'main( )'.

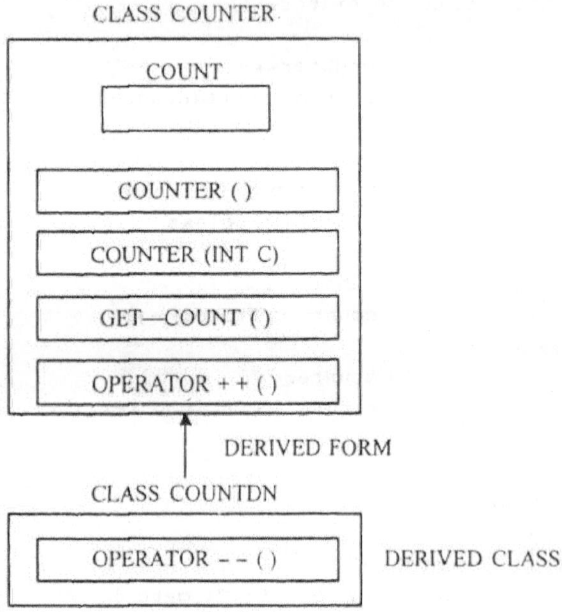

Fig. 11.1. Class Hierarchy in our example.

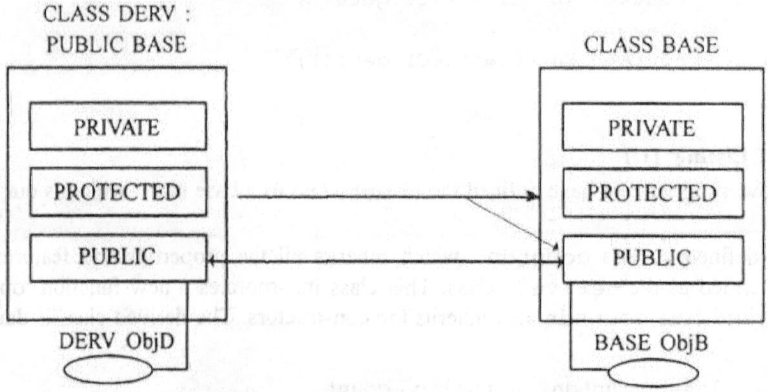

Fig. 11.2. Access Specifiers with Inheritance.

11.3 Class Hierarchies

Here, we demonstrate the class hierarchy by defining one base class called 'employee' and three derived classes from base class which are 'manager', 'scientist' and 'laborer'.

Listing 11.2 :

```
//demonstrates class hirarchies
#include<iostream.h>
class employee
    {
        Private:
        char name[100];
        int number;
        public:
        void getdata()
            {
                cout<<''\n Enter your name:'';
                cin>>name; cin>>number;
            }
        void putdata()
            {
                cout<<''\n Name:''<<name;
                cout<<''\n Number:''<<number;
            }
    }
        Class manager:public employee
            {
                private:
                char title[80];
                int dues;
                public:
                void getdata()
            {
                employee::getdata();
                cout<<''Enter title:'';
                cin>>title;
                cout<<''\n Enter dues:'';
                cin>>dues;
            }
        void putdata()
            {
                employee::putdata()
                cout<<''\n Title:''<<title;
                cout<<''\n Dues:''<<dues;
            }
    };
```

```
        class scientist:public employee
            {
                private:
                int p;                          //publications
                public:
                void getdata()
            {
                employee::getdata()
            {
                cout<<''\n Enter number of publications:'';
                cin>>p;
            }
    };
        void putdata()
            {
                employee::putdata();
                cout<<''/n No. of publications:<<p;
            }
    };
        class laborer:public employee
            {
            };
void main()
    {
        manager m1;
        scientist s1;
        laborer l1;
        cout<<''\n Enter data for manager'';
            m1.getdata();
        cout<<''\n Enter data for scientist'';
            s1.getdata();
        cout<<''\n Enter data for laborers'';
            l1.getdata();
        cout<<''\n Data for manager'';
            m1.putdata();
        cout<<''\n Data for scientist'';
            s1.putdata();
        cout<<''\n Data for laborer'';
            l1.putdata();
    }
```

Explanation of Listing 11.2

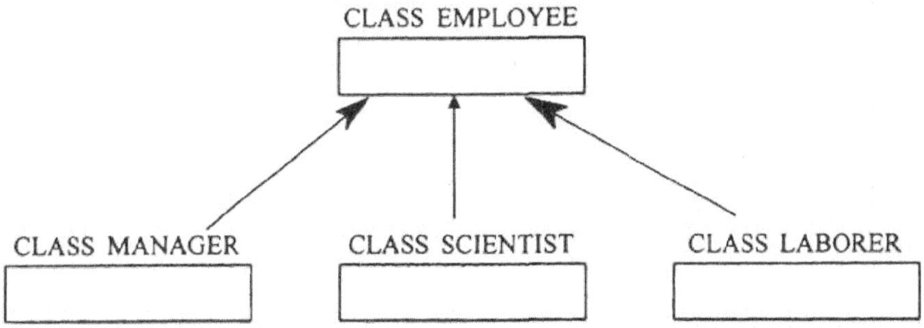

Fig. 11.3. Class Hierarchies

In the above program, we have defined a base class 'employee' and three derived classes, 'manager', 'scientist' and 'laborer' from the base class. The two member functions `putdata( )` and `getdata( )` are defined in base class and all the derived classes.

So the two member functions have same name in both base class and derived class but with different arguments. Then, how the compiler knows when to use which function in `main( )` program when different derived classes call the member function ?

Suppose, the class 'manager' calls its own member functions, `getdata( )` and `putdata( )`, then the compiler would call the appropriate inherited member classes of derived class 'manager' by the statement.

```
employee: :getdata( );  and
employee: :putdata( );
```

These statements specify that, the two member functions are inherited from base class 'employee' and the code appropriate to derived class and its function should be executed since the object is of derived class 'manager' in 'main( )' program.

"Abstract" Base Class

In the program, we have not defined any object of class 'employee'. We use this as a general class whose sole purpose is to act as a base class from which other classes, 'manager', 'scientist' and 'laborer' are derived.

The 'laborer' class operates identically to the 'employee' class, since it contains no additional data and functions.

So the base used only for deriving other classes is called an 'abstract' class.

Public and Private Inheritance

In the above program, we inherited a class by statement.

```
class manager : public employee;
```

The keyword *public* is used to specify that the objects of derived classes are able to access public member functions of base class.

Instead of *public, private* keyword is used for not allowing the access of public member functions of base class by the objects of derived classes.

Access Combinations

Table 11.1

Access Specifier	*Accessible from own class*	*Derived class*	*Objects outside class*
public	yes	yes	yes
protected	yes	yes	no
private	yes	no	no

11.4 Multiple Inheritance

When a class is derived from more than one base class, it is called 'multiple inheritance'.

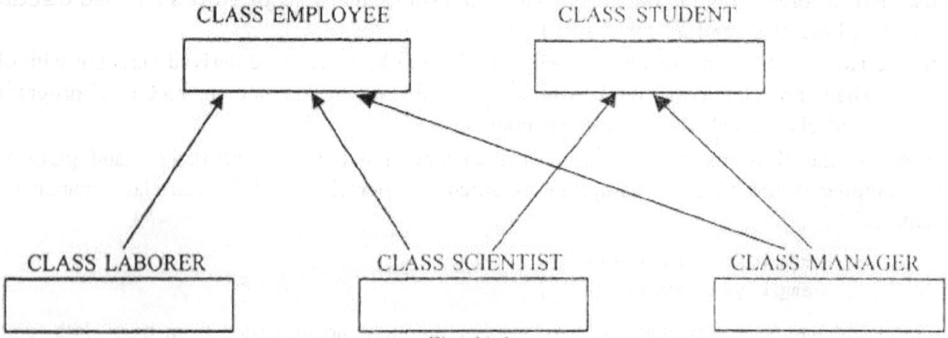

Fig. 11.4

Listing 11.3 :

```
//demonstrates multiple inheritance
#include<iostream.h>
Class student
    {
        private:
        char school[100];                 //name of school
        public:
        void geted()
            {
                cout<<''Enter name of school:'';
                cin>>school;
            }
        void puted()
            {
                cout<<''school is:''<<school;
            }
    };
```

```
    class employee
        {
            private:
            char name[100];
            int number;
            public:
            void getdata()
        {
            cout<<''\n Enter your name'';
            cin>>name;
            cout<<''\n Enter the number'';
            cin>>number;
        }
    void putdata()
        {
            cout<<''\n Name:''<<name;
            cout<<''\n Number:''number;
        }
};
    class manager:private employee, private student
        {
            private:
            char title[80];
                int dues;
            public:
            void getdata()
        {
            employee::getdata();
            cout<<''\n Enter title:'';
            cin>>title;
            cout<<''\n Enter dues:'';
            cin>dues;
            student::geted();
        }
    void putdata()
        {
            employee::putdata();
            cout<<''\n Title:''<<title;
            cout<<''\n Dues:''<<dues;
            student::puted();
        }
};
    class laborer:public employee
    {
    };
```

```
void main()
    {
        manager m1;
        laborer l1;
        cout<<''\n Enter data for manager'';
            m1.getdata();
        cout<<''\n Enter data for laborer'';
            l1.getdata();
        cout<<''\n Data for manager:'';
            m1.putdata();
        cout<<''\n Data for laborer:'';
            l1.putdata();
    }
```

Explanation of Listing 11.3

The two modifications we have done from the program in listing 11.2 are : we introduced one more base class 'student' and secondly we made the access specifier of inheritance as 'private'.

When the compiler encounters the statement,

```
class manager : private employee, private student
```

What does it mean ?

It means that the class 'manager' is derived from two base classes, one after the another by keeping the access specifier as 'private'. They are privately derived from two base classes because object of 'manager' never call routines in 'employee' and 'student' base classes.

The only thing which is added to previous program in derived class 'manager' are statements,

```
student : : geted( ); and
student : : puted( );
```

which calls to function in 'student' class. This completes the explanation.

11.5 Containers

What is containership ?

Earlier, we saw how one class can be derived from one or more base classes that inherits all the features and properties of base class.

But there is another kind of relationship, called as 'has a' relationship or 'containership'. This is a property in which object of one or more base classes are 'contained' in the base or derived classes.

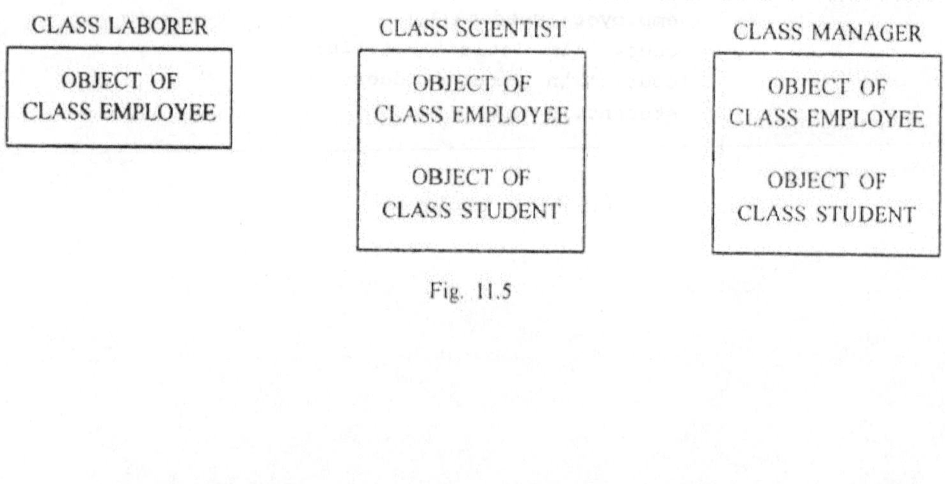

Fig. 11.5

Listing 11.4 :

Here we take the same previous program, but with a concept of containers. If we match this program with the previous one, we will see the difference between inheritance and containers.

```
//demonstrates containership
#include<iostream.h>
class student
    {
        Private:
        char school[100];
        Public:
        void geted()
            {
                cout<<''\n Enter name of school'';
                cin>>school;
            }
        void puted()
            {
                cout<<''school is:''<<school;
            }
    };
        class employee
            {
                private:
                char name[100];
                int number;
                public:
        void getdata()
            {
                cout<<''\n Enter your name'';
                cin>>name;
                cout<<''\n Enter the number'';
                cin>>number;
            }
        void putdata()
            {
                cout<<''\n Name:''<<name;
                cout<<''\n Number:''<<number;
            }
    };
        class manager
            {
                private:
                char title[80];
                int dues;
                employee e;            //object of class employee
                student s;             //object of class student
```

```
                public:
                void getdata()
            {
                e.getdata();
                cout<<''\n Enter title'';
                cin>>title;
                cout<<''\n Enter dues'';
                cin>>dues;
                s.geted();
            }
        void putdata()
            {
                e.putdata();
                cout<<''\n Title:''<<title;
                cout<<''\n Dues:''<<dues;
                s.puted();
            }
    };
        class laborer
            {
                private:
                employee e;
                public:
                void getdata()
            {
                e.getdata();
            }
        void putdata()
            {
                e.putdata();
            }
    };
void main()
    {
        manager m1;
        laborer l1;
        cout<<''\n Enter data for manager'';
        m1.getdata();
        cout<<''\n Enter data for laborer'';
        l1.getdata();
        cout<<''\n Data for manager'';
        m1.putdata();
        cout<<''\n Data for laborer'';
        l1.putdata();
    }
```

Explanation of Listing 11.4

The logic and explanation is the same as in previous program listing except one difference. Look at the derived class 'manager'. In the class, we have two functions `getdata( )` and `putdata( )` which were not inherited as in the previous program. Secondly, we defined the objects of base classes 'employee' and 'students' as an variable in derived class 'manager'.

Then we used the functions as the members of that base classes in the statements.

```
e.getdata( );
s.geted( );
e.putdata( );   and
s.puted( );
```

so the base class objects are 'contained' in their derived class and this is called as 'containership'.

Often the 'inheritance' relationship is simpler to implement and offers a clearer conceptual framework.

SUMMARY

In 'inheritance' we can define two classes 'base' class and 'derived' class. The derived class inherits all the properties and features of base class while new properties and features can be added additionally to derived class.

Accessibility of base class members from derived classes and its objects can be done, if they have 'public' or 'protected' access specifier. But objects of privately derived class cannot access 'private', 'public' or 'protected' members and functions.

A class can be derived from more than one base class which is called the 'multiple inheritance'. A class can also be 'contained' within another class.

It permits the reusability of software which leads to new flexibility in software development process, and to a wider range of roles for software developers.

EXERCISES

1. Rewrite the listing 11.2 with constructors.
2. Rewrite the listing 11.2 by using multiple inheritance.
3. Rewrite the listing 11.3 with constructors using the concept of multiple inheritance.
4. Modify above program with the concept of containers.
5. Write the program, whose base class is sales. Derived classes are publication, book and tape. All has the functions putdata( ) and getdata( ). Alter the book and tape classes so they are derived from both publication and sales classes. Write a main( ) function to create a book object and exercise their input/output capabilities. Variables can be of programmers or users choice.

12

Virtual and Friend Functions

Virtual Functions

What is a virtual function ?

'Virtual' means existing in effect but not in reality. So a 'virtual function' is the one that does not really exist but appears real to some parts of program.

Then, you will think why virtual functions are needed ?

Suppose you have a number of objects of different classes but if you put them on list and perform a particular operation using the same function call, the action will be different every time.

So, virtual functions prove to be an important example of 'polymorphism', giving different meanings to same thing.

Now, lets start with a short program and proceed further to understand virtual functions.

Normal Member Functions

First we take an example where a base class and derived classes have functions with same name and access it using pointers.

Listing 12.1 :

```
//demonstrates normal functions
#include<iostream.h>
class base
    {
        public:
        void show()
            {
                cout<<''\n Base'';
            }
    };
        class derived1: public base
```

```
            {
                public:
                void show()
            {
                cout<<''\n Derived is'';
            }
        };
            class derived2: public base
            {
                public:
                void show()
            {
                cout<<''\n Derived to'';
            }
        };
    void main()
        {
            derived1 d1;
            derived2 d2;
            base*p;                         //pointer to base class
            p=&d1;
            p→show();                       //execute show()
            p=&d2;
            p→show();
        }
```

Explanation of Listing 12.1

We have two class `derived 1` and `derived 2` from base class `base`, all having the member function `show( )`.

In `main( )` we create objects of class `derived 1` and `derived 2` and a pointer to class `base`. Then we put the address of derived class object in base class pointer by the statement :

```
p = & d1;
```

Here we can do this because according to the rule, pointers to objects of derived class are type compatible with pointers to objects of base class. But when we execute the line,

```
p → show( );
```

which function will be called ? Whether the compiler will call member function of base class or derived class ? If you see the output of program, you will come to know that, the function in base class is always executed and function in derived class is always ignored.

12.1 Virtual Functions

To overcome the above problem, let's make a single change in our listing. We will just add a keyword `virtual` in front of declarator for `show( )` function only in the base class.

Listing 12.2 :

```
//demonstrates virtual functions
#include<iostream.h>
clacs base
    {
       public:
       virtual void show()               //virtual function
          {
             cout<<''\n Base'';
          }
    };
       class derived1:public base
          {
             public:
             void show()
          {
             cout<<''\n Derived is'';
          }
    };
       class derived2:public base
          {
             public:
             void show()
          {
             cout<<''\n Derived to'';
          }
    };
void main()
    {
       derived1 d1;
       derived2 d2;
       base*p;                           //pointer to base
       p=&d1;
       p→show();                         //execute show()
       p=&d2;
       p→show();
    }
```

Explanation of Listing 12.2

If you see the output of the above program, you will notice that the member functions of derived classes are executed as opposed to execution of base class as in the previous program. We change the contents of pointer p from address of `derived 1` to that of `derived 2`. Particular instance of `show( )` that is executed also changes.

Thus, the same function call,

```
p → show( );
```

executes different functions, depending on contents of pointer p since compiler selects the function based on the contents of p, not on the type of p as in the previous program.

Here, the compiler doesn't know what class the contents of p contains. The compiler knows at run time, what class is pointed to by p and it is executed appropriately. This is called *late* or *dynamic* binding.

This enhances the power of flexibility.

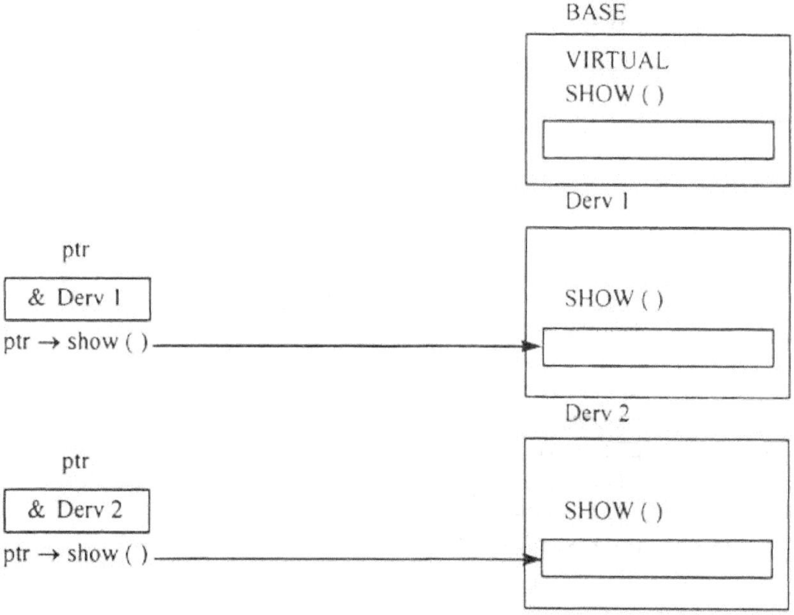

Fig. 12.1

Pure Virtual Functions

A pure virtual function is a function with no body. Since the function in base class is never executed, the body of member function in base class is removed, and the notation = 0 is added to function declaration.

Listing 12.3 :

```
//demonstrates pure virtual function
#include<iostream.h>
class base
    {
        public:
            {
                virtual void show()=0;      //pure virtual function
            }
    };
        class derived1:public base
```

```
            public:
            void show()
          {
            cout<<''\n Derived is'';
          }
      };
        class derived2:public base
          {
            public:
            void show()
          {
            cout<<''\n Derived to'';
          }
      };
   void main()
      {
        base*p[2];                          //list of pointers to base
                                            //class
        derived1 d1;
        derived2 d2;
        p[0]=&d1;
        p[1]=&d2;
        p[0]→show();
        p[1]→show();
      }
```

Explanation of Listing 12.3

In the above program, we declared the pure virtual function in our base class as,

```
virtual void show( ) = 0;
```

Here in this statement, equal sign doesn't denote assignment statement, since value 0 is not assigned to anything. But =0 syntax is simply to tell the compiler that function is pure without body and is declared just to allow the derived class to inherit it.

But remember, if one doesn't declare a virtual function at all in base function, then the functions in derived class will not work at all because the pointers in p[ ] array must point to members of class base. The output of this program will be same as of the previous program.

Virtual Base Classes

The last element in virtual programming is 'virtual base classes'.

Consider the code in which we have a base class 'professor', two derived classes 'Lecturer 1' and 'Lecturer 2' and fourth class 'student' derived from two derived classes.

```
   //demonstrates virtual base classes
   class professor
      {
        protected:
```

```
            int  data;
        };
    class  lecturer1:virtual  public  professor
        {};
    class  lecturer2:virtual  public  professor
        {};
    class  student:public  lecturer1,  public  lecturer2
        {
            public:
1           int  getdata()
                {
                    return  data;
                }
        };
```

To make access of member function in the 'student' class to the data or functions in the 'professor' class, we use a keyword 'virtual' in two derived classes.

The keyword allows two classes to share a single common sub-object of their base class 'professor'. So now, there is only one copy of 'data' which is referred to in the 'student' class.

12.2 Friend Functions

As we know, encapsulation and data-hiding concept of 'OOPS' dictates that, the non-member function should not be allowed to access on objects private or protected data.

But, sometimes the condition arises where we have to violate this rule.

Imagine that, you want a function to operate on object of two different classes as different arguments and operate on their private data. If two classes are inherited from same base class, no problem arises, since you may be able to put the function in base class.

But what if classes are unrelated to each other ?

Here is the condition where we have to violate the rule of data encapsulation. To perform, we have to use the concept of 'friend' function.

Listing 12.4 :

```
    Example  of  'friend'  function:
    //demonstration  of  friend  functions
    #include<iostream.h>
    class  gamma;                                    //needed  for  friendfunc.
    class  delta
        {
            private:
            int  data;
            public:
            delta()
                {
                    data=6;
                }
```

```
        friend int friendfunc(delta, gamma);
    };
class gamma
    {
        private:
        int data;
        public:
        gamma()
            {
                data=15;
            }
        friend int friendfunc.(delta,gamma);
    };
int friendfunc.(delta a, gamma b)
    {
        return(a.data+b.data);
    }
void main()
    {
        delta d;
        gamma g;
        cout<<friendfunc.(d, g);
    }
```

Explanation of Listing 12.4

In the above program, we have defined two classes *delta* and *gamma* and constructors are used to initialize their values.

Here, we want the function `friendfunc.` to have access to the private data of both the classes. In order to do that we make it a `friend function` by attaching the *friend* keyword in both the classes, as in statement.

```
friend int friendfunc.(delta, gamma);
```

This declaration can be placed anywhere in the class either in 'private' or 'public' section.

An object of class is passed as an argument to friend function and it accesses the 'private' data of both the classes through arguments.

In our program, it adds the data and displays it.

Remember that a class can't be referred to until it has been declared first.

So in order to declare class *'gamma'* inside the class *'delta'*, we declared class 'gamma' at the beginning of the program.

Friend Classes

To make the member functions of one class access the *'private'* data of other class, we can make the entire class as a friend. We take an example to get a clear understanding.

Listing 12.5 :

```
//demonstrates friend classes
#include<iostream.h>
class gamma;
class delta
    {
        private:
        int data;
        public:
        delta()
            {
                data=100;
            }
        friend gamma;                          //gamma is friend class
    };
class gamma
    {
        public:
        void f1(delta a)
            {
                cout<<''\n data=''<<a.data;
            }
        void f2(delta a)
            {
                cout<<''\n data=''<<a.data;
            }
    };
void main()
    {
        delta a;
        gamma b;
        f.f1(a);
        f.f2(a);
    }
```

Explanation of Listing 12.5

Here, in class *delta*, the entire class *gamma* is proclaimed as a *friend*. So, now all the member functions of *gamma* can access the private data of *'delta'*.

12.3 Static Functions

We already know about the static data. If you recall, a static data is not duplicated for each object but shared by all objects of a class. We extend this concept to function also.

We will demonstrate a program which will keep record of how many objects are created and then destructor is introduced to destroy that objects.

Listing 12.6 :

```
//demonstrates static functions
#include<iostream.h>
class delta
    {
        private:
        static int data;                    //total objects of class
        int id;                             //ID number of object
        public:
        delta()
            {
                count++;
                id=count;
            }
        ~delta()
            {
                count--;
                cout<<''\n Destroying ID=''<<id;
            }
        static void showcount()             //static function
            {
                cout<<''\n Total count is''<<count;
            }
        void showid()
            {
                cout<<''\n ID is''<<id;
            }
    };
void main()
    {
        cout<<''Program started\n'';
        delta d1;
        delta::showcount();
        delta d2, d3, d4;
        delta::showcount();
        d1.showid();
        d2.showid();
        d3.showid();
        d4.showid();
        cout<<''Program ended'';
    }
```

Explanation of Listing 12.6

In the above program, we have a static data `'count'` which keeps track of number of objects in a class. The objects are incremented by constructor and decremented by destructor.

But if we want to access the `count` from outside the class, we construct the function `showcount( )` that prints the value of `count`.

But, how to access the function ? To access the function using class name only, we declare the function as `static` and access from the class using a scope resolution operator.

The `showid( )` function prints out the ID of object and when destructors destroy the objects to free the memory, it prints it respectively and finally end of the program is printed.

Note that, the destructors destroy the objects in order of 'last-in-first-out' basis.

12.4 The 'this' Pointer

The 'this' pointer is a magic pointer, which points to the object itself. Every member functions of the object has access to it, thus it can find out the address of the object.

We demonstrate this by taking a small program which is listed below.

Listing 12.7 :

```
#include<iostream.h>
class address
    {
        private:
        char array[20];                          //occupies 20 bytes
        public:
        void reveal()
            {
                cout<<''\n Objects address''<<this;
            }
    };
void main()
    {
        address col, co2;
        col.reveal();
        co2.reveal();
    }
```

Explanation of Listing 12.7

The `main( )` program in our example creates two objects of class address which ask each object to print its address using the member function `reveal( )`.

This function prints out the address using the `this` pointer which is used in the function itself.

When you see the output, you will come to know that the objects are spaced 20 bytes apart in memory and address will be in hexadecimal code which can differ from machine to machine.

Member Data and this

One can use the `this` pointer like any other pointer to a object to access the data in the object it points to.

Listing 12.8 :

```
//demonstrates this pointer referring to data
#include<iostream.h>
class data
    {
        private:
        int d;
        public:
        void test()
            {
                this→d=15;                    //same as d=15
                cout<<this→d;
            }
    };
void main()
    {
        data a;
        a.test();
    }
```

Explanation of Listing 12.8

This program simply prints the value 15. So when one calls the member function `test( )`, it comes into existence with the value of `this` which access the variable d as

`this → d = 15;`

This is exactly same as referring to `d` directly.

This Pointer for Returning Values

Till now, we were not returning the object by reference, because the object was local to the function, returning it and thus destroyed (,) when the function returned.

To make the object return by reference of which a function is a member, we use 'this' pointer.

Using this concept we can also overload the operators.

Here we take an example of an array which overloads the assignment operator and the copy constructor.

Listing 12.9 :

```
#include<iostream.h>
class array
    {
        private:
        int*p;                            //pointer to array
        int s;                            //size of array
        Public:
        array()
            { }
```

```
        array(int  a)
            {
                s=a;
                p=new  int[a];
            }
        array(array  &)                          //copy  constructor
        ~array()                                 //destructor
            {
                delete  p;
            }
        int &operator[](int  i)                  //overloaded
            {                                    //subscript
                return*(p+i);
            }
        array&operator=(array  &);               //overloaded  '='
    };
        array::array(array&or)                   //copy  constructor
            {
                s=a.s;                           //new  one  of  same  size
                p=new  int[s];                   //get  space  for  contents
                for(int  i=0;  i<s;  i++)
                *(p+i)=*(ar.p+i);                //copy  contents
            }
        array&array::operator=(array&ar)
            {
                s=ar.s;
                p=new  int[s];
                for(i=0;  i<s;  i++)
                *(p+i)=*(ar.p+i);
                return*this;                     //return  this  object
            }
void  main()
    {
        const  int  SIZE=20;                     //size  of  array
        array  ar1(SIZE);                        //make  array
        for(int  i=0;  i<SIZE;  i++)
        ar1[i]=i*i;
        array  ar2(ar1);                         //use  copy  constructor
        cout<<endl;
        cout<<endl;
        for(i=0;  i<SIZE;  i++)
        cout<<ar2[i]<<''  '';
        array  ar3;
        ar3=ar1;                                 //use  assignment  operator
        for(i=o;  i<SIZE;  i++)
        cout<<ar3[i]<<''  '';
    }
```

Explanation of Listing 12.9

In the above program, we used the declaration

```
array & operator = (array &);
```

in class array, which returns the object by reference. If we want to return this same object by value, we have to declare it as

```
array operator = (array &);
```

Then we encounter the last statement

```
return*this;
```

in function of 'assignment' operator overloading. Since `this` pointer is a pointer to object of which the function is a member, `*this` is that object itself, and statement returns it by reference.

We should note that the `this` pointer is not available in static member functions, since they are not associated with a particular object.

SUMMARY

Virtual functions provide a way to the programs to make the function work according to different kinds of object and this decision is taken at the runtime. This provides the flexibility to the software.

Typically a function is declared virtual in base class and other functions with same name are declared in derived classes. A pure virtual function has no body in base class.

A 'friend' function is used to access the 'private' data of a class, even though it is not a member function of class. This is useful when one function must have access to two or more unrelated classes.

The 'this' pointer is used in member functions to point to object of which the function is a member. It is useful to return the object by reference.

EXERCISES

1. Imagine a publishing company with a base class publication and two derived classes : book and tape each having a function 'putdata( )' and 'getdata( )'.

   Have this as a virtual function in base class as pure. The data can be of user's choice.
2. Create an overload '*' and '– –' operators. Make it an friend function so that you can use expressions as,

   dist1 = 8*dist2;

   dist– –;

   You'll need one argument constructor to convert integer values to distance values of class distance. Write a main( ) program to test the operators.

   The distance prototype program is as in listing 10.4 in chapter 10 of this book.
3. Write a program to copy the string by overloading '=' operator using 'this' pointer.

13

File Management

When one comes to real life programming, it becomes an acute necessity to write and read the programs from disk files.

'C++' provides the stream classes and features in order to enable the programmers to implement the read and write data to disk files.

C programmers will note that the approach to disk I/O used in 'C++' is quite different from 'C'. The old functions of C, `'fread( )'`, `'fwrite( )'` etc. still work in 'C++' environment but are not well-suited to the object-oriented environment.

13.1 Streams

The new approach in 'C++' consisting of 'streams' makes file input and output considerably cleaner and easier.

A 'stream' is a general name given to the flow of data. Different streams are used to represent different kinds of data flow.

Streams	*Used for*
ifstream	Input files
ofstream	Output files
fstream	Both input and output files
istream	Extraction operator (>>)
streams	Used for
ostream	Insertion operator (<<)

The `iostream.h` class is derived from `istream.h` and `ostream.h` by multiple inheritance.

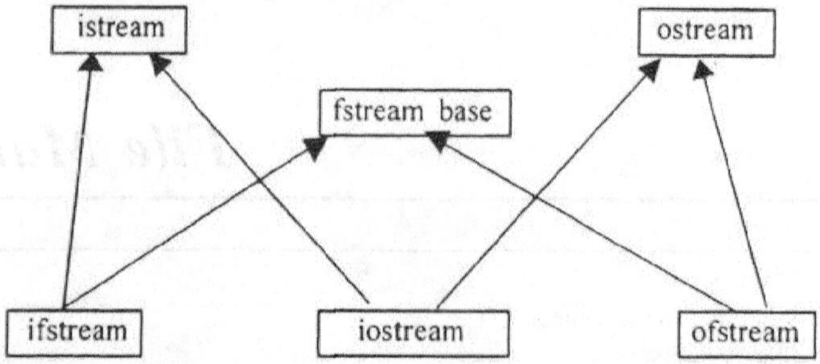

Fig. 13.1

The `fstream.h` class contains `ifstream.h`, `ofstream.h`, `fstream.h` and `iostream.h`.

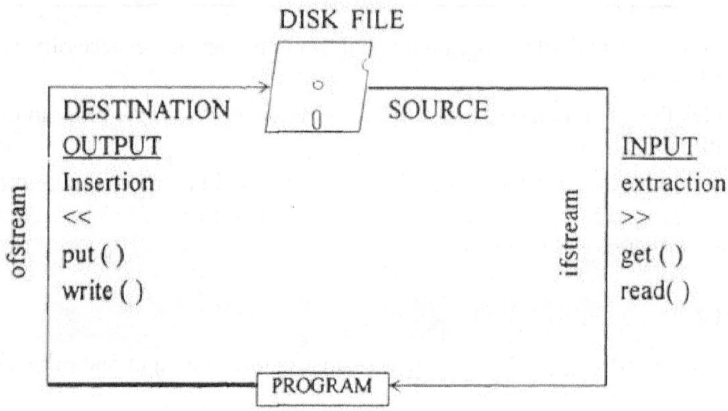

Fig. 13.2. File input and output.

Thus, when the programmer declares `fstream.h` as a header file, there is no need to declare explicitly any other file for file management features.

String I/O

Let us look at a simple program that reads and writes the data to the file.

Listing 13.1 :

```
//demonstrates file input and output
#include<fstream.h>
void main()
    {
        char str[100];              //character buffer
        ifstream infile(''In.Txt'');
        while(infile)
            {
                cin>>str;
                infile.getline(str, 100);
            }
```

```
          ofstream  outfile(''In.Txt'');
          while(outfile)
              {
                  outfile<<''string:''<<str<<endl;
              }
      }
```

Explanation of Listing 13.1

In the above program, the user inputs the string using `cin` function.

Then, we read the text from the file, one line at a time using the `getline()` function. This function reads the characters until it encounters the '\n' character, and places the resulting string in 'str' which is supplied as an argument.

The file is created for input using the object `infile` of class `ifstream`. Similarly, the file for output is created by defining an object called `outfile` to be a member of `ofstream` class and at same time, we initialize it to file named `''In.Txt''`. This sets aside various resources for file and accesses the file of that name on disk.

When the program terminates, the `outfile` goes out of scope which calls destructor to close the file. So, we don't need to close the file explicitly.

End of file

In the above program, `while` loop checks for end-of-file function, which is a signal sent to the program from hardware when a read or write operation has reached the end of file. When this function is encountered, the read or write operation discontinues and loop is exited.

13.2 Read and Write Objects

Since C++ is an object-oriented language, it is reasonable to allow the objects to be written on disk and read from it. Here we demonstrate a program to write and read a object from disk file.

Listing 13.2 :

```
//demonstrates object I/O
#include<fstream.h>
class person
    {
        protected:
        char name[30];                  //person's name
        int tel;                        //person's telephone no.
        public:
        void getdata(void)
            {
                cout<<''Enter name:'';
                cin>>name;
                cout<<''Enter telephone number:'';
                cin>>tel;
            }
```

```
            void showdata(void)
                {
                    cout<<''\n  Name:''<<name;
                    cout<<''\n  Tel:''<<tel;
                }
        };
    void main()
        {
            person p;
            p.getdata();
            ofstream  outfile(''Info.dot'');
            outfile.write((char*)&p,  size  of(p));
            ifstream  infile(''Info.dot'');
            infile.read((char*)&p,  size  of(p));
            p.showdata();
        }
```

Explanation of Listing 13.2

In the above program, we have called the member function `getdata( )`, which it places in the object `p` ; the contents of which are then written in a file using `write( )` function.

The syntax, we have used is

```
outfile.write((char*)&p,  size  of(p));
```

It indicates that `write( )` function is written on the file which is pointed by the pointer `outfile`. `write( )` function takes two arguments first, the address of the object to be written and length of the object in bytes. We have used the `size of` operator to find the length of the object p. Address of object must be cast to type pointer to `char`.

Then we created the same file for reading using the class `ifstream`. That file is read using the `read( )` member function which calls the `showdata( )` function from class `person`.

Binary Files

Note that, here we used `write( )` function instead of `get( )` as in previous program in order to write file in binary format instead of character format.

Similarly, the `read( )` function is used to read the file which is written using `write( )` function as it reads the file in binary form only.

The advantage of this is that, the file can be read inside the application only and cannot be read outside that application or in any other application. This type of examples can be seen in 'microsoft word' application whose file with doc extension can be viewed inside the word application only.

Input and Output with Multiple Objects

In our next example, we will open a file and write as many objects as user wants. Then it reads and displays the content of file.

Listing 13.3 :

```
//demonstrates  multiple  objects  I/O
#include<fstream.h>
```

```
class person
    {
        protected:
        char name[30];                  //person's name
        int tel;                        //person's telephone no.
        public:
        void getdata(void)
            {
                cout<<''Enter name:'';
                cin>>name;
                cout<<''Enter telephone number:'';
                cin>>tel;
            }
        void showdata(void)
            {
                cout<<''\n Name:''<<name;
                cout<<''\n Tel:''<<tel;
            }
    };
void main()
    {
        person p;                       //create person object
        char ch;
        fstream file;                   //create file for I/O
        file.open(''Test.Txt'', ios::app|ios::out|ios::in);
        do
            {
                cout<<''\n Enter your data:'';
                p.getdata();
                file.write((char*)&p, size of(p));
                cout<<''want to enter another data''<<''(y/n)?'';
                cin>>ch;
            }
        while(ch= ='y'||ch= ='y');
        file.seekg(0);                  //reset to start file
        file.read((char*)&p, size of(p));
        while(!file.cof())
            {
                cout<<''\n Person is:'';
                p.showdata();
                file.read((char*)&p, size of(p));
            }
    }
```

Explanation of Listing 13.3

In this program, we have created a file that can be used for both input and output, which requires an object `file` of `fstream` class. To open the file, we used `open( )` function, which is a member of `fstream( )` class in statement.

```
file.open(''Test.Txt'',  ios::app|ios::out|ios::in);
```

We used `app` for append function, `out` for output of data on file and `in` for input in file. The vertical bars between the flags cause the bits representing the flags to be logically ORed together, so that several flags can apply simultaneously.

Remaining things are same as in previous example, and therefore need not be explained.

Table 13.1

Mode Bits for open( ) function

Mode bit	*Result*
in	open for reading
out	open for writing
app	start reading or writing at end of file (append)
ate	erase file before reading or writing
nocreate	error when opening if file doesn't exist
noreplace	error when opening for output if file already exists
binary	open file in binary mode

13.3 File Pointers

Each file object has associated with it, two integer values called *get pointer* and *put pointer* which give the current position of the pointer. These value specify the byte number in file where writing or reading takes place.

In order to set and examine the get pointer, `seekg( )` and `tellg( )` functions are used. Similarly, for put pointer, `seek p( )` and `tellp( )` functions are used.

In `seekg( )` function, one can specify two arguments, where first represents an offset from particular location in file, and second specifies the location from which offset is measured.

In second argument, there are three possibilities :

`'beg'` (—) beginning of file.

`'cur'` (—) current pointer position

`'end'` (—) end of file.

Here, we take an example, which displays the size of the file.

Listing 13.4 :

```
//demonstrates file pointers
#include<fstream.h>
#include<process.h>                    //for exit()
void main(int argc, char**argv)
    {
if(argc!=2)
```

```
    {
        arr<<''\n  Format:filesize  filename'';
        exit(-1);
    }
ifstream  infile;
infile.open(argv[1]);                       //open  file
if(!infile)
    {
        arr<<''\n  can't  open'';
        exit(-1);
    }
infile.seekg(0,  ios::end);
cout<<''size  of  file:''<<argv[1]<<''is''<<infile.tellg();
    }
```

Explanation of Listing 13.4

We have written the above program using command line arguments. It will be explained later in this chapter. Here, we concentrate only on file pointers.

The statement, `infile.seekg(0, ios::end);` means that the get pointer is positioned at the end of file until the end of file is not encountered. Then the size of filc in total number of bytes is displayed by `tellg( )` function in the last statement, which returns the current position of get pointer.

13.4 Redirection

Till now, we have read or written files using the objects `cout` and `cin`. These predefined objects normally represent display and keyboard. But if we want, we can redirect the input, output or both to other files instead to standard input or output.

Here we demonstrate it using a program which we give a name, `redirect.cpp`.

Listing 13.5 :

```
//redirect.cpp
//demonstrates  redirection
#include<iostream.h>
#include<iomanip.h>                         //for  resetiosflags()
void  main()
    {
        char  c;
        while(!cin.eof())                   //quit  on  EOF
            {
                cin>>resetiosflags(ios::skipws)>>c;
                                            //read  from  std  input
                cout<<c;                    //send  to  std  output
            }
    }
```

Explanation of Listing 13.5

Here, in our program, we reset the `skipws` flag while getting the input from `cin` because `cin` normally skips white spaces, newlines and EOFs. Since we want to read these characters, we disable the white space skipping by resetting the ios flags.

We can redirect the keyboard input to file name `Test.dat` to your screen by typing the command

`redirect>Test.dot.`

Before typing above command, compile your `redirect.cpp` file to `redirect.exe` file.

Similarly you can redirect both input and output file simultaneously by typing the command

`redirect<Test.dot>dest.dot.`

Nothing will be displayed, but you will find that `Test.dot` has been copied to `dest.dot.`

All `.dot` files are example files. The users can use other files of their choice also.

13.5 Command-Line Arguments

You shall be familiar with command-line arguments in DOS programs.

Today, we will make one DOS command just to let you know, how it can be made. If you understand this program thoroughly, you shall able to make many DOS and alike commands by applying similar type of logic.

We demonstrate here the *copy* command of DOS. Here we make a command in our own way.

Listing 13.6 :

```
#include<fstream.h>
#include<process.h>                        //for exit()
void main(int argc, char**argv)
    {
        if(argc!=3)
            {
                eerr<<''\n syntax:kopy source dest'';
                exit(-1);
            }
        char c;
        ifstream infile;                   //create file
        infile.open(argv[1]);              //open file
        if(!infile)
            {
                eerr<<''\n can't open''<<argv[1];
                exit(-1);
            }
        ofstream outfile;
        outfile.open(argv[2], ios::noreplace);
        if(!outfile)
            {
                eerr<<''\n can't open''<<argv[2];
                exit(-1);
            }
```

```
            while(infile)
                {
                    infile.get(c);              //read  character
                    outfile.put(c);             //write  character
                }
        }
```

Explanation of Listing 13.6

If you notice carefully, you will see that there is a difference between the main( ) function of this program and previous chapter's program.

Here, we have passed two arguments to main( ) function in order to make the program as command-line program. The first argument is argc (argument count) which represents the total number of arguments in command line. The first command line argument is always the pathname of current program (Krpy in our case) and remaining arguments are those typed by the user.

The system stores the command line arguments as strings in memory and creates an array of pointers which points to these strings. This array is argv which is passed as a second argument in main( ) function. Individual strings are accessed through appropriate functional pointer, so first string (pathname) is argv[0], the second is argv[1] (source file name), and third is argv[2] (destination file name). So the total number of arguments are 3 which is argc.

Finally in 'while' loop, the program reads the file character by character from source file and writes it to destination file until end of file (EOF) is reached.

13.6 Printer Output

Sending data to printer is similar as sending data to disk file.

Here, we have a special filenames for hardware devices.

Name	*Device*
Con	Console
Aux or Com1	First serial port
Com2	Second serial port
PRN OR LPT1	First parallel printer
LPT2	Second parallel printer
LPT3	Third parallel printer
NUL	Dummy device

In most systems, the printer is connected to port LPT1. So we take that part as a default while writing a program.

But you can substitute the appropriate port name if your system is configured differently.

Listing 13.7 :

```
//cprint.cpp
//demonstrates print command of DOS
#include<fstream.h>
#include<process.h>                          //for exit()
```

```
void main(int argc, char**argv);
    {
        if(argc!=2)
            {
                eerr<<''\n Format:cprint<filename>'';
                exit(-1);
            }
        char c;
        ifstream infile;                    //create file to read
        infile.open(argv[1]);               //open file
        if(!infile)
            {
                eerr<<''\n can't open:''<<argv[1];
                exit(-1);
            }
        ofstream outfile;
        outfile.open(''PRN'');              //open for printer
        while(infile.get(c)!=0)
        outfile.put(c);
    }
```

Explanation of Listing 13.7

In our program, first we checked the syntax so that the program will execute only if number of arguments in command line are correct.

We opened the file for reading and checked for errors. If there are errors, it will not open displaying the message on the screen.

Then we created a file for output, which is opened to printer.

Thus, 'while' loop reads character by character from input file and prints it to printer, until the end of file is not reached. So this completes our discussion about the concept of file management.

SUMMARY

In this chapter, we have seen disk file I/O using 'ifstream' for 'input', 'ofstream' for 'output' and 'fstream' for both.

Then, we saw read( )' and 'write( )' functions which work in binary mode and 'get( )', 'put( )' functions which work in character mode.

Finally, we learnt about 'file pointers', 'command-line arguments' and 'redirection'.

EXERCISES

1. Write a program that display the file according to options you give with display command at command line. The options are :

u—underline,

l—lowercase (all characters)

U—upper case(all characters)

Z—should show 15 lines and then pause.

The format of display command should be display [–u] [–l] [–u] [–l] <filename>.

2. Create a file which automatically should have extension '.txt' after its creation.
3. Write type command.
4. Write file at command. in which data of two files are merged into third file and display that file.
5. Overload the '<<' and '>>' operators.

14
Graphics

Turbo C++ and Borland C++ include an extensive collection of graphics-oriented library functions.

With these functions, you can make almost any type of graphics and sound in 'DOS' mode. You can also make objects with the help of object-oriented programming.

Here we do not cover all Turbo C++ graphics functions. Our aim is to show most important functions and how they work. If you are interested in more functions, you can refer 'Turbo C++ Bible.'

Here all graphics functions with their description and syntax are explained one by one. So, the program of graphics will be taken towards the end of the chapter after completing the explanation of major graphic syntaxes.

14.1 Text-Mode Graphics

When the computer is started, it is usually in text mode. In this mode, the screen is divided into 80 columns and 25 rows. Remember that, all text-mode and graphics library functions are portable only to MS-DOS environment. This is the only drawback of 'TC++' compiler.

Let us we take a tour to text-mode functions :

The window( ) function :

The `window( )` is a key library function for text-mode. This function requires `conio.h` header file.

```
syntax  :  window  (left,  top,  right,  bottom).
```

This function takes four coordinates of screen as mentioned in syntax.

Here, columns runs from 1 to 80 and rows runs from 1 to 25.

This function doesn't draw border or outline around the window, but makes window in logical memory.

The cputs( ) function :

This function is especially made to put the text inside window which is made from 'window( )'.

```
syntax  :  cputs( ).
```

The clrscr( ) function :

The function is used to erase what is there on screen.

```
syntax : clrscr( ).
```

The gotoxy( ) function :

This library function positions the cursor on the specified x-coordinate and y-coordinate.

```
syntax : gotoxy (x-cord, y-coord)
```

The textcolor( ) function :

This library function is used to display the color of the text which is displayed on screen.

```
syntax : textcolor(color number).
```

Table 14.1

Text-Mode Colors

Colour Numbers	*Color Constant*
0	Black
1	Blue
2	Green
3	Cyan
4	Red
5	Magenta
6	Brown
7	Light Grey
8	Dark Grey
9	Light Blue
10	Light Green
11	Light Cyan
12	Light Red
13	Light Magenta
14	Yellow
15	White
128	Blink

14.2 Setting Graphics Mode

To switch your computer from text-mode to graphics mode, you will have to perform two steps :

(1) Include header file ``graphics.h''.

(2) Install graphics driver.

Graphics driver

To install the graphics driver in your program, you will have to use `initgraph( )` function. This library function must be executed before any other graphics-mode functions can be used.

```
syntax : initgraph(&driver, &mode, ``\\tc\\bgi\\''.
```

In this syntax, the driver and mode are automatically selected and taken from the system by `initgraph()` function.

The path given is almost general but you can modify according to your system configuration if necessary.

14.3 Shapes, Line, Color, Pattern, Sound

The circle( ) function :

This library function is used to draw the circle of your desired shape. It takes three arguments : x-coordinate, y-coordinate and radius.

```
syntax : circle(x-coord, y-coord, rad)
```

The closegraph( ) function :

This function is used to close graphics mode and return to previous video mode. It releases the memory which graphics system was using.

```
syntax : closegraph().
```

The setcolor( ) function :

This function is used to set the color for drawing lines and outlines. The color code is given in Table 14.1.

```
syntax : setcolor(color number).
```

The setlinestyle( ) function :

This library function is used to specify the lines styles.

```
syntax : setlinestyle(line style)
```

Table 14.2

Line Styles

0	Solid-Line
1	Dotted-Line
2	Center-Line
3	Dashed-Line
4	Userbit-Line

The setfillstyle( ) function :

This library function is used to specify the pattern of line with color of it.

```
syntax : setfillstyle(line pattern, line color).
```

The color names and their codes are already given in Table 14.1.

The table of patterns is :

Table 14.3

Patterns

Pattern Code	*Pattern*	*Use*
0	Empty-Filll	Background color
1	Solid-Fill	Solid color
2	Line-Fill	Horizontal lines

3	LTslash-Fill	SW-NE light lines
4	Slash-Fill	SW-NE heavy lines
5	Bkslash-Fill	NW-SE heavy lines
6	LTBkslash-Fill	NW-SE light lines
7	Hatch-Fill	Light cross lines
8	Xhatch-Fill	Heavy cross lines
9	Interleave-Fill	Interleave
10	Wide-Dot-Fill	Wide-spaced dots
11	Close-Dot-Fill	Close-spaced dots
12	User-Fill	User-defined

The rectangle( ) function :

This library function draws the outline of rectangle.

```
syntax : rectangle(left, top, right, bottom);
```

The line( ) function :

This library function is used to specify and draw a line. It requires wo arguments of function to specify x and y coordinates of lines at starting point, and last two arguments to specify at end point.

```
syntax : line(x1, y1, x2, y2);
```

Sound Functions

The sound( ) function :

This library function sets the sound generator to a specific frequency in 'hertz'. Once this function is executed, the sound remains on until specifically stopped with `nosound( )` function.

```
syntax : sound(number);
```

The delay( ) function :

This library function is used to control how long sound will continue. So if you want, the sound to be delayed by half a second, you should enter 500 to function parameter number.

```
syntax : delay(number);
```

14.4 Text in Graphics Mode

The settextstyle( ) function :

This library function is used to modify the font, direction and size of the text.

```
syntax : settextstyle(font, direction, size);
```

The settextjustify( ) function :

This library function is used to specify, where text will be displayed relative to current pointer.

```
syntax : settextjustify(horzjustify, vertjustify);
```

Table 14.4

Horizontal Justification	
Left Text	Current pointer on left end of text
Center Text	Current pointer in horizontal center of text
Right Text	Current pointer on right end of text

Vertical Justification

Top-Text	Current pointer on top of text
Center-Text	Current pointer in vertical center of text
Bottom-Text	Current pointer on bottom of text.

The outtext( ) function :

This library function is used display the string in graphic format.

```
syntax : outtext(string);
```

Since, we have seen many functions of graphics above, now we will put that knowledge in creating a program below.

We program a code of class car which has various shapes.

Listing 14.1 :

```
//demonstrates graphics
#include<graphics.h>                         //for graphics functions
#include<conio.h>                            //for getch()
class shape
   {
      protected:
        int x, y;                            //coordinates of center
        int w, h;                            //width, height
        int line color;                      //color of outline
        int fillcolor;                       //color of interior
      public:
        shape()                              //constructor
          {
             x=0; y=0; w=0; h=0;
             linecolor=white;
             fillcolor=white;
          }
      void set(int x1, int y1, int w1, int h1, int l, int f)
          {
             x=x1; y=y1; w=w1; h=h1;
             linecolor=l;
             fillcolor=f;
          }
      void draw()
          {
             setcolor(linecolor);
             setlinestyle(solid-line, 0, thick-width);
             setfillstyle(solid-fill, fillcolor);
          }
   };
      class ball: public shape
```

```
        {
            public:
            ball:shape()
            {}
    void set(int x, int y, int r, int l, int f)
        {
            shape::set(x1, y1, r, r, l, f);
        }
    void draw()
        {
            shape::draw();                      //set colors
            circle(x, y, w/2);                  //draw circle
            floodfill(x, y, line color);        //fill circle
        }
};
    class rect: public shape
        {
            public:
            rect:shape()
            {}
    void set(int x1, int y1, int w1, int h1, int l, int f)
        {
            shape::set(x1, y1, w1, h1, l, f);
        }
    void draw()
        {
            shape::draw();              //set colors
            rectangle(x-w/2, y-h/2, x+w/2, y+h/2);
            floodfill(x, y, linecolor);
        }
};
    class car
        {
            private:
            rect window;                //create top part of car
            rect body;                  //create bottom part of car
            ball wheel1, wheel2;        //create wheels
            public:
    void set(int x, int y)
        {
            window.set(x+10, y, 40, 20, Yellow, Blue);
            body.set(x+30, y+25, 100, 30, Yellow, Blue);
            wheel1.set(x, y+42, 27, Yellow, Brown);
            wheel2.set(x+60, y+42, 27, Yellow, Brown);
        }
```

```
            void draw()
                {
                    window.draw();
                    body.draw();
                    wheel1.draw();
                    wheel2.draw();
                }
        };
    void main()
        {
            int driver, mode;
            driver=DETECT;                             //set best graphic mode
            initgraph(&driver, &mode, ''\\tc\\bgi'');
            car c1, c2;
            c1.set(100, 100);
            c2.set(300, 300);
            c1.draw();
            c2.draw();
            getch();
            closegraph();                              //close graphics system
        }
```

This completes the static model of a car program.

14.5 Stand-Alone Graphics System

The above program will run fine as long as it is on your PC. But suppose, you want that, your program should run anywhere and on any computer system, you will have to make your above program, a 'stand-alone' graphic program. To create a stand-alone program you have to add some code inside the main( ) function immediately after opening the brace of the 'main( )' function.

The code will remain same for any graphic program.

```
registerbgidriver(EGAVGA-driver);
registerbgifont(sansserif-font);
int driver, mode;
driver=DETECT;
initgraph(&driver, &mode, '' '');
   //initialize the graphic system.
```

After adding this code, you will have to link drivers and font files to your application. But to link, you have to convert these files to object form by using utility `BGIOBJ.EXE`.

The command is :

```
C:\>bgiolj egavga and
C:\>bgiobj sans.
```

After doing this, link these object files to your application by going to *'Compile'* menu and click the option *'Build all'*.

SUMMARY

We have seen the text function which is in header file <conio.h>. Then functions for graphics, sound and text in graphic mode are seen. We have used function 'window' The 'initgraph( )' and 'closegraph( )' functions are used for initializing the graphics and closing the graphics.

Library functions can write lines, circles, squares etc. One can use different colors, shapes, colors fills etc.

The graphic objects can be conceptualized by using the graphic functions.

EXERCISES

1. Write a program that have three wheels, which moves when you press a 'spacebar' key and stops when you press another time. It should also generate a sound.
2. Make a keyboard piano.
3. Write a program that makes any shape of a polygon by entering a specific key. *e.g.*, when key 'R' is pressed, rectangle should be formed.

15

Large Programs

In previous chapters, we have seen each and every aspect of C++ including graphics.

However, all the programs in previous chapters consist of a single file. But in real-life applications, all the programs not necessarily consist of single file only. So here, we introduce the concept of programming using 'multifiles'.

Designing a Project

In this chapter, we are designing an application of a calculator. Here we go step by step starting from designing a calculator logic to the compilation of an entire project consisting of multifiles.

Steps to design a Pocket Calculator

Step I : Thinking of Logic

You have planned to write a program that models a four function pocket calculator, placing a picture of calculator on screen.

Step II : Thinking of Output

The buttons on calculator appear to push in when activated, which is an optical illusion. Different kinds of buttons are coloured differently. Digits have black background, blue arithmetic operators and red clear button.

Simulate the action of mouse, using keyboard keys. So, when you type a digit, for instance, the corresponding button on screen appears to push in accompanying the clicking noise.

Step III : Files included in project

Here, we code each file turn by turn. Here, first we code the header file ''calc.h''.

```
//calc.h
//header file for calculator application
#include<string.h>                          //for strcpy()
#include<graphics.h>                        //for graphics
#include<conio.h>                           //for getche()
#include<dos.h>                             //for delay(), sound() etc.
#include<stdio.h>                           //for sprintf()
#include<math.h>                            //for atof()
class window;                               //for building screen
window*const SCREEN=(window*)0;
enum bottomstatus {unpushed, pushed};
enum boolean {false, true};
```

```
class window
    {
        protected:
        window*ptrowner;                    //address of window
        int left, top, right, bot;          //edges of rectangle
        int delta;                          //distance between borders
        int deltacolor;                     //color between borders
        int centercolor;                    //color within border
        public:                             //constructor
        window(window*ptr, int l, int t, int r, int b,
               int dc=BLUE, int cc=DARK GRAY): window(ptr,
               l, t, r, b, dc, cc)
        { }
    };
        class Button:public window          //push button
            {
               private:
               char text[20];               //characters on button
               button status b;
               public:
               Button(window*ptr, int l, int t, int r, int b,
                     int cc=BLACK, char*tx='' ''):window(ptr, l,
                     t, r, b, BLACK, cc)
            {
               strcpy(text, tsc);
               b=unpushed;
            }
        void click(void);
        void display(void);
    };
        //so create a output window
            {
               private:
               char text[100];
               public :
               output(window*ptr, int l, int t, int r, int b,
                     int dc=BLUE, int cc=WHITE):window(ptr, l,
                     t, r, b, dc, cc)
               { }
        void text(char*);                   //display text
        void number (double);               //display number
    };
```

Now, we create another file `'calc.cpp'` which contains the number functions to build a calculator

```
//calc.cpp
#include''calc.h''                          //include header
//file, which we had coded previously
window::window(window*ptr, int l, int t, int r, int b,
               int dc, int cc)
    {
        ptrowner=ptr; left=l; top=t;
        right=r;      bot=b;   deltacolor=dc;
        centercolor=cc;
        //calculate delta
        delta=((right-left)+(bot-top))/150+3;
        if(ptrowner!=SCREEN)
            {
                left+=ptrowner→left;
                right+=ptrowner→left;
                top+=ptrowner→top;
                bot+=ptrowner→top;
            }
    }
//To display the window:
void window::Display(void)
    {
        setcolor(WHITE);
        intp[10];
        //draw outer rectangle and fill it by
        //using a fillpoly()function
         p[0]=left;  p[1]=top;
         p[2]=right; p[3]=top;
         p[4]=right; p[5]=bot;
         p[6]=left;  p[7]=bot;
         p[8]=left;  p[9]=top;
        setfillstyle(SOLID_FILL, deltacolor);
        fillpoly(5, p);
        //now draw inner rectangle
        rectangle(left+delta+1, top+delta, right-delta-1, bot-delta);
        setfillstyle(SOLID_FILL, centercolor);
        floodfill(left+(right-left)/2, top+delta+1, WHITE);
    }
//Now, code for clicking the button
void button::click(void);
    {
        b=pushed;                             //push it
        Button::Display();
        sound(500);
        delay(20);
        nosound();
```

```
        delay(270);
        b=unpushed;
        Button::Display();
        sound(500);
        delay(20);
        nosound();
    }
        //Now, code to display the button
        Window::Display();
        moveto(left+(right-left)/2+1,  top+(bot-top)/2);
        settextjustify(CENTER_TEXT,  CENTER_TEXT);
        settextstyle(Sans-serif-font,  Horiz-dir,  User-chor-size);
        setusercharsize(5, 8, 2, 3);       //5/8 width,  2/3 height
        setcolor(white);
        outtext(text);
        moveto(left,  top);                //upper left diagonal
        lineto(left+delta,  top+delta);
        moveto(right,  top);               //upper right diagonal
        lineto(right-delta,  top+delta);
        moveto(left,  bot);                //lower left diagonal
        lineto(left+delta,  bot-delta);
        moveto(right,  bot);               //lower right diagonal
        lineto(right-delta,  bot-delta);
        setfillstyle(solid-fill,  lightgray);
        if(b==unpushed);
            {
                floodfill(left+(right-left)/2,  top+1,  white);
                floodfill(right-1,  top+(bot-top)/2,  white);
            }
    }
        //code for displaying text
        void  Output::Text(char*ptrs);
            {
                display();
                moveto(right-delta,  top+(bot-top)/2);
                settextjustify(Right-Text,  Center-Text);
                settextstyle(Sans-serif-font, Horiz-dir, User-char-size);
                setusercharsize(5,  8,  1,  1);
                setcolor(BLACK);
                outtext(ptrs);             //insert string
            }
        //code to display number
        void  Output::Number(double  d)
            {
                char  buffer[100];
                sprintf(buffer,  ''%16.2f'',d);
```

```
                Output::Text(buffer);}
//Now, this is code which uses the various
//classes to create calculator
//calculator.cpp uses calc.cpp
#include''calc.h''
void main()
   {
       int driver, mode;
       driver=DETECT;
       initgraph(&driver, &mode, ''\\tc\\bgi'');
       //this section defines buttons.
       Border  border1(SCREEN, 240, 30, 480, 330);
       Output  output1(&border1, 20, 20, 220, 60, BLUE, WHITE);
       Button  button0(&border1, 30, 230, 65, 265, BLACK, ''0'');
       Button  button1(&border1, 30, 180, 65, 215, BLACK, ''1'');
       Button  button2(&border1, 78, 180, 113, 215, BLACK, ''2'');
       Button  button3(&border1, 127, 180, 162, 275, BLACK, ''3'');
       Button  button4(&border1, 30, 130, 65, 165, BLACK, ''4'');
       Button  button5(&border1, 78, 130, 113, 165, BLACK, ''5'');
       Button  button6(&border1, 127, 130, 162, 165, BLACK, ''6'');
       Button  button7(&border1, 30, 80, 65, 115, BLACK, ''7'');
       Button  button8(&border1, 78, 80, 113, 115, BLACK, ''8'');
       Button  button9(&border1, 127, 80, 162, 115, BLACK, ''9'');
       Button  buttond(&border1, 175, 80, 210, 115, BLUE, ''/'');
       Button  buttonm(&border1, 175, 130, 210, 165, BLUE, ''*'');
       Button  buttons(&border1, 175, 180, 210, 215, BLUE, ''-'');
       Button  buttondot(&border1, 78, 230, 113, 265, BLACK, ''.'');
       Button  buttonc(&border1, 127, 230, 162, 265, RED, ''c'');
       Button  buttona(&border1, 175, 230, 210, 265, BLUE, ''+='');
       //this section displays buttons
       border1.display();
       output1.display();
       button7.display();    button8.display();
       button9.display();    button4.display();
       button5.display();    button6.display();
       button1.display();    button2.display();
       button3.display();    buttons.display();
       buttond.display();    buttonm.display();
       buttona.display();    button0.display();
       buttondot.display();  buttonc.display();
       output1.number(0.0);             //display0.0;
       //this section of code handles keyboard
       //and activates display
       const char ESC=27;               //escape key
       char dstring[100];               //string for display
       char temp[100];
```

```
        int  chars=0;
        char  ch;                              //character  read  from
                                               //keyboard
        char  open;                            //operator:/, *, -, +
        boolean  first=true;                   //first  operator
        boolean  chain=false;                  //chaining  to  next  numbers
        double  n1,  n2;                       //1st  and  2nd  numbers
        double  ans;                           //answer  on  screen
        while(ch=getch())!=ESC)
            {
                if((ch>='0'&&ch<='9')          //ch=='.')
            {
                switch(ch)                     //click  button
            {
                case'0':  button0.click();    break;
                case'1':  button1.click();    break;
                case'2':  button2.click();    break;
                case'3':  button3.click();    break;
                case'4':  button4.click();    break;
                case'5':  button5.click();    break;
                case'6':  button6.click();    break;
                case'7':  button7.click();    break;
                case'8':  button8.click();    break;
                case'9':  button9.click();    break;
                case'-':  buttondot.click();  break;
            }
        dstring[chars++]=ch;
        dstring[chars]='\0';                   //put  null  at  end
                                               //of  string
        if(atof(dstring)>999999999.99||chars>)
            {
                delay(200);
                sound(300);
                delay(200);
                nosound();
                dstring[--chars]='/0';
            }
        output1.text(dstring);}
//if  it's  a  valid  math  character
else  if(ch=='/'||ch=='*'||ch=='-'||ch=='+'||ch=='=')
    {
        strcpy(temp,  dstring);
        chars=0;
        dstring[chars]='\0';
        output1.text(dstring);                 //display  empty
                                               //buffer
```

```
if(first)
    {
        n1=(chain)?ans:atof(temp);
        first=false;                //next op will be second
        switch(ch);
    {
        case'/':buttond.click();
                oper='/'; break;
        case'*':buttonm.click();
                oper='*'; break;
        case'-':buttons.click();
                oper='-'; break;
        case'+':
        case'=':buttona.click();
                oper='+'; break;
    }
}
    else
    buttona.click(),                //assume as'='
    n2=atof(temp);
    swtich(oper)
    {
        case'/':ans=n1/n2;  break;
        case'*':ans=n1*n2;  break;
        case'-':ans=n1-n2;  break;
        case'+':ans=n1+n2;  break;
    }
    if(ans>999999999.99)
    output1.text(''overflow'');
    else
    {
        output1.number(ans);
        n1=ans;
    }
    first=true;
    chain=true;
    }
}
    else  if(ch=='c'||ch=='c')      //if clear
    {
        buttonc.click();
        first=true;
        chain=false;
        chars=0;
        dstring[chars]='\0';
        output1.number(0.0);
```

```
                }
            else
                {
                    delay(200);
                    sound(300);
                    delay(200);
                    nosound();
                }
        }
        closegraph();
    }
```

This completes the entire coding of the 'calculator' application.

Now, we move ahead about discussing, how to compile the multiple files into a single `'.exe'` file.

Step IV : Compilation of a Project

We have already made the programs of the calculator. At present we have the files, `''calc.cpp''` and `''calculator.cpp''` each of which is included the header file `''calc.h''`.

Steps to form `'calculator.exe'` file :

(1) Open a project named `'calculator.prj'`.

(2) Add the files `''calc.cpp''`, `''calculator.cpp''` and `''calc.h''` inside the project by clicking 'add items' of project window.

(3) Then press Enter.

(4) Then goto the *'compile'* menu and select `'make.Exe.'`

(5) Then press 'Ctrl-F9' to run the program.

This completes your creation of project and running of a application of a calculator.

SUMMARY

Vendor-provided object libraries are often distributed as a '.lib' library file.

The Turbo C++ project feature can be used to combine several source or object files into a single executable file. The project feature simplifies keeping track of what files need to be compiled. It compiles any source file that has been modified since last linking and links resulting object files.

Appendices

A : ASCII Table
B : Turbo C++ Keywords
C : Bibliography

A : ASCII Table

Decimal	*Symbol (ASCII)*	*Key*
0	NULL	ctrl-2
1	⊖	ctrl A
2	●	ctrl B
3	♥	ctrl C
4	♦	ctrl D
5	♣	ctrl E
6	♠	ctrl F
7	.	ctrl G
8	◙	book space
9	o	tab
10	▯	ctrl J
11	♂	ctrl K
12	♀	ctrl L
13	♪	Enter
14	♫	ctrl N
15	Π	ctrl O
16	►	ctrl P
17	◄	ctrl Q
18	↕	ctrl R
19	!!	ctrl S
20	*q*	ctrl T
21	■	ctrl U
22		ctrl V
23	↨	ctrl W
24	↑	ctrl X
25	↓	ctrl Y
26	→	ctrl Z
27	←	Esc
28	L	

(Table Contd.)

Decimal	*Symbol (ASCII)*	*Key*
29	↔	**ctrl]**
30	▲	**ctrl 6**
31	▼	**ctrl -**
32	space	**spacebar**
33	!	!
34	"	"
35	#	#
36	$	$
37	%	%
38	&	&
39	'	'
40	(	(
41	)	)
42	*	*
43	+	+
44	,	,
45	-	-
46	.	.
47	/	/
48	0	0
49	1	1
50	2	2
51	3	3
52	4	4
53	5	5
54	6	6
55	7	7
56	8	8
57	9	9
58	:	:
59	;	;
60	<	<
61	=	=
62	>	>
63	?	?
64	@	@
65	A	A
66	B	B
67	C	C
68	D	D
69	E	E

(Table Contd.)

Decimal	*Symbol (ASCII)*	*Key*
70	F	F
71	G	G
72	H	H
73	I	I
74	J	J
75	K	K
76	L	L
77	M	M
78	N	N
79	O	O
80	P	P
81	Q	Q
82	R	R
83	S	S
84	T	T
85	U	U
86	V	V
87	W	W
88	X	X
89	Y	Y
90	Z	Z
91	[	[
92	\	\
93	]	]
94	^	^
95	_	_
96	`	`
97	a	a
98	b	b
99	c	c
100	d	d
101	e	e
102	f	f
103	g	g
104	h	h
105	i	i
106	j	j
107	k	k
108	l	l
109	m	m
110	n	n

(Table Contd.)

Decimal	*Symbol (ASCII)*	*Key*
111	o	o
112	p	p
113	q	q
114	r	r
115	s	s
116	t	t
117	u	u
118	v	v
119	w	w
120	x	x
121	y	y
122	z	z
123	{	{
124	|	|
125	}	}
126	~	~
127	Δ	Alt ←
128	ç	Alt 128
129	ù	Alt 129
130	é	Alt 130
131	á	Alt 131
132	ä	Alt 132
133	â	Alt 133
134	ã	Alt 134
135	Ç	Alt 135
136	ê	Alt 136
137	ë	Alt 137
138	è	Alt 138
139	ï	Alt 139
140	î	Alt 140
141	ì	Alt 141
142	Ä	Alt 142
143	Å	Alt 143
144	É	Alt 144
145	æ	Alt 145
146	Æ	Alt 146
147	ô	Alt 147
148	ö	Alt 148
149	ò	Alt 149
150	û	Alt 150
151	ù	Alt 151

(Table Contd.)

Decimal	*Symbol (ASCII)*	*Key*
152	ÿ	**Alt 152**
153	Ö	**Alt 153**
154	Ü	**Alt 154**
155	¢	**Alt 155**
156	£	**Alt 156**
157	¥	**Alt 157**
158	Pt	**Alt 158**
159	ƒ	**Alt 159**
160	á	**Alt 160**
161	í	**Alt 161**

Turbo C++ Keywords

asm
auto
break
case
catch
char
class
const
continue
-cs
default
do
double
else
enum
extern

–far
float
for
friend
huge
inline
interrupt
long
near
new
operator
pascal
private
protected
public
register

–public
return
seg
short
signed
sizeof
static
struct
switch
template
this
typedof
union
unsigned
virtual
void

Bibliography

1. *Armotated C++ Reference Manual* — Margaret Ellis.
2. *Turbo C++ Bible* — Nabajyoti Barkakati.
3. *Programming in Turbo C++* — Robert Zafore.
4. *Teach yourself* C++ — Al Stevens.

Index

A

B

C

D

E

F

G

H

I

K

L

M

N

O

P

R

S

T

U

V

W

List of Programs

Project—Library Management System

INTRODUCTION

A library is a place from where you borrow books, read them and then return them. For all this you have to give a fee for joining or becoming a member. After getting a book issued, you may read it for a fixed time, which is allotted to you by the Librarian or his assistant. If you are not able to finish the book in that stipulated time, you can get it re-issued. If some other member has already made a request for the book, then you have to return it and then get it re-issued later, when the book returns to the library.

In case you forget to return the book in time, there is every chance that you would be forced to pay a fine. This fine usually varies from library to library.

For providing the reading services, library purchases books from the market. When books arrive in the library, they are physically inspected and if they are found in order, they are taken into account, also they else they are rejected. Details of the books are noted in the acquisition register. After these formalities, book can be issued to the readers on their request.

When a member requests for a book, librarian searches it in the library according to the acquisition number and the accession number of the book. If it is present (not issued to other member) then it is issued to the member and details of the issue are noted down in a register called issue register.

After reading the book, members return the book to the librarian. At the time of return of the book, librarian check if the book is being returned within due date of return. If yes then he takes the book back else he calculates the amount of fine. Fine amount is collected from the member and issue details are striked off from the issue register.

Time to time librarian scans through the issue register and finds out list of books which are overdue.

Followings are the activities of librarian of READER'S PARADISE library:

- Acquisition of books
- Membership maintenance
- Book issue
- Book return
- Renewal of membership
- Answer management queries

Acquisition of Books

Purchase department of the library purchases various books. After purchase, these books are inspected and if found is order a unique number called acquisition number is assigned to each book. Purchase department then sends these books to librarian. Based on the subject, author of the books etc., librarian assigns a code to the book. This code is called as accession number. He also enters various details regarding a book in Acquisition register. He changes entires of the acquisition register, if some change in book information takes place.

Membership Maintenance

A person who wants to be a member of the library, has to fill an application form and give it to the librarian along with membership fee and caution money. Librarian assigns a unique membership number to him and enters the details of this member in membership register. After some time, if any member wants to retude or increase his caution money, librarian makes changes accordingly in the membership modification form. If a member want to discontinue in between, librarian strikes off his entry from the membership register and returns the caution meney.

Book Issue

Librarian issues only one book at a time to a member. Members fill a requisition slip and requests the librarian to issue the book to him. Format of the requisition slip is checked by the librarian and the librarian first checks in member register, whether his membership is still cintinuing. If not, he does not accept the request else he physically checks for the presence of the book in the library. If not present, he rejects the request of the member, otherwise he issues the book to member. Librarian note down the detaisl in Issue register.

Book Return

When a member returns a book, librarian first checks whether the member is returning the book on time or not. If it is late return then the charges file @ Rs. 1.00 per day from the member. He updates the fine register by entering the date of actual return from the schedule return date and fine collected (if charged).

Renewal of Membership

As explained before, librarian provides membership only for one year duration. After this, if members wants to continue their membership, they have to give an application to the librarian requesting hem to extend their membership for next year duration. This application has to be supported by appropriate amount of renewal fee. On receiving the application librarian makes appropriate entries in the Membership register and renews the membership so that members can avail various facilities of the library, for next year also.

SOURCE PROGRAM: LIBRARY.CPP

```
*/
// Declaration of header files
#include <iostream.h>
#include <fstream.h>
#include <process.h>
#include <string.h>
#include <stdio.h>
#include <ctype.h>
#include <conio.h>
#include <dos.h>
#include <stdlib.h>
#include <iomanip.h>

// Function to find the expire dates of members
int date_expire(int, int, int);

// Function to find the no of days in between two dates
int no_of_days(int, int, int, int, int, int);

// Function to return the total days in a month
```

```
int month_days(int);

// class lib_class
class BOX_CLASS
{
    public:
        void DRAW_LINE(int, int, int, char);
        void DRAW_VER(int, int, int, char);
        void DRAW_BOX(int, int, int, int, char);
};

// Class for main control
class control
{
    public:
        void lib_SCREEN(void);
    private:
        void MENU_EDIT(void);
};


// Information regarding to library acquisition
class Library
{
    int acq_no;  // Acquisition number
    int acc_no;  // Accession number
    char title[30];
    char author1[30], author2[30];     // Authors
    char publisher[30]; // Name of the publisher
    float price; // Price of the book
    int dd, mm, yy; // Date of purchase
    int pages;    // Total pages in book
    char status; // Present status of book
    public:
        void Menu_console(void); // Menu for add, modify and delete of library
books
        void new_library(void);  // Function to enter new library books through
the acquisition number
        void NEW_lib(int, int, char s_title[30], char s_author1[30], char
s_author2[30], char s_publisher[30], float s_price, int sdd, int smm, int syy,
int s_pages, char s_status);
        void Lib_delete(int, int); // Deleting library information from data file
        void Left_clear(int, int); // Function to perform a left clear on specified
row from a specified column
        void Clear_area(int, int, int, int); // Function to clear a specified
area in the screen
        void Right_clear(int, int); // Function to perform a right clear on
specified row from a specified column
        void Change_library(void);     // Function to change the library
information
        // Function to rewrite the library contents at its original location
        void Replace(int, int, char s_title[30], char s_author1[30], char
s_author2[30], char s_publisher[30], float s_price, int sdd, int smm, int syy,
int s_pages, char s_status);
        int recordno(int, int);  // Function to find the position in file
        void Delete_Accno(void); // Function to delete records from library
        void Record_delete(int, int);  // Function to delete the record by copy
method
        void Book_Issue(void);  // Function to issue books to members
        void Book_display(int, int); // Function to display the book information
at return time
```

```
        // Report functions on Library of purchase department
        void Report_Menu(void); // Function to display various option on related
  to report for answer to management queires
        void Acqu_Register(void);       // Acquisition register for report
  };

  // Class contains information containing the member details
  class Member
  {

     public:
        void Memb_console(void); // Menu for add, modify and delete of Membership
        void new_member(void); // Function to select addition of members
        // Deletes the same record after creating its position
        void Memb_delete(int);
        void Memb_modify(int); // Library member modification function
        int Memb_Check(int);     // Membership check
        int Expire_Check(int); // Function to check membership date expired or
  not
        void Change_member(void);       // Function to change the members
  information
        void Display_member(int);       // Function to display the existing
  information for modification
        // Function to rewrite the Member contents at its original location
        void Replace(int, char s_name[30], char s_address[30], int, int, int,
  int, int, int, float, float);
        int recordno(int);   // Function to find the position in file
        void Delete_member(void); // Function to delete member from MEMBER.dat
  data file
        void Member_Renewal(void);      // Function to renewal of membership
        void Renewal_member(int);       // Function where the membership date is
  modified
        // Reporting function for member
        void Memb_Register(void); // Function to display the membership register
  globally
        void Expire_Register(void); //Function to display the expired membership
  register

     private:
        // Function to simply add records
        void NEW_memb(int, char s_name[30], char s_address[30], int, int, int,
  int, int, int, float, float);

        int memb_no; // Membership number
        char name[30];   // Name of the member
        char address[30]; // Address of the employee
        int mdd, mmm, myy;   // Membership date
        int edd, emm, eyy; // Expire date
        float memb_fee; // Membership fee
        float caut_fee;  // Caution money

  };

  // Information related to issue of books and issue register
  class Issue
  {
     public:
        int Issue_Check(int, int); // Function to check the book is issued or not
  while deleting a library book
        void Issue_Add(int, int, int, int, int, int, int, int, int);
        void Issue_Delete(int s_acq_no, int s_acc_no, int s_memb_no, int s_idd,
  int s_imm, int s_iyy, int s_rdd, int s_rmm, int s_ryy);
```

```
        int Issue_memb_check(int); // Function to issue member check
        void Book_Return(void); // Function to return books
        void Return_Issue(int); // Function for displaying the returned books
information
        void Issue_member_delete(int); // Function to delete the issued book of
member from MASTER.dat data file
        void Issue_Register(void);          // Function to display the issued
books in library
        void OverDue_Book(void); // Function for overdue books

        void Read_issue(void);
    private:
        int acq_no;  // Aquisition number
        int acc_no;  // Accession no
        int memb_no; // Member number
        int idd, imm, iyy;       // Issue date
        int rdd, rmm, ryy;       // Return date

};

// Information related to fine register
class Fine
{
    int memb_no; // Member number
    intacq_no;   // fine acquisition no
    int acc_no;  // fine accession no

    int idd, imm, iyy; // Book issue date

    int rdd, rmm, ryy; // Book purposed return date

    int cdd, cmm, cyy; // Returned date
    int finfee;
    public:
        void Fine_add(int, int, int, int, int, int, int, int, int, int, int, int,
int);
        void Fine_Register(void);        // Function to display the fine collection
register
};

// Function for horizontal line draw
void BOX_CLASS::DRAW_LINE(int column1, int column2, int row, char c)
{
    for (column1; column1 <= column2; column1++)
    {
        gotoxy(column1, row);
        cout << c;
    }
}

// Function for vertical line draw
void BOX_CLASS::DRAW_VER(int row1, int row2, int column, char c)
{
    for (row1; row1 <= row2; row1++)
    {
        gotoxy(column, row1);
        cout << c;
    }
}

void BOX_CLASS::DRAW_BOX(int column1, int row1, int column2, int row2, char c)
{
```

```
    char ch = 218;
    char c1, c2, c3, c4;
    char l1 = 196, l2 = 179;
    if (c == ch)
    {
        c1 = 218;
        c2 = 191;
        c3 = 217;
        c4 = 217;
        l1 = 196;
        l2 = 179;
    }
    else
    {
        c1 = c;
        c2 = c;
        c3 = c;
        c4 = c;
        l1 = c;
        c2 = c;
    }
    gotoxy(column1, row1);
    cout << c1;
    gotoxy(column2, row1);
    cout << c2;
    gotoxy(column1, row2);
    cout << c3;
    gotoxy(column2, row2);
    cout << c4;
    column1++;
    column2--;
    DRAW_LINE(column1, column2, row1, l1); //Horizontal line
    DRAW_LINE(column1, column2, row2, l1);
    column1--;
    column2++;
    row1++;
    row2--;
    DRAW_VER(row1, row2, column1, l2); // Vertical line
    DRAW_VER(row1, row2, column2, l2);
}

// Function to clear a row from left of the screen
void Library::Left_clear(int col, int row)
{
    for (int j = col; j <= 39; j++)
    {
        gotoxy(j, row);
        cout << " ";
    }
}

// Function to clear a row from right of the screen
void Library::Right_clear(int col, int row)
{
    for (int j = col; j <= 79; j++)
    {
        gotoxy(j, row);
        cout << " ";
    }
}

// Function to clear a specified area in the screen
```

```
void Library::Clear_area(int row, int till, int col, int tcol)
{
    for (int p = row; p <= till; p++)
    {
        int xcol = col;
        for ( xcol = xcol; xcol <= tcol; xcol++)
        {
            gotoxy(xcol, p);
            cout << " ";
        }
    }
}

// Function for main menu for library management system
void control::lib_SCREEN(void)
{
    char ch;
    while (ch <= '6')
    {
        clrscr();

        int xdd, xmm, xyy;
        struct date d;    // For extracting system date
        getdate(&d);
        xdd = d.da_day;
        xmm = d.da_mon;
        xyy = d.da_year;

        BOX_CLASS s;
        s.DRAW_BOX(10, 5, 71, 21, 219);
        s.DRAW_BOX(9, 4, 72, 22, 218);
        textcolor(BLACK);
        textbackground(LIGHTGRAY);
        gotoxy(10, 3);
        cout << "Date: "<< xdd << "-" << xmm << "-" << xyy;

        gotoxy(65, 3);
        cout << "<0>=Exit";
        gotoxy(27, 25);
        cout << "Developed by Author & Her Team";
        gotoxy(15,7);
        cprintf(" L I B R A R Y  M A N A G E M E N T  S Y S T E M ");
        gotoxy(28,9);
        cout << "1. Acquisition Section";
        gotoxy(28, 10);
        cout << "2. Membership Maintenance";
        gotoxy(28, 11);
        cout << "3. Book Issue";
        gotoxy(28, 12);
        cout << "4. Book Return";
        gotoxy(28, 13);
        cout << "5. Renewal of Membership";
        gotoxy(28, 14);
        cout << "6. Answer Management Queries";

        gotoxy(28, 17);
        cprintf("Enter Your Choice ");
        ch = getche();
        switch (ch)
        {
            case '0':
                clrscr();
```

```
                exit(0); // Option to exit from main menu
                break;
            case '1':
            {
                Library lib;
                lib.Menu_console(); // Library books into LIB.dat
                break;
            }
            case '2':
            {
                Member Memb;
                Memb.Memb_console(); // Members management in MEMFILE.dat
                break;
            }
            case '3':
            {
                Library lib;
                lib.Book_Issue(); // Function to issue books
                break;
            }
            case '4':
            {
                Issue Iss;
                Iss.Book_Return(); // Function to return books
            }
            case '5':
            {
                Member Memb;
                Memb.Member_Renewal();
                break;
            }
            case '6':
            {
                Library lib;
                lib.Report_Menu(); // Function for displaying report menu
                break;
            }
        }
    }
}
```

LIBRARY MANAGEMENT SYSTEM

1. Acquisition Section
2. Membership Maintenance
3. Book Issue
4. Book Return
5. Renewal of Membership
6. Answer Management Queries

Enter Your Choice . . .

```
// Function for Adding, modifying and deleting from LIB.dat data file
void Library::Menu_console(void)
{
    char ch;
```

```
while (1)
{
    clrscr();
    gotoxy(65, 3);
    cout << "<0>=Exit";

    BOX_CLASS s;
    s.DRAW_BOX(10, 5, 71, 21, 219);
    s.DRAW_BOX(9, 4, 72, 22, 218);
    textcolor(BLACK);
    textbackground(WHITE);
    gotoxy(22, 8);
    cprintf("L I B R A R Y  C O N S O L E");
    textcolor(LIGHTGRAY);
    textbackground(BLACK);
    gotoxy(25, 12);
    cout << "1: Keeping New Record";
    gotoxy(25, 13);
    cout << "2. Changing Existing Record";
    gotoxy(25, 14);
    cout << "3. Deleting Library Record";

    gotoxy(25, 16);
    cout << "0. Return";
    gotoxy(25, 18);
    cout << "Enter your choice : ";
    ch = getche();
    if (ch == 27)
        break;
    else
        if (ch == '1')
        {
            new_library();
        }
        else
            if (ch == '2')
            {
                Change_library();
                break;
            }
            else
                if (ch == '3')
                {
                    Delete_Accno();
                    break;
                }
                else
                    if (ch == '0')
                        break;
    }
}

// Function to append a record into LIB.dat data file
void Library::NEW_lib(int s_acq_no, int s_acc_no, char s_title[30], char
s_author1[30], char s_author2[30], char s_publisher[30], float s_price, int sdd,
int smm, int syy, int s_pages, char s_status)
{
    acq_no = s_acq_no;
    acc_no = s_acc_no;
    strcpy(title, s_title);
    strcpy(author1, s_author1);
    strcpy(author2, s_author2);
    strcpy(publisher, s_publisher);
```

LIBRARY CONSOLE

1. Keeping New Record
2. Changing Existing Record
3. Deleting Library Record

0. Return

Enter Your Choice . . .

```
    price  =  s_price;
    dd  =  sdd;
    mm  =  smm;
    yy  =  syy;
    pages  =  s_pages;
    status  =  s_status;

    fstream  sfile;

    // Append  the  new  record  into  LIB.dat  data  file
    sfile.open("LIB.dat",  ios::out|ios::app);
    sfile.write((char  *)this,  sizeof(Library));
    sfile.close();
}

// Function  to  delete  a  selected  record  from  LIB.dat  data  file
void Library::Lib_delete(int  s_acq_no,  int  s_acc_no)
{
    fstream  file;
    file.open("LIB.dat",  ios::in);
    fstream  temp;
    temp.open("TEMP.dat",  ios::out);
    file.seekg(0,ios::beg);

    // Delete  the  record  using  copy  method  into  temporaty  file
    while  (!file.eof())
    {
        file.read((char  *)this,  sizeof(Library));
        if  (file.eof())
            break;
        if  ((acq_no  !=  s_acq_no)  &&  (acc_no  !=  s_acc_no))
            temp.write((char  *)this,  sizeof(Library));
    }
    file.close();
    temp.close();
    file.open("LIB.dat",  ios::out);
    temp.open("TEMP.dat",  ios::in);
    temp.seekg(0,  ios::beg);

    // Overwrites  the  temporay  contents  into  original  LIB.dat  data  file
    while  (!temp.eof())
    {
        temp.read((char  *)this,  sizeof(Library));
        if  (temp.eof())
            break;
```

```
        if ((acq_no != s_acq_no) && (acc_no != s_acc_no))
            file.write((char *)this, sizeof(Library));
    }
    file.close();
    temp.close();
}

// Function for main menu to append new library books LIB.dat
/* In an acquisition no. there may be more than one books which contains several
accession numbers */
void Library::new_library(void)
{
    char ch;
    int i, valid;
    clrscr();

    gotoxy(3, 3);
    for (i = 1; i<= 76; i++)
        cprintf(" ");

    textbackground(BLACK);
    textcolor(BLACK+BLINK);
    textbackground(WHITE);
    gotoxy(30, 3);
    cprintf("Library Acquisition Entry");
    textcolor(LIGHTGRAY);
    textbackground(BLACK);
    gotoxy(65, 3);
    cout << "<0>=Exit";

    BOX_CLASS s;
    s.DRAW_BOX(10, 5, 71, 21, 219);
    s.DRAW_BOX(9, 4, 72, 22, 218);
    textcolor(BLACK);
    textbackground(LIGHTGRAY);

    int s_acq_no;// Acquisition number

    do
    {
        // Function to clear a specified input box from the screen
        Clear_area(6, 18, 11, 70);

        int s_acc_no;// Accession number
        char s_title[30];
        char s_author1[30], s_author2[30];    // Authors
        char s_publisher[30];    // Name of the publisher
        float s_price;    // Price of the book
        int sdd, smm, syy;  // Date of purchase
        int s_pages; // Total pages in book
        char s_status;   // Present status of book

        struct date d;     // For extracting system date
        getdate(&d);
        sdd = d.da_day;
        smm = d.da_mon;
        syy = d.da_year;

        gotoxy(50, 7);
        cout << "Date: " << sdd << '-' << smm << '-' << syy;

        gotoxy(10, 23);
```

```
        cout << "Enter the Acquisition number";
        gotoxy(13, 7);
        cout << "Acquisition No. "
        gotoxy(29, 7);
        cin >> s_acq_no;
        Left_clear(10, 23);
        Right_clear(39, 23);

        gotoxy(11, 8);
        for (i = 1; i <= 60; i++)
        cout << "=";

        do
        {
            // Function to clear a specified input box from the screen
            Clear_area(9, 18, 11, 70);

            gotoxy(10, 23);
            cout << "Enter the Accession number";
            gotoxy(13, 9);
            cout << "Accession No. ";
            gotoxy(28, 9);
            cin >> s_acc_no;
            Left_clear(10, 23);
            Right_clear(39, 23);

            if (s_acq_no == 1)
            {
                // Creates a temporaty space in LIB.dat data tile
                NEW_lib(s_acq_no, s_acc_no, "aaa", "bbb", "ccc", "ddd", 0, 0, 0,
0, 0, 'x');
                // Deletes the same record after creating its position
                Lib_delete(s_acq_no, s_acc_no);
            }
            if ((s_acq_no == 0) || (s_acc_no == 0))
                return;

            gotoxy(13, 10);
            cout << "Title : ";
            gotoxy(13, 12);
            cout << "Author(s) : ";
            gotoxy(13, 14);
            cout << "Publisher : ";
            gotoxy(13, 15);
            cout << "Price : ";
            gotoxy(13, 16);
            cout << "Pages : ";
            gotoxy(13, 17);
            cout << "Status : ";

            do
            {
                Left_clear(10, 23);
                gotoxy(10, 23);
                cout << "Enter Title of the Book";
                valid = 1;
                gotoxy(22, 10);
                gets(s_title);
                strupr(s_title);
                if (s_title[0] == '0')
                    return;
                if (strlen(s_title) == 0 || strlen(s_title) > 30)
```

```
    {
        valid = 0;
        gotoxy(10, 23);
        cout << "\7Title should not greater than 30";
        getch();
    ;
} while (!valid);
Left_clear(5, 23);
Right_clear(39, 23);

do
{
    gotoxy(10, 23);
    cout << "Enter Author of the Book ";
    valid = 1;
    gotoxy(26, 12);
    gets(s_author1);
    strupr(s_author1);
    if (s_author1[0] == '0')
        return;
    if (strlen(s_author1) == 0 || strlen(s_author1) > 30)
    {
        valid = 0;
        gotoxy(10, 23);
        cout << "\7Author should not greater than 30";
        getch();
    }
} while (!valid);
Left_clear(10, 23);
Right_clear(39, 23);

gotoxy(10, 23);
cout << "Enter second author if there";
// Second author
gotoxy(26, 13);
gets(s_author2);
strupr(s_author2);
Left_clear(5, 23);
Right_clear(39, 23);

do
{
    Left_clear(10, 23);
    Right_clear(39, 23);

    gotoxy(10, 23);
    cout << "Enter name of the Publisher";
    valid = 1;
    gotoxy(26, 14);
    gets(s_publisher);
    strupr(s_publisher);
    if (s_publisher[0] == '0')
        return;
    if (strlen(s_publisher) == 0 || strlen(s_publisher) > 30)
    {
        valid = 0;
        gotoxy(10, 23);
        cout << "\7Publisher should not greater than 30";
        getch();
    }
} while (!valid);
Left_clear(10, 23);
Right_clear(39, 23);
```

```
            gotoxy(10, 23);
            cout << "Enter selling price of the book";
            gotoxy(22, 15);
            cin >> s_price;
            Left_clear(10, 23);
            Right_clear(39, 23);

            gotoxy(10, 23);
            cout << "Enter Total pages in the book";
            gotoxy(22, 16);
            cin >> s_pages;
            Left_clear(10, 23);
            Right_clear(39, 23);

            // The status is automatically fill as "Y", because the accession is
entering
            // fresh books

            gotoxy(22, 17);
            s_status = 'Y';
            cout << s_status;

            do
            {
                valid = 1;
                gotoxy(10, 23);
                cout << "Do you want to save the record <Y/N>: ";
                ch = getche();
                if (ch == '0')
                    return;
                ch = toupper(ch);
            }while (ch != 'N' && ch != 'Y');
            if (ch == 'N')
                return;
            NEW_lib(s_acq_no, s_acc_no, s_title, s_author1, s_author2, s_publisher,
s_price, sdd, smm, syy, s_pages, s_status);
            Left_clear(10, 23);
            Right_clear(39, 23);

            gotoxy(12, 23);
            cout << "Any Accession <Y/N>: ";
            ch = getche();
            if (ch == '0')
                return;
            Left_clear(12, 23);
            Right_clear(12, 23);

            ch = toupper(ch);
        } while (ch == 'Y');

        gotoxy(12, 23);
        cout << "Any Acquisition <Y/N>: ";
        ch = getche();
        if (ch == '0')
            return;
        Left_clear(12, 23);
        Right_clear(12, 23);

        ch = toupper(ch);
    } while (ch == 'Y');

}
```

Library Acquisition Entry <0>=Exit

Acquisition No. 01 Date: 10-12-2008

Accession No. 10
Title: VB.NET Traning Guide
Author(s): Andrew S. Tanenbaum
Publisher: Pearsons
Price: 350
Pages: 1000
Status: Y
Do you want to save the record <Y/N>: Y

```
// Function to count the total number of records in LIB.dat data file for
// counting the modification record till found
int Library::recordno(int s_acq_no, int s_acc_no)
{
    fstream file;
    file.open("LIB.dat", ios::in);
    file.seekg(0, ios::beg);
    int count = 0;

    // Counts the total records in DETAILS.dat data file
    while (file.read((char *)this, sizeof(Library)))
    {
        count++;
        if ((s_acq_no == acq_no) && (s_acc_no == acc_no))
            break;
    }
    file.close();
    return count;
}

// Modification function for library record
void Library::Replace(int s_acq_no, int s_acc_no, char s_title[30], char
s_author1[30], char s_author2[30], char s_publisher[30], float s_price, int sdd,
int smm, int syy, int s_pages, char s_status)
{
    int recno;
    recno = recordno(s_acq_no, s_acc_no);
    fstream file;
    file.open("LIB.dat", ios::out|ios::ate);

    acq_no = s_acq_no;
    acc_no = s_acc_no;
    strcpy(title, s_title);
    strcpy(author1, s_author1);
    strcpy(author2, s_author2);
    strcpy(publisher, s_publisher);
    price = s_price;
    dd = sdd;
    mm = smm;
    yy = syy;
    pages = s_pages;
```

```
    status = s_status;

    // Finding the location in file
    int location;
    location = (recno-1) * sizeof(Library);

    // Search the position in file
    file.seekp(location);

    // Re-write the contents in DETAILS.dat data file
    file.write((char *)this, sizeof(Library));
    file.close();
    return;
}

// Function for main menu to change the existing recrod in LIB.dat
/* In the library the searching can only happen through the acquisition no
and the accession number, because in one acquisition number there may be more
than
library books */

void Library::Change_library(void)
{
    char ch;
    int i, valid;
    clrscr();

    gotoxy(3, 3);
    for (i = 1; i<= 76; i++)
        cprintf(" ");

    textbackground(BLACK);
    textcolor(BLACK+BLINK);
    textbackground(WHITE);
    gotoxy(30, 3);
    cprintf("Library Modification");
    textcolor(LIGHTGRAY);
    textbackground(BLACK);
    gotoxy(65, 3);
    cout << "<0>=Exit";

    BOX_CLASS s;
    s.DRAW_BOX(10, 5, 71, 21, 219);
    s.DRAW_BOX(9, 4, 72, 22, 218);
    textcolor(BLACK);
    textbackground(LIGHTGRAY);

    int s_acq_no = 0;   // Acquisition number

    do
    {
        // Function to clear a specified input box from the screen
        Clear_area(6, 18, 11, 70);

        int s_acc_no = 0;// Accession number
        char s_title[30];
        char s_author1[30], s_author2[30];     // Authors
        char s_publisher[30];    // Name of the publisher
        float s_price;    // Price of the book
        int sdd, smm, syy;         // Date of purchase
        int s_pages; // Total pages in book
        char s_status;    // Present status of book
```

```
struct date d;    // For extracting system date
getdate(&d);
sdd = d.da_day;
smm = d.da_mon;
syy = d.da_year;

gotoxy(50, 7);
cout << "Date: " << sdd << '-' << smm << '-' << syy;

gotoxy(10, 23);
cout << "Enter the Acquisition number";
gotoxy(13, 7);
cout << "Acquisition No. " ;
gotoxy(29, 7);
cin >> s_acq_no;
Left_clear(10, 23);
Right_clear(39, 23);

gotoxy(11, 8);
for (i = 1; i <= 60; i++)
cout << "=";

do
{
    // Function to clear a specified input box from the screen
    Clear_area(9, 18, 11, 70);

    gotoxy(10, 23);
    cout << "Enter the Accession number";
    gotoxy(13, 9);
    cout << "Accession No. ";
    gotoxy(28, 9);
    cin >> s_acc_no;
    Left_clear(10, 23);
    Right_clear(39, 23);
    if ((s_acq_no == 0) || (s_acc_no == 0))
        return;

    fstream file;
    file.open("LIB.dat", ios::in);
    file.seekg(0,ios::beg);

    // Search the record for further modification
    while (file.read((char *)this, sizeof(Library)))
    {
        if ((s_acq_no == acq_no) && (s_acc_no == acc_no))
        {
            gotoxy(13, 10);
            cout << "Existing Information";
            gotoxy(13, 11);
            cout << "Title : ";
            gotoxy(13, 12);
            cout << "Author(s) : ";
            gotoxy(13, 14);
            cout << "Publisher : ";
            gotoxy(13, 15);
            cout << "Price : ";
            gotoxy(13, 16);
            cout << "Pages : ";
            gotoxy(13, 17);
            cout << "Status : ";
            gotoxy(22, 11);
```

```
            puts(title);

            gotoxy(26, 12);
            puts(author1);

            gotoxy(26, 13);
            puts(author2);
            gotoxy(26, 14);
            puts(publisher);
            gotoxy(22, 15);
            cout << price;

            gotoxy(22, 16);
            cout << pages;
            gotoxy(22, 17);
            cout << status;
            break;
        }
    }
    file.close();
    gotoxy(45, 10);
    cout << "New Information";

    do
    {
        Left_clear(10, 23);
        gotoxy(10, 23);
        cout << "Enter New Title of the Book";
        valid = 1;
        gotoxy(45, 11);
        gets(s_title);
        strupr(s_title);
        if (s_title[0] == '0')
            return;
        if (strlen(s_title) == 0 || strlen(s_title) > 30)
        {
            valid = 0;
            gotoxy(10, 23);
            cout << "\7Title should not greater than 30";
            getch();
        }
    } while (!valid);
    Left_clear(5, 23);
    Right_clear(39, 23);

    do
    {
        gotoxy(12, 23);
        cout << "Enter New Author of the Book ";
        valid = 1;
        gotoxy(45, 12);
        gets(s_author1);
        strupr(s_author1);
        if (s_author1[0] == '0')
            return;
        if (strlen(s_author1) == 0 || strlen(s_author1) > 30)
        {
            valid = 0;
            gotoxy(10, 23);
            cout << "\7Author should not greater than 30";
            getch();
        }
```

```
} while (!valid);
Left_clear(10, 23);
Right_clear(39, 23);

gotoxy(10, 23);
cout << "Enter second author if there";
// Second author
gotoxy(45, 13);
gets(s_author2);
strupr(s_author2);
Left_clear(5, 23);
Right_clear(39, 23);

do
{
    Left_clear(10, 23);
    Right_clear(39, 23);

    gotoxy(10, 23);
    cout << "Enter name of the Publisher";
    valid = 1;
    gotoxy(45, 14);
    gets(s_publisher);
    strupr(s_publisher);
    if (s_publisher[0] == '0')
        return;
    if (strlen(s_publisher) == 0 || strlen(s_publisher) > 30)
    {
        valid = 0;
        gotoxy(10, 23);
        cout << "\7Publisher should not greater than 30";
        getch();
    }
} while (!valid);
Left_clear(10, 23);
Right_clear(39, 23);

gotoxy(10, 23);
cout << "Enter selling price of the book";
gotoxy(45, 15);
cin >> s_price;
Left_clear(10, 23);
Right_clear(39, 23);

gotoxy(10, 23);
cout << "Enter Total pages in the book";
gotoxy(45, 16);
cin >> s_pages;
Left_clear(10, 23);
Right_clear(39, 23);

// The status is automatically fill as "Y", because the accession is
entering
// fresh books

gotoxy(45, 17);
s_status = 'Y';
cout << s_status;

do
{
    valid = 1;
```

```
                gotoxy(10, 23);
                cout << "Do you want to Overwrite the record <Y/N>: ";
                ch = getche();
                if (ch == '0')
                    return;
                ch = toupper(ch);
            }while (ch != 'N' && ch != 'Y');
            if (ch == 'N')
                return;
            Replace(s_acq_no, s_acc_no, s_title, s_author1, s_author2, s_publisher,
s_price, sdd, smm, syy, s_pages, s_status);
            Left_clear(10, 23);
            Right_clear(39, 23);

            gotoxy(12, 23);
            cout << "Any Accession <Y/N>: ";
            ch = getche();
            if (ch == '0')
                return;
            Left_clear(12, 23);
            Right_clear(12, 23);

            ch = toupper(ch);
        } while (ch == 'Y');

        gotoxy(12, 23);
        cout << "Any Acquisition <Y/N>: ";
        ch = getche();
        if (ch == '0')
            return;
        Left_clear(12, 23);
        Right_clear(12, 23);

        ch = toupper(ch);
    } while (ch == 'Y');

}
```

Library Modification <0>=Exit

Acquisition No. 01 **Date: 10-12-2008**

Accession No. 10	
Existing Information	New Information
Title: VB.NET Training Guide	ASP.NET Training Guide
Author(s): Andrew S. Tanenbaum	Andrew S. Tanenbaum
Publisher: Pearsons	Pearsons
Price: 350	400
Pages: 1000	1000
Status: Y	Y

Do you want to Overwrite the record <Y/N>: Y

```
// Function to find the acquisition number and accession number is exists or not
int Issue::Issue_Check(int s_acq_no, int s_acc_no)
{
```

```
    int tflag = 0;
    fstream file;
    file.open("MASTER.dat", ios::in);
    file.seekg(0,ios::beg);

    // Search the record for further modification
    while (file.read((char *)this, sizeof(Issue)))
    {
        if ((s_acq_no == acq_no) && (s_acc_no == acc_no))
        {
            tflag = 1;
            break;
        }
    }
    file.close();
    return (tflag);
}

// Function to check member for issue
int Issue::Issue_memb_check(int s_memb_no)
{
    int mflag = 0;
    fstream file;
    file.open("MASTER.dat", ios::in);
    file.seekg(0,ios::beg);

    // Search the record for further modification
    while (file.read((char *)this, sizeof(Issue)))
    {
        if (s_memb_no == memb_no)
        {
            mflag = 1;
            break;
        }
    }
    file.close();
    return (mflag);
}

// Function to find the MEMFILE.dat file that the member has EXISTS or not
int Member::Memb_Check(int s_memb_no)
{
    int mflag = 0;
    fstream file;
    file.open("MEMFILE.dat", ios::in);
    file.seekg(0,ios::beg);

    // Search the record for further modification
    while (file.read((char *)this, sizeof(Member)))
    {
        if (s_memb_no == memb_no)
        {
            mflag = 1;
            break;
        }
    }
    file.close();
    return (mflag);
}

// Function to delete record from LIB.dat data file by the matching acquition
no. and accession no.
```

```
void Library::Record_delete(int s_acc_no, int s_acc_no)
{
    fstream file;
    file.open("LIB.dat", ios::in);
    fstream temp;
    temp.open("TEMP.dat", ios::out);
    file.seekg(0,ios::beg);

    // Delete the record using copy method into temporaty file
    while (!file.eof())
    {
        file.read((char *)this, sizeof(Library));
        if (file.eof())
            break;
        if ((s_acq_no != acc_no) && (s_acc_no != acc_no))
            temp.write((char *)this, sizeof(Library));
    }
    file.close();
    temp.close();
    file.open("LIB.dat", ios::out);
    temp.open("TEMP.dat", ios::in);
    temp.seekg(0, ios::beg);

    // Overwrites the temporay contents into original DETAILS.dat data file
    while (!temp.eof())
    {
        temp.read((char *)this, sizeof(Library));
        if (temp.eof())
            break;
        if ((s_acq_no != acc_no) && (s_acc_no != acc_no))
            file.write((char *)this, sizeof(Library));
    }
    file.close();
    temp.close();
}

// Function for main menu to Delete the existing recrod in LIB.dat
/* In the library the searching can only happen through the acquisition no
and the accession number, because in one acquisition number there may be more
than
library books */

void Library::Delete_Accno(void)
{
    char ch;
    int i;
    clrscr();

    int flag = 0;
    int tflag = 0;
    gotoxy(3, 3);
    for (i = 1; i<= 76; i++)
        cprintf(" ");

    textbackground(BLACK);
    textcolor(BLACK+BLINK);
    textbackground(WHITE);
    gotoxy(30, 3);
    cprintf("Library Deletion");
    textcolor(LIGHTGRAY);
    textbackground(BLACK);
```

```
gotoxy(65, 3);
cout << "<0>=Exit";

BOX_CLASS s;
s.DRAW_BOX(10, 5, 71, 21, 219);
s.DRAW_BOX(9, 4, 72, 22, 218);
textcolor(BLACK);
textbackground(LIGHTGRAY);

int s_acq_no = 0;  // Acquisition number

do
{
   // Function to clear a specified input box from the screen
   Clear_area(6, 18, 11, 70);

   int s_acc_no = 0;// Accession number
   char s_title[30];
   char s_author1[30], s_author2[30];    // Authors
   char s_publisher[30];    // Name of the publisher
   float s_price;  // Price of the book
   int sdd, smm, syy;       // Date of purchase
   int s_pages; // Total pages in book
   char s_status;  // Present status of book

   struct date d;   // For extracting system date
   getdate(&d);
   sdd = d.da_day;
   smm = d.da_mon;
   syy = d.da_year;

   gotoxy(50, 7);
   cout << "Date: " << sdd << '-' << smm << '-' << syy;

   gotoxy(10, 23);
   cout << "Enter the Acquisition number";
   gotoxy(13, 7);
   cout << "Acquisition No. " ;
   gotoxy(29, 7);
   cin >> s_acq_no;
   Left_clear(10, 23);
   Right_clear(39, 23);

   gotoxy(11, 8);
   for (i = 1; i <= 60; i++)
   cout << "=";

   do
   {
      // Function to clear a specified input box from the screen
      Clear_area(9, 18, 11, 70);

      gotoxy(10, 23);
      cout << "Enter the Accession number";
      gotoxy(13, 9);
      cout << "Accession No. ";
      gotoxy(28, 9);
      cin >> s_acc_no;
      Left_clear(10, 23);
      Right_clear(39, 23);
      if ((s_acq_no == 0) || (s_acc_no == 0))
         return;
```

```
fstream file;
file.open("LIB.dat", ios::in);
file.seekg(0,ios::beg);

// Search the record for further modification
while (file.read((char *)this, sizeof(Library)))
{
    if ((s_acq_no == acq_no) && (s_acc_no == acc_no))
    {
        flag = 1;
        gotoxy(15, 11);
        cout << "Title : ";
        gotoxy(15, 12);
        cout << "Author(s) : ";
        gotoxy(15, 14);
        cout << "Publisher : ";
        gotoxy(15, 15);
        cout << "Price : ";
        gotoxy(15, 16);
        cout << "Pages : ";
        gotoxy(15, 17);
        cout << "Status : ";
        gotoxy(26, 11);
        puts(title);

        gotoxy(26, 12);
        puts(author1);

        gotoxy(26, 13);
        puts(author2);
        gotoxy(26, 14);
        puts(publisher);
        gotoxy(26, 15);
        cout << price;

        gotoxy(26, 16);
        cout << pages;
        gotoxy(26, 17);
        cout << status;
        break;
    }
}
file.close();

Issue Iss;
tflag = Iss.Issue_Check(s_acq_no, s_acc_no);
if (tflag == 0)
{
    do
    {
        gotoxy(10, 23);
        cout << "Are you you sure to Delete this record <Y/N>: ";
        ch = getche();
        if (ch == '0')
            return;
        ch = toupper(ch);
    }while (ch != 'N' && ch != 'Y');
}
else
{
    gotoxy(12, 23);
    cout << "The is already Issued ...";
```

```
            }
            Left_clear(10, 23);
            Right_clear(39, 23);

            if ((ch == 'Y') && (flag == 1))
            {
               Record_delete(s_acq_no, s_acc_no);
            }
            if (flag == 1)
            {
               gotoxy(57, 23);
               cout << "Record Deleted !";
               getch();
            }
            Left_clear(10, 23);
            Right_clear(39, 23);

            gotoxy(12, 23);
            cout << "Any Accession <Y/N>: ";
            ch = getche();
            if (ch == '0')
               return;
            Left_clear(12, 23);
            Right_clear(12, 23);

            ch = toupper(ch);
         } while (ch == 'Y');

         gotoxy(12, 23);
         cout << "Any Acquisition <Y/N>: ";
         ch = getche();
         if (ch == '0')
            return;
         Left_clear(12, 23);
         Right_clear(12, 23);

         ch = toupper(ch);
      } while (ch == 'Y');

}
```

Library Deletion <0>=Exit

Acquisition No. 01 Date: 10-12-2008

Accession No. 11

Title: ASP.NET Training Guide

Author(s): Andrew S. Tanenbaum

Publisher: Pearsons

Price: 400

Pages: 1000

Status: Y

Are you sure to Delete the record <Y/N>: Y

```
// Function to append a record into MEMFILE.dat data file
void Member::NEW_memb(int s_memb_no, char s_name[30], char s_address[30], int
s_mdd, int s_mmm, int s_myy, int s_edd, int s_emm, int s_eyy, float s_memb_fee,
float s_caut_fee)
{
    memb_no = s_memb_no;
    strcpy(name, s_name);
    strcpy(address, s_address);
    mdd = s_mdd;
    mmm = s_mmm;
    myy = s_myy;
    edd = s_edd;
    emm = s_emm;
    eyy = s_eyy;
    memb_fee = s_memb_fee;
    caut_fee = s_caut_fee;

    fstream sfile;

    // Append the new record into MEMFILE.dat data file
    sfile.open("MEMFILE.dat", ios::out|ios::app);
    sfile.write((char *)this, sizeof(Member));
    sfile.close();
}

// Function to delete a selected record from MEMFILE.dat data file
void Member::Memb_delete(int s_memb_no)
{
    fstream file;
    file.open("MEMFILE.dat", ios::in);
    fstream temp;
    temp.open("TEMP.dat", ios::out);
    file.seekg(0,ios::beg);

    // Delete the record using copy method into temporaty file
    while (!file.eof())
    {
        file.read((char *)this, sizeof(Member));
        if (file.eof())
            break;
        if (memb_no != s_memb_no)
            temp.write((char *)this, sizeof(Member));
    }
    file.close();
    temp.close();
    file.open("MEMFILE.dat", ios::out);
    temp.open("TEMP.dat", ios::in);
    temp.seekg(0, ios::beg);

    // Overwrites the temporay contents into original MEMFILE.dat data file
    while (!temp.eof())
    {
        temp.read((char *)this, sizeof(Member));
        if (temp.eof())
            break;
        if (memb_no != s_memb_no)
            file.write((char *)this, sizeof(Member));
    }
    file.close();
    temp.close();
}
```

```
// Function for main menu to append new members in MEMFILE.dat
void Member::new_member(void)
{
    char ch;
    int i, valid;

    Library lib;
    clrscr();
    gotoxy(65, 2);
    cout << "<0>=Exit";
    BOX_CLASS s;
    s.DRAW_BOX(10, 5, 71, 21, 219);
    s.DRAW_BOX(9, 4, 72, 22, 218);
    textcolor(BLACK);
    textbackground(LIGHTGRAY);

    gotoxy(3,3);
    for (i = 1; i<= 76; i++)
        cprintf(" ");

    textbackground(BLACK);
    textcolor(BLACK+BLINK);
    textbackground(WHITE);
    gotoxy(35, 4);
    cprintf("Membership Form");
    textcolor(LIGHTGRAY);
    textbackground(BLACK);

    do
    {
        lib.Clear_area(6, 18, 12, 70);
        int s_memb_no;   // Membership number
        char s_name[30]; // Name of the member
        char s_address[30]; // Address of the employee
        int s_mdd, s_mmm, s_myy;  // Membership date
        int s_edd, s_emm, s_eyy; // Expire date
        float s_memb_fee; // Membership fee
        float s_caut_fee; // Caution money

        struct date d;   // For extracting system date
        getdate(&d);
        s_mdd = d.da_day;
        s_mmm = d.da_mon;
        s_myy = d.da_year;

        gotoxy(12, 7);
        cout << "Date: " << s_mdd << '-' << s_mmm << '-' << s_myy;
        gotoxy(12, 23);
        cout << "Enter new membership no.";
        gotoxy(12, 9);
        cout << "Membership No. " ;
        gotoxy(27, 9);
        cin >> s_memb_no;
        lib.Left_clear(12, 23);
        lib.Right_clear(12, 23);

        if (s_memb_no == 1)
        {
            // Creates a temporaty space in MEMFILE.dat data tile
            NEW_memb(s_memb_no, "aaa", "bbb", 0, 0, 0, 0, 0, 0, 0.0, 0.0);
            // Deletes the same record after creating its position
            Memb_delete(s_memb_no);
```

```
}
if (s_memb_no == 0)
    return;

gotoxy(12, 11);
cout << "Name : ";
gotoxy(12, 14);
cout << "Address : ";
gotoxy(12, 15);
cout << "Memb. Dat : ";
gotoxy(12, 16);
cout << "Exp. Date : ";
gotoxy(12, 17);
cout << "Memb. Fees : ";
gotoxy(12, 18);
cout << "Caution Money : ";

do
{
    lib.Left_clear(12, 23);
    gotoxy(12, 23);
    cout << "Enter Name of the Member";
    valid = 1;
    gotoxy(19, 11);
    gets(s_name);
    strupr(s_name);
    if (s_name[0] == '0')
        return;
    if (strlen(s_name) == 0 || strlen(s_name) > 30)
    {
        valid = 0;
        gotoxy(12, 23);
        cprintf("\7Name should not greater than 30");
        getch();
    }
} while (!valid);
lib.Left_clear(12, 23);
lib.Right_clear(12, 23);

do
{
    lib.Left_clear(12, 23);
    gotoxy(15, 23);
    cout << "Enter Address of the Member ";
    valid = 1;
    gotoxy(23, 14);
    gets(s_address);
    strupr(s_address);
    if (s_address[0] == '0')
        return;
    if (strlen(s_address) == 0 || strlen(s_address) > 30)
    {
        valid = 0;
        gotoxy(12, 23);
        cprintf("\7Address should not greater than 30");
        getch();
    }
} while (!valid);
lib.Left_clear(12, 23);
lib.Right_clear(12, 23);

gotoxy(12, 23);
```

```
        cout << "Enter the membership date";
        gotoxy(25, 15);
        cin >> s_mdd;
        gotoxy(27, 15);
        cout << '-';
        gotoxy(28, 15);
        cin >> s_mmm;
        gotoxy(30, 15);
        cout << '-';
        gotoxy(31, 15);
        cin >> s_myy;
        lib.Left_clear(12, 23);
        lib.Right_clear(12, 23);

        // Calculation of expire date according to a validation of 1 year for
        // membership from membership date and will be calculated in s_edd, s_emm,
s_eyy
        s_edd = s_mdd;
        s_emm = s_mmm;
        s_eyy = s_myy + 1; // Added 1 with the membership year to know the expire
date

        gotoxy(25, 16);
        cout << s_edd;
        gotoxy(27, 16);
        cout << '-';
        gotoxy(28, 16);
        cout << s_emm;
        gotoxy(30, 16);
        cout << '-';
        gotoxy(31, 16);
        cout << s_eyy;

        gotoxy(12, 23);
        cout << "Enter membership fees for a member";
        gotoxy(25, 17);
        cin >> s_memb_fee;
        lib.Left_clear(12, 23);
        lib.Right_clear(12, 23);

        gotoxy(12, 23);
        cout << "Enter caution money ";
        gotoxy(28, 18);
        cin >> s_caut_fee;
        lib.Left_clear(12, 23);
        lib.Right_clear(12, 23);

        do
        {
            valid = 1;
            gotoxy(12, 23);
            cout << "Do you want to save the record <Y/N>: ";
            ch = getche();
            if (ch == '0')
                return;
            ch = toupper(ch);
        } while (ch != 'Y');
        if (ch == 'N')
            return;

        NEW_memb(s_memb_no, s_name, s_address, s_mdd, s_mmm, s_myy, s_edd, s_emm,
s_eyy, s_memb_fee, s_caut_fee);
```

```
        lib.Left_clear(12, 23);
        lib.Right_clear(12, 23);
        gotoxy(12, 23);
        cout << "Do You Want New Record <Y/N>: ";
        ch = getche();
        if (ch == '0')
            return;
        lib.Left_clear(12, 23);
        lib.Right_clear(12, 23);

        ch = toupper(ch);
    } while (ch == 'Y');
}
```

Membership Form <0>=Exit

Date: 10-10-2008

Membership No. 428

Name: Shah Rukh Khan

Address: 112 Jor Bagh

Membership Date: 8-12-2007

Exp. Date: 7-12-2008

Membership Fee: 100

Caution Money: 500

Do you want to save the record <Y/N>: Y

```
// Function to count the total number of records in MEMBER.dat data file for
// counting the modification record till found
int Member::recordno(int s_memb_no)
{
    fstream file;
    file.open("MEMFILE.dat", ios::in);
    file.seekg(0, ios::beg);
    int count = 0;

    // Counts the total records in MEMBER.dat data file
    while (file.read((char *)this, sizeof(Member)))
    {
        count++;
        if (memb_no == s_memb_no)
            break;
    }
    file.close();
    return (count);
}

// Modification function for member information
void Member::Replace(int s_memb_no, char s_name[30], char s_address[30], int
s_mdd, int s_mmm, int s_myy, int s_edd, int s_emm, int s_eyy, float s_memb fee,
float s_caut_fee)
{
    int recno = 0;
```

```
    recno = recordno(s_memb_no);

    memb_no = s_memb_no;
    strcpy(name, s_name);
    strcpy(address, s_address);
    mdd = s_mdd;
    mmm = s_mmm;
    myy = s_myy;
    edd = s_edd;
    emm = s_emm;
    eyy = s_eyy;
    memb_fee = s_memb_fee;
    caut_fee = s_caut_fee;

    fstream file;
    file.open("MEMFILE.dat", ios::out|ios::ate);

    // Finding the location in file
    int location;
    location = (recno-1) * sizeof(Member);

    // Search the position in file
    file.seekp(location);

    // Re-write the contents in DETAILS.dat data file
    file.write((char *)this, sizeof(Member));
    file.close();
    return;
}

// Function to display the existing member in screen to change the further
information
void Member::Display_member(int s_memb_no)
{
        fstream file;
        file.open("MEMFILE.dat", ios::in);
        file.seekg(0, ios::beg);
        while (file.read((char *)this, sizeof(Member)))
        {
            if (memb_no == s_memb_no)
            {
                gotoxy(12, 11);
                cout << "Name : ";
                gotoxy(19, 11);
                puts(name);

                gotoxy(12, 14);
                cout << "Address : ";
                gotoxy(23, 14);
                puts(address);

                gotoxy(12, 15);
                cout << "Memb. Dat : ";
                gotoxy(25, 15);
                cout << mdd;
                gotoxy(27, 15);
                cout << '-';
                gotoxy(28, 15);
                cout << mmm;
                gotoxy(30, 15);
                cout << '-';
                gotoxy(31, 15);
                cout << myy;
```

```
            gotoxy(12, 16);
            cout << "Exp. Date : ";
            gotoxy(25, 16);
            cout << edd;
            gotoxy(27, 16);
            cout << '-';
            gotoxy(28, 16);
            cout << emm;
            gotoxy(30, 16);
            cout << '-';
            gotoxy(31, 16);
            cout << eyy;

            gotoxy(12, 17);
            cout << "Memb. Fees : ";
            gotoxy(25, 17);
            cout << memb_fee << setw(15)      // setwidth
                 << setprecision(2)      // set position of decimal point
                 << setiosflags(ios::left)     // set left justified output
                 << setiosflags(ios::showpoint)   // always show decimal point
                 << setiosflags(ios::fixed);      // set fixed notation for
display

            gotoxy(12, 18);
            cout << "Caution Money : ";
            gotoxy(28, 18);
            cout << caut_fee << setw(15)
                 << setprecision(2)
                 << setiosflags(ios::left)
                 << setiosflags(ios::showpoint)
                 << setiosflags(ios::fixed)
;
            break;
        }
    }
    file.close();
}

// Function for main menu to Change member informations in MEMFILE.dat
void Member::Change_member(void)
{
    char ch;
    int i, valid;

    Library lib;
    clrscr();
    gotoxy(65, 2);
    cout << "<0>=Exit";
    BOX_CLASS s;
    s.DRAW_BOX(10, 5, 71, 21, 219);
    s.DRAW_BOX(9, 4, 72, 22, 218);
    textcolor(BLACK);
    textbackground(LIGHTGRAY);

    gotoxy(3,3);
    for (i = 1; i<= 76; i++)
        cprintf(" ");

    textbackground(BLACK);
    textcolor(BLACK+BLINK);
    textbackground(WHITE);
    gotoxy(35, 4);
    cprintf("Membership Form");
```

```
textcolor(LIGHTGRAY);
textbackground(BLACK);

do
{
    lib.Clear_area(6, 18, 12, 70);
    int s_memb_no;   // Membership number
    char s_name[30]; // Name of the member
    char s_address[30]; // Address of the employee
    int s_mdd, s_mmm, s_myy;   // Membership date
    int s_edd, s_emm, s_eyy; // Expire date
    float s_memb_fee; // Membership fee
    float s_caut_fee; // Caution money

    struct date d;    // For extracting system date
    getdate(&d);
    s_mdd = d.da_day;
    s_mmm = d.da_mon;
    s_myy = d.da_year;

    gotoxy(12, 7);
    cout << "Date: " << s_mdd << '-' << s_mmm << '-' << s_myy;
    gotoxy(12, 23);
    cout << "Enter new membership no.";
    gotoxy(12, 9);
    cout << "Membership No. " ;
    gotoxy(27, 9);
    cin >> s_memb_no;
    lib.Left_clear(12, 23);
    lib.Right_clear(12, 23);

    if (s_memb_no == 0)
        return;

    Display_member(s_memb_no);
    do
    {
        lib.Left_clear(12, 23);
        gotoxy(12, 23);
        cout << "Enter New Name of the Member";
        valid = 1;
        gotoxy(45, 11);
        gets(s_name);
        strupr(s_name);
        if (s_name[0] == '0')
            return;
        if (strlen(s_name) == 0 || strlen(s_name) > 30)
        {
            valid = 0;
            gotoxy(12, 23);
            cprintf("\7Name should not greater than 30");
            getch();
        }
    } while (!valid);
    lib.Left_clear(12, 23);
    lib.Right_clear(12, 23);
    do
    {
        lib.Left_clear(12, 23);
        gotoxy(15, 23);
        cout << "Enter New Address of the Member ";
        valid = 1;
        gotoxy(45, 14);
```

```
            gets(s_address);
            strupr(s_address);
            if (s_address[0] == '0')
                return;
            if (strlen(s_address) == 0 || strlen(s_address) > 30)
            {
                valid = 0;
                gotoxy(12, 23);
                cprintf("\7Address should not greater than 30");
                getch();
            }
        } while (!valid);
        lib.Left_clear(12, 23);
        lib.Right_clear(12, 23);

        gotoxy(12, 23);
        cout << "Enter New the membership date";
        gotoxy(45, 15);
        cin >> s_mdd;
        gotoxy(47, 15);
        cout << '-';
        gotoxy(48, 15);
        cin >> s_mmm;
        gotoxy(50, 15);
        cout << '-';
        gotoxy(51, 15);
        cin >> s_myy;
        lib.Left_clear(12, 23);
        lib.Right_clear(12, 23);

        // Calculation of expire date according to a validation of 1 year for
        // membership from membership date and will be calculated in s_edd, s_emm,
s_eyy
        s_edd = s_mdd;
        s_emm = s_mmm;
        s_eyy = s_myy + 1; // Added 1 with the membership year to know the expire
date

        gotoxy(45, 16);
        cout << s_edd;
        gotoxy(47, 16);
        cout << '-';
        gotoxy(48, 16);
        cout << s_emm;
        gotoxy(50, 16);
        cout << '-';
        gotoxy(51, 16);
        cout << s_eyy;

        gotoxy(12, 23);
        cout << "Enter membership fees for a member";
        gotoxy(45, 17);
        cin >> s_memb_fee;

        lib.Left_clear(12, 23);
        lib.Right_clear(12, 23);

        gotoxy(12, 23);
        cout << "Enter caution money ";
        gotoxy(45, 18);
        cin >> s_caut_fee;
        lib.Left_clear(12, 23);
        lib.Right_clear(12, 23);
```

```
        do
        {
            valid = 1;
            gotoxy(12, 23);
            cout << "Do you want to Modify the record <Y/N>: ";
            ch = getche();
            if (ch == '0')
                return;
            ch = toupper(ch);
        } while (ch != 'Y');
        if (ch == 'N')
            return;

        Replace(s_memb_no, s_name, s_address, s_mdd, s_mmm, s_myy, s_edd, s_emm,
s_eyy, s_memb_fee, s_caut_fee);
        lib.Left_clear(12, 23);
        lib.Right_clear(12, 23);
        gotoxy(12, 23);
        cout << "Do You Want New Record <Y/N>: ";
        ch = getche();
        if (ch == '0')
            return;
        lib.Left_clear(12, 23);
        lib.Right_clear(12, 23);

        ch = toupper(ch);
    } while (ch == 'Y');
}
```

Membership Form <0>=Exit

Date: 10-10-2008

Membership No. 428

Name: Shah Rukh Khan	Shah Rukh Khan
Address: 112 Jor Bagh	112 Jor Bagh
Membership Date: 8-12-2007	8-12-2007
Exp. Date: 7-12-2008	7-12-2008
Membership Fee: 100	200
Caution Money: 500	700

Do you want to Mofify the record <Y/N>: Y

```
// Function to delete a member from MEMBER.dat data file.
/* While executing the procedure it first displays the member information and
checks in the MASTER.dat data file whether the member is issued any book or not.
If
the member issued any book then the record cannot be deleted, otherwise the
record will
be deleted from MEMBER.dat data file */

void Member::Delete_member()
{
    char ch;
    int i, flag = 0;
```

```
Library lib;
clrscr();
gotoxy(65, 2);
cout << "<0>=Exit";
BOX_CLASS s;
s.DRAW_BOX(10, 5, 71, 21, 219);
s.DRAW_BOX(9, 4, 72, 22, 218);
textcolor(BLACK);
textbackground(LIGHTGRAY);

gotoxy(3,3);
for (i = 1; i<= 76; i++)
    cprintf(" ");

textbackground(BLACK);
textcolor(BLACK+BLINK);
textbackground(WHITE);
gotoxy(35, 4);
cprintf("Membership Deleted Form");
textcolor(LIGHTGRAY);
textbackground(BLACK);

do
{
    lib.Clear_area(6, 18, 12, 70);
    int s_memb_no;   // Membership number
    char s_name[30]; // Name of the member
    char s_address[30]; // Address of the employee
    int s_mdd, s_mmm, s_myy;   // Membership date
    int s_edd, s_emm, s_eyy; // Expire date
    float s_memb_fee; // Membership fee
    float s_caut_fee; // Caution money

    struct date d;    // For extracting system date
    getdate(&d);
    s_mdd = d.da_day;
    s_mmm = d.da_mon;
    s_myy = d.da_year;

    gotoxy(12, 7);
    cout << "Date: " << s_mdd << '-' << s_mmm << '-' << s_myy;
    gotoxy(12, 23);
    cout << "Enter membership no. to delete";
    gotoxy(12, 9);
    cout << "Membership No. " ;
    gotoxy(27, 9);
    cin >> s_memb_no;
    lib.Left_clear(12, 23);
    lib.Right_clear(12, 23);

    if (s_memb_no == 0)
        return;

    Display_member(s_memb_no);
    Issue Iss;
    flag = Iss.Issue_memb_check(s_memb_no);

    if (flag == 1)
    {
        gotoxy(12, 23);
        cout << "Member has already a book. Can't Delete ...!";
        getch();
```

```
            lib.Left_clear(12, 23);
            lib.Right_clear(12, 23);
        }
        else
        {
            gotoxy(12, 23);
            cout << "Are You Sure to delete <Y/N>: ";
            ch = getche();
            ch = toupper(ch);
            if (ch == 'Y')
            {
                Memb_delete(s_memb_no);
                gotoxy(12, 23);
                cout << "Member Deleted";
                getch();
                lib.Left_clear(12, 23);
                lib.Right_clear(12, 23);
            }
        }
        gotoxy(12, 23);
        cout << "Do you want to Delete any Record <Y/N>: ";
        ch = getche();
        if (ch == '0')
            return;
        lib.Left_clear(12, 23);
        lib.Right_clear(12, 23);

        ch = toupper(ch);
    } while (ch == 'Y');
}
```

Membership Deleted Form <0>=Exit

Date: 10-10-2008

Membership No. 428

Name: Shah Rukh Khan

Address: 112 Jor Bagh

Membership Date: 8-12-2007

Exp. Date: 7-12-2008

Membership Fee: 100

Caution Money: 500

MEMBER DELETED

```
// Function to display the existing member and renewal the membership date
void Member::Renewal_member(int s_memb_no)
{
        char s_name[30]; // Name of the member
        char s_address[30]; // Address of the employee
        int s_mdd, s_mmm, s_myy;  // Membership date
        int s_edd, s_emm, s_eyy; // Expire date
        float s_memb_fee; // Membership fee
        float s_caut_fee; // Caution money
```

```
fstream file;
file.open("MEMFILE.dat", ios::in);
file.seekg(0, ios::beg);
while (file.read((char *)this, sizeof(Member)))
{
    if (memb_no == s_memb_no)
    {
        strcpy(s_name, name);
        strcpy(s_address, address);
        s_mdd = mdd;
        s_mmm = mmm;
        s_myy = myy;

        s_edd = edd;
        s_emm = emm;
        s_eyy = eyy;

        s_memb_fee = memb_fee;
        s_caut_fee = caut_fee;

        gotoxy(12, 11);
        cout << "Name : ";
        gotoxy(19, 11);
        puts(s_name);

        gotoxy(12, 14);
        cout << "Address : ";
        gotoxy(23, 14);
        puts(s_address);

        gotoxy(12, 15);
        cout << "Memb. Dat : ";
        gotoxy(25, 15);
        cout << s_mdd;
        gotoxy(27, 15);
        cout << '-';
        gotoxy(28, 15);
        cout << s_mmm;
        gotoxy(30, 15);
        cout << '-';
        gotoxy(31, 15);
        cout << s_myy;

        gotoxy(12, 16);
        cout << "Exp. Date : ";
        gotoxy(25, 16);
        cout << s_edd;
        gotoxy(27, 16);
        cout << '-';
        gotoxy(28, 16);
        cout << s_emm;
        gotoxy(30, 16);
        cout << '-';
        gotoxy(31, 16);
        cout << s_eyy;

        gotoxy(12, 17);
        cout << "Memb. Fees : ";
        gotoxy(25, 17);
        cout << s_memb_fee << setw(15)
               << setprecision(2)
               << setiosflags(ios::left)
```

```
                        << setiosflags(ios::showpoint)
                        << setiosflags(ios::fixed);

                gotoxy(12, 18);
                cout << "Caution Money : ";
                gotoxy(28, 18);
                cout << s_caut_fee << setw(15)
                        << setprecision(2)
                        << setiosflags(ios::left)
                        << setiosflags(ios::showpoint)
                        << setiosflags(ios::fixed);

                gotoxy(40, 15);
                cout << "Renewal. Dat : ";
                gotoxy(55, 15);
                cin >> s_mdd;
                gotoxy(58, 15);
                cout << '-';
                gotoxy(59, 15);
                cin >> s_mmm;
                gotoxy(61, 15);
                cout << '-';
                gotoxy(62, 15);
                cin >> s_myy;

                // Membership contain for 1 year valid after renewal date
                s_edd = s_mdd;
                s_emm = s_mmm;
                s_eyy = s_myy + 1;

                gotoxy(40, 16);
                cout << "Exp. Date : ";
                gotoxy(55, 16);
                cout << s_edd;
                gotoxy(58, 16);
                cout << '-';
                gotoxy(59, 16);
                cout << s_emm;
                gotoxy(61, 16);
                cout << '-';
                gotoxy(62, 16);
                cout << s_eyy;

                break;
            }
        }
        file.close();
        if (s_eyy > 0)
            Replace(s_memb_no, s_name, s_address, s_mdd, s_mmm, s_myy, s_edd, s_emm,
s_eyy, s_memb_fee, s_caut_fee);
}

// Function for main menu to renewal of membership
void Member::Member_Renewal(void)
{
    char ch;
    int i, valid;

    Library lib;
    clrscr();
    gotoxy(65, 2);
    cout << "<0>=Exit";
```

```
    BOX_CLASS s;
    s.DRAW_BOX(10, 5, 71, 21, 219);
    s.DRAW_BOX(9, 4, 72, 22, 218);
    textcolor(BLACK);
    textbackground(LIGHTGRAY);

    gotoxy(3,3);
    for (i = 1; i<= 76; i++)
        cprintf(" ");

    textbackground(BLACK);
    textcolor(BLACK+BLINK);
    textbackground(WHITE);
    gotoxy(35, 4);
    cprintf("Membership Renewal Form");
    textcolor(LIGHTGRAY);
    textbackground(BLACK);

    do
    {
        lib.Clear_area(6, 18, 12, 70);
        int s_memb_no;   // Membership number
        char s_name[30]; // Name of the member
        char s_address[30]; // Address of the employee
        int s_mdd, s_mmm, s_myy;   // Membership date
        int s_edd, s_emm, s_eyy; // Expire date
        float s_memb_fee; // Membership fee
        float s_caut_fee; // Caution money

        struct date d;    // For extracting system date
        getdate(&d);
        s_mdd = d.da_day;
        s_mmm = d.da_mon;
        s_myy = d.da_year;

        gotoxy(12, 7);
        cout << "Date: " << s_mdd << '-' << s_mmm << '-' << s_myy;
        gotoxy(12, 23);
        cout << "Enter new membership no.";
        gotoxy(12, 9);
        cout << "Membership No. " ;
        gotoxy(27, 9);
        cin >> s_memb_no;
        lib.Left_clear(12, 23);
        lib.Right_clear(12, 23);

        if (s_memb_no == 0)
            return;

        Renewal_member(s_memb_no);

        ch = toupper(ch);
    } while (ch == 'Y');
}

// Function for Adding, modifying and deleting from MEMFILE.dat data file
void Member::Memb_console(void)
{
    char ch;
    while (1)
    {
        clrscr();
        gotoxy(65, 3);
```

Membership Renewal Form <0>=Exit

Date: 10-10-2008

Membership No. 428

Name: Shah Rukh Khan

Address: 112 Jor Bagh

Membership Date: 8-12-2007 Renewal Date: 8-12-2008

Exp. Date: 7-12-2008

Membership Fee: 100

Caution Money: 500

```
        cout << "<0>=Exit";

        BOX_CLASS s;
        s.DRAW_BOX(10, 5, 71, 21, 219);
        s.DRAW_BOX(9, 4, 72, 22, 218);
        textcolor(BLACK);
        textbackground(WHITE);
        gotoxy(22, 8);
        cprintf("M E M B E R S H I P  C O N S O L E");
        textcolor(LIGHTGRAY);
        textbackground(BLACK);
        gotoxy(25, 12);
        cout << "1: Recording New Member";
        gotoxy(25, 13);
        cout << "2. Changing Member Data";
        gotoxy(25, 14);
        cout << "3. Deleting Member Record";

        gotoxy(25, 17);
        cout << "0. Return";
        gotoxy(25, 18);
        cout << "Enter your choice : ";
        ch = getche();
        if (ch == 27)
           break;
        else
           if (ch == '1')
           {
              new_member();
           }
           else
              if (ch == '2')
              {
                 Change_member();
                 break;
              }
              else
                 if (ch == '3')
                 {
                    Delete_member();
                    break;
```

```
                }
                else
                    if (ch == '0')
                        break;
        }
}
```

MEMBERSHIP CONSOLE

1. Recording New Member
2. Changing Member Data
3. Deleting Member Record

0. Return

Enter Your Choice . . .

```
// Function to add issued books into MASTER.dat data file
void Issue::Issue_Add(int s_acq_no, int s_acc_no, int s_memb_no, int s_idd, int
s_imm, int s_iyy, int s_rdd, int s_rmm, int s_ryy)
{
    acq_no = s_acq_no;
    acc_no = s_acc_no;
    memb_no = s_memb_no;
    idd = s_idd;
    imm = s_imm;
    iyy = s_iyy;

    rdd = s_rdd;
    rmm = s_rmm;
    ryy = s_ryy;
    fstream sfile;

    // Append the new record into MASTER.dat data file
    sfile.open("MASTER.dat", ios::out|ios::app);
    sfile.write((char *)this, sizeof(Issue));
    sfile.close();
}

// Function to delete a selected record from MASTER.dat data file
void Issue::Issue_Delete(int s_acq_no, int s_acc_no, int s_memb_no, int s_idd,
int s_imm, int s_iyy, int s_rdd, int s_rmm, int s_ryy)
{
    fstream file;
    file.open("MASTER.dat", ios::in);
    fstream temp;
    temp.open("TEMP.dat", ios::out);
    file.seekg(0,ios::beg);

    // Delete the record using copy method into temporaty file
    while (!file.eof())
    {
        file.read((char *)this, sizeof(Issue));
        if (file.eof())
            break;
```

```
        if ((acq_no != memb_no) && (acc_no != s_acc_no))
            temp.write((char *)this, sizeof(Issue));
    }
    file.close();
    temp.close();
    file.open("MASTER.dat", ios::out);
    temp.open("TEMP.dat", ios::in);
    temp.seekg(0, ios::beg);

    // Overwrites the temporay contents into original MASTER.dat data file
    while (!temp.eof())
    {
        temp.read((char *)this, sizeof(Issue));
        if (temp.eof())
            break;
        if (memb_no != s_memb_no)
            file.write((char *)this, sizeof(Issue));
    }
    file.close();
    temp.close();
}

// Function to find the expire dates of members
int date_expire(int s_edd, int s_emm, int s_eyy)
{
    int s_cdd, s_cmm, s_cyy;    // Current date
    int pdays = 0;
    struct date td;
    getdate(&td);
    s_cdd = td.da_day;
    s_cmm = td.da_mon;
    s_cyy = td.da_year;
    // when expire day less than current day, expire month equal to current
month
    // and expire year equal to current year
    if ((s_edd < s_cdd) && (s_emm == s_cmm) && (s_eyy == s_cyy))
        pdays = 1;
    else

    // when expire day less than current day, expire month less than current
month
    // and expire year equal to current year

    if ((s_edd < s_cdd) && (s_emm < s_cmm) && (s_eyy == s_cyy))
        pdays = 1;
    else

    // when expire day less than current day, expire month less than current
month
    // and expire year less than current year

    if ((s_edd < s_cdd) && (s_emm < s_cmm) && (s_eyy < s_cyy))
        pdays = 1;
    else

    // when expire day greater than current day, expire month less than current
month
    // and expire year equal to current year

    if ((s_edd > s_cdd) && (s_emm < s_cmm) && (s_eyy == s_cyy))
        pdays = 1;
    else
```

```
    // when expire day greater than current day, expire month less than current
month
    // and expire year less current year

    if ((s_edd > s_cdd) && (s_emm < s_cmm) && (s_eyy < s_cyy))
        pdays = 1;
    else

    // when expire day greater than current day, expire month equal to current
month
    // and expire year less than current year

    if ((s_edd > s_cdd) && (s_emm == s_cmm) && (s_eyy < s_cyy))
        pdays = 1;
    else

    // when expire day greater than current day, expire month greater than current
month
    // and expire year less than current year

    if ((s_edd > s_cdd) && (s_emm > s_cmm) && (s_eyy < s_cyy))
        pdays = 1;
    else

    // when expire day equal to current day, expire month equal to current month
    // and expire year less than current year

    if ((s_edd == s_cdd) && (s_emm == s_cmm) && (s_eyy < s_cyy))
        pdays = 1;
    else

    // when expire day less than current day, expire month equal to current
month
    // and expire year less than to current year

    if ((s_edd < s_cdd) && (s_emm == s_cmm) && (s_eyy < s_cyy))
        pdays = 1;
    else

    // when expire day equal to current day, expire month less than current
month
    // and expire year less than current year

    if ((s_edd == s_cdd) && (s_emm < s_cmm) && (s_eyy < s_cyy))
        pdays = 1;
    else

    // when expire day less than current day, expire month greater than current
month
    // and expire year less than to current year

    if ((s_edd < s_cdd) && (s_emm > s_cmm) && (s_eyy < s_cyy))
        pdays = 1;
    else

    // when expire equal to current day, expire month greater than current month
    // and expire year less than current year

    if ((s_edd == s_cdd) && (s_emm > s_cmm) && (s_eyy < s_cyy))
        pdays = 1;
    return (pdays);
}
```

```
// Function to check membership date expired or not
int Member::Expire_Check(int s_memb_no)
{
    int xflag = 0;

    fstream file;
    file.open("MEMFILE.dat", ios::in);
    file.seekg(0, ios::beg);
    while (file.read((char *)this, sizeof(Member)))
    {
        if (s_memb_no == memb_no)
        {
            xflag = date_expire(edd, emm, eyy);
            break;
        }
    }
    file.close();
    return (xflag);
}

// Function to issue books to members
void Library::Book_Issue()
{
    char ch;
    int i, tflag = 0; //, valid;
    int mday = 0;
    clrscr();
    gotoxy(65, 3);
    cout << "<0>=Exit";
    BOX_CLASS s;
    s.DRAW_BOX(10, 5, 71, 21, 219);
    s.DRAW_BOX(9, 4, 72, 22, 218);
    textcolor(BLACK);
    textbackground(LIGHTGRAY);

    gotoxy(3,3);
    for (i = 1; i<= 76; i++)
        cprintf(" ");

    textbackground(BLACK);
    textcolor(BLACK+BLINK);
    textbackground(WHITE);
    gotoxy(35, 4);
    cprintf("Issue Form");
    textcolor(LIGHTGRAY);
    textbackground(BLACK);

    int s_acq_no = 0;   // Acquisition number

    int s_acc_no = 0;   // Accession number
    char s_title[30];
    char s_author1[30], s_author2[30]; // Authors
    char s_publisher[30]; // Name of the publisher
    float s_price;   // Price of the book
    int s_idd, s_imm, s_iyy;    // Date of Issue
    int s_rdd, s_rmm, s_ryy;    // Date of return
    int s_pages; // Total pages in book
    char s_status;   // Present status of book

    int s_memb_no;   // Member number for issuing books

    struct date d;      // For extracting system date
```

```
getdate(&d);

s_idd = d.da_day;
s_imm = d.da_mon;
s_iyy = d.da_year;

// Steps to find the return date of issued book
mday = month_days(s_imm);

s_rdd = s_idd + 3;
if (s_rdd <= mday)
{
    s_rdd = s_rdd;
    s_rmm = s_imm;
    s_ryy = s_iyy;
}
else
{
    s_rdd = 3 - (mday - s_idd);
    if (s_imm == 12)
    {
        s_rmm = 1;
        s_ryy = s_iyy + 1;
    }
    else
    {
        s_rmm = s_imm + 1;
        s_ryy = s_iyy;
    }
}

gotoxy(48, 7);
cout << "Issue date: " << s_idd << '-' << s_imm << '-' << s_iyy;
gotoxy(48, 8);
cout << "Return date: " << s_rdd << '-' << s_rmm << '-' << s_ryy;

gotoxy(10, 23);
cout << "Enter the Acquisition number";
gotoxy(13, 7);
cout << "Acquisition No. " ;
gotoxy(29, 7);
cin >> s_acq_no;
Left_clear(10, 23);
Right_clear(39, 23);

gotoxy(11, 8);
for (i = 1; i <= 60; i++)
    cout << "=";

gotoxy(10, 23);
cout << "Enter the Accession number";
gotoxy(13, 9);
cout << "Accession No. ";
gotoxy(28, 9);
cin >> s_acc_no;
Left_clear(10, 23);
Right_clear(39, 23);

if ((s_acq_no == 0) || (s_acc_no == 0))
{
    Issue Iss;
    Iss.Issue_Add(0, 0, 0, 1, 1, 1, 1, 1, 1);
```

```
        Iss.Issue_Delete(0, 0, 0, 1, 1, 1, 1, 1, 1);
        return;
    }

    fstream file;
    file.open("LIB.dat", ios::in);
    file.seekg(0,ios::beg);

    // Search the record to display before issue
    while (file.read((char *)this, sizeof(Library)))
    {
        if ((s_acq_no == acq_no) && (s_acc_no == acc_no))
        {
            gotoxy(15, 11);
            cout << "Title : ";
            gotoxy(15, 12);
            cout << "Author(s) : ";
            gotoxy(15, 14);
            cout << "Publisher : ";
            gotoxy(15, 15);
            cout << "Price : ";
            gotoxy(15, 16);
            cout << "Pages : ";
            gotoxy(15, 17);
            cout << "Status : ";
            gotoxy(26, 11);
            puts(title);

            gotoxy(26, 12);
            puts(author1);

            gotoxy(26, 13);
            puts(author2);
            gotoxy(26, 14);
            puts(publisher);
            gotoxy(26, 15);
            cout << price;

            gotoxy(26, 16);
            cout << pages;
            gotoxy(26, 17);
            cout << status;

            // Function check whether this book is already issued or not to any
member
            Issue Iss;
            tflag = Iss.Issue_Check(s_acq_no, s_acc_no);

            if (tflag == 1)
            {
                gotoxy(12, 23);
                cout << "This book is aleardy issued";
                getch();
                Left_clear(10, 23);
                Right_clear(39, 23);
                return;
            }
            else
            {
                tflag = 0;
                gotoxy(45, 9);
                cout << "Membership No. ";
```

```
                gotoxy(64, 9);
                cin >> s_memb_no;

                // Function to check such a member is their in MEMBER.dat data
file or not
                Member Memb;
                tflag = Memb.Memb_Check(s_memb_no);

                if (tflag == 1)
                {
                    tflag = 0;
                    // Function to check membership expired or not
                    tflag = Memb.Expire_Check(s_memb_no);

                    if (tflag == 0)
                    {
                        tflag = 0;
                        // Function to check whether the member already book issued
or not by tflag
                        tflag = Iss.Issue_memb_check(s_memb_no);

                        if (tflag == 0)
                        {
                            // Function to append the issued book into MASTER.dat
data file
                            Iss.Issue_Add(s_acq_no, s_acc_no, s_memb_no, s_idd, s_imm,
s_iyy, s_rdd, s_rmm, s_ryy);
                            gotoxy(12, 23);
                            cout << "Book Issued";
                            getch();
                            Left_clear(10, 23);
                            Right_clear(39, 23);
                        }
                        else
                        {
                            gotoxy(12, 23);
                            cout << "The member has already a book";
                            getch();
                        }
                    }
                    else
                    {
                        gotoxy(12, 23);
                        cout << "The membership Expired";
                        getch();
                    }
                }
                else
                {
                    gotoxy(12, 23);
                    cout << "The member does not exists";
                    getch();
                }
            }
            break;
        }
    }
    file.close();
}

// Function to add fines if return date is exceeds
void Fine::Fine_add(int s_memb_no, int s_acq_no, int s_acc_no, int s_idd, int
```

Issue Form

Acquisition No. 01 **Date: 10-12-2008**

Accession No. 11

Title: ASP.NET Training Guide
Author(s): Andrew S. Tanenbaum
Publisher: Pearsons
Price: 400
Pages: 1000
Status: Y

BOOK ISSUED

```
s_imm, int s_iyy, int s_rdd, int s_rmm, int s_ryy, int s_cdd, int s_cmm, int
s_cyy, int s_finfee)
{
    memb_no = s_memb_no;
    acq_no = s_acq_no;  // fine acquisition no
    acc_no = s_acc_no;  // fine accession no

    idd = s_idd;      // Book issue date
    imm = s_imm;
    iyy = s_iyy;

    rdd = s_rdd; // Book purposed return date
    rmm = s_rmm;
    ryy = s_ryy;

    cdd = s_cdd;      // Returned date
    cmm = s_cmm;
    cyy = s_cyy;

    finfee = s_finfee;
    fstream sfile;

    // Append the fined record into FINE.dat data file if the member returns the
book after due date
    sfile.open("FINE.dat", ios::out|ios::app);
    sfile.write((char *)this, sizeof(Fine));
    sfile.close();
}

// Function to display the book information at return time
void Library::Book_display(int s_acq_no, int s_acc_no)
{
    fstream file;
    file.open("LIB.dat", ios::in);
    file.seekg(0,ios::beg);

    // Search the record for displaying the book information
    while (file.read((char *)this, sizeof(Library)))
    {
        if ((s_acq_no == acq_no) && (s_acc_no == acc_no))
```

```
        {
            gotoxy(40, 8);
            cout << "Title : ";
            gotoxy(40, 9);
            cout << "Author(s) : ";
            gotoxy(40, 11);
            cout << "Publisher : ";
            gotoxy(40, 15);
            cout << "Price : ";
            gotoxy(40, 16);
            cout << "Pages : ";
            gotoxy(40, 17);
            cout << "Status : ";
            gotoxy(49, 8);
            puts(title);

            gotoxy(53, 9);
            puts(author1);

            gotoxy(53, 10);
            puts(author2);
            gotoxy(53, 11);
            puts(publisher);
            gotoxy(52, 15);
            cout << price;

            gotoxy(52, 16);
            cout << pages;
            gotoxy(52, 17);
            cout << status;
            break;
        }
    }
    file.close();
}

// Function to return the total days in a month
int month_days(int s_cmm)
{
    int dmon = 0;
    switch (s_cmm)
    {
        case 1: dmon = 31; break;
        case 2: dmon = 28; break;
        case 3: dmon = 31; break;
        case 4: dmon = 30; break;
        case 5: dmon = 31; break;
        case 6: dmon = 30; break;
        case 7: dmon = 31; break;
        case 8: dmon = 31; break;
        case 9: dmon = 30; break;
        case 10: dmon = 31; break;
        case 11: dmon = 30; break;
        case 12: dmon = 31; break;
    }
    return (dmon);
}

// Function to find the days in between two dates
int no_of_days(int s_cdd, int s_cmm, int s_cyy, int s_rdd, int s_rmm, int s_ryy)
{
    int mdays = 0;
```

```
    int pdays = 0;
    mdays = month_days(s_rmm);
    if ((s_rdd < s_cdd) && (s_rmm == s_cmm) && (s_ryy == s_cyy))
        pdays = s_cdd - s_rdd;
    else
    if ((s_rdd < s_cdd) && (s_rmm < s_cmm) && (s_ryy == s_cyy))
        pdays = (mdays - s_rdd) + s_cdd + ((s_cmm-1) - s_rmm) * 30;
    else
    if ((s_rdd < s_cdd) && (s_rmm < s_cmm) && (s_ryy < s_cyy))
        pdays = (mdays - s_rdd) + s_cdd + ((s_cmm-1) - s_rmm) * 30 + (s_cyy -
s_ryy) * 12 * 30;
    else
    if ((s_rdd > s_cdd) && (s_rmm < s_cmm) && (s_ryy == s_cyy))
        pdays = (mdays - s_rdd) + s_cdd + ((s_cmm-1) - s_rmm) * 30;
    else
    if ((s_rdd > s_cdd) && (s_rmm < s_cmm) && (s_ryy < s_cyy))
        pdays = (mdays - s_rdd) + s_cdd + ((s_cmm-1) - s_rmm) * 30 + (s_cyy -
s_ryy) * 12 * 30;
    else
    if ((s_rdd > s_cdd) && (s_rmm == s_cmm) && (s_ryy < s_cyy))
        pdays = (mdays - s_rdd) + s_cdd + ((s_cmm-1) - s_rmm) * 30 + (s_cyy -
s_ryy) * 12 * 30;
    else
    if ((s_rdd > s_cdd) && (s_rmm > s_cmm) && (s_ryy < s_cyy))
        pdays = (mdays - s_rdd) + s_cdd + ((s_cmm-1) - s_rmm) * 30 + (s_cyy -
s_ryy) * 12 * 30;
    else
    if ((s_rdd == s_cdd) && (s_rmm == s_cmm) && (s_ryy < s_cyy))
        pdays = (s_cyy - s_ryy) * 12 * 30;
    else
    if ((s_rdd < s_cdd) && (s_rmm == s_cmm) && (s_ryy < s_cyy))
        pdays = (s_cdd - s_rdd) + (s_cyy - s_ryy) * 12 * 30;
    else
    if ((s_rdd == s_cdd) && (s_rmm < s_cmm) && (s_ryy < s_cyy))
        pdays = (s_cmm - s_rmm) * 30 + (s_cyy - s_ryy) * 12 * 30;
    else
    if ((s_rdd < s_cdd) && (s_rmm > s_cmm) && (s_ryy < s_cyy))
        pdays = (mdays - s_rdd) + s_cdd + (12 - s_rmm) * 30 + (s_cmm - 1) * 30
+ ((s_cyy - (s_ryy+1)) * 12 * 30) ;
    else
    if ((s_rdd == s_cdd) && (s_rmm > s_cmm) && (s_ryy < s_cyy))
        pdays = (12 - s_rmm) * 30 + (s_cmm) * 30 + ((s_cyy - (s_ryy+1)) * 12 *
30) ;
    cout << pdays;
    return (pdays);
}

// Function display the books at the time of return
void Issue::Return_Issue(int s_memb_no)
{
    fstream file;
    file.open("MASTER.dat", ios::in);
    file.seekg(0,ios::beg);
    int s_acq_no, s_acc_no;
    int s_idd, s_imm, s_iyy;    // Issue date
    int s_rdd, s_rmm, s_ryy;    // Return date
    int s_cdd, s_cmm, s_cyy;    // Current date

    int s_finfee; // Fine amount
    struct date d;       // For extracting system date
    getdate(&d);
    s_cdd = d.da_day;
```

```
    s_cmm = d.da_mon;
    s_cyy = d.da_year;
    int tdays = 0;  // Variable store the date difference
    // Search the record for further displaying the issue and return dates
    while (file.read((char *)this, sizeof(Issue)))
    {
        if (s_memb_no == memb_no)
        {
            s_acq_no = acq_no;
            s_acc_no = acc_no;
            s_idd = idd;
            s_imm = imm;
            s_iyy = iyy;

            s_rdd = rdd;
            s_rmm = rmm;
            s_ryy = ryy;

            // Function to display the book information at the time of return
            Library lib;
            lib.Book_display(s_acq_no, s_acc_no);

            gotoxy(12, 19);
            cout << "Issue Date: " << s_idd << "-" << s_imm << "-" << s_iyy;
            gotoxy(40, 19);
            cout << "Return Date: " << s_rdd << "-" << s_rmm << "-" << s_ryy;

            // The function no_of_days() calculate the difference betwee
            // return date and current date
            tdays = no_of_days(s_cdd, s_cmm, s_cyy, s_rdd, s_rmm, s_ryy);
            if (tdays > 0)
            {
                s_finfee = tdays;
                cout << s_finfee;
                // Function add a fine record if the member returned the book
after due date
                Fine fin;
                fin.Fine_add(s_memb_no, s_acq_no, s_acc_no, s_idd, s_imm, s_iyy,
s_rdd, s_rmm, s_ryy, s_cdd, s_cmm, s_cyy, s_finfee);
            }
            break;
        }
    }
    file.close();
}

// Function to delete member data from MASTER.dat data file
void Issue::Issue_member_delete(int s_memb_no)
{
    fstream file;
    file.open("MASTER.dat", ios::in);
    fstream temp;
    temp.open("TEMP.dat", ios::out);
    file.seekg(0,ios::beg);

    // Delete the record using copy method into temporaty file
    while (!file.eof())
    {
        file.read((char *)this, sizeof(Issue));
        if (file.eof())
            break;
        if (memb_no != s_memb_no)
```

```
            temp.write((char *)this, sizeof(Issue));
    }
    file.close();
    temp.close();
    file.open("MASTER.dat", ios::out);
    temp.open("TEMP.dat", ios::in);
    temp.seekg(0, ios::beg);

    // Overwrites the temporay contents into original MASTER.dat data file
    while (!temp.eof())
    {
        temp.read((char *)this, sizeof(Issue));
        if (temp.eof())
            break;
        if (memb_no != s_memb_no)
            file.write((char *)this, sizeof(Issue));
    }
    file.close();
    temp.close();
}

// Function to return books in library
// The user has to enter the member no and the screen will display the details
of the book which is returning
void Issue::Book_Return(void)
{
    char ch;
    int i, flag = 0;

    Library lib;
    clrscr();
    gotoxy(65, 3);
    cout << "<0>=Exit";
    BOX_CLASS s;
    s.DRAW_BOX(10, 5, 71, 21, 219);
    s.DRAW_BOX(9, 4, 72, 22, 218);
    textcolor(BLACK);
    textbackground(LIGHTGRAY);

    gotoxy(3,3);
    for (i = 1; i<= 76; i++)
        cprintf(" ");

    textbackground(BLACK);
    textcolor(BLACK+BLINK);
    textbackground(WHITE);
    gotoxy(35, 4);
    cprintf("Book Return Form");
    textcolor(LIGHTGRAY);
    textbackground(BLACK);

    do
    {
        lib.Clear_area(6, 18, 12, 70);
        int s_memb_no;   // Membership number
        char s_name[30]; // Name of the member
        char s_address[30]; // Address of the employee
        int s_mdd, s_mmm, s_myy;   // Membership date
        int s_edd, s_emm, s_eyy; // Expire date
        float s_memb_fee; // Membership fee
        float s_caut_fee; // Caution money

        struct date d;    // For extracting system date
```

```
        getdate(&d);
        s_mdd = d.da_day;
        s_mmm = d.da_mon;
        s_myy = d.da_year;

        gotoxy(12, 7);
        cout << "Date: " << s_mdd << '-' << s_mmm << '-' << s_myy;
        gotoxy(12, 23);
        cout << "Enter membership no. to Return Book";
        gotoxy(12, 9);
        cout << "Membership No. " ;
        gotoxy(27, 9);
        cin >> s_memb_no;
        lib.Left_clear(12, 23);
        lib.Right_clear(12, 23);

        if (s_memb_no == 0)
            return;

        // Function to display members information at the time of book return
        Member Memb;
        Memb.Display_member(s_memb_no);
        // Function to find the fine and display the issue and return dates
        Return_Issue(s_memb_no);

        // Function to check whether the member takes book or not
        flag = Issue_memb_check(s_memb_no);

        if (flag == 1)
        {
            // Member deleted from MASTER.dat data file i.e., book returned
            Issue_member_delete(s_memb_no);
            // Return_function displays the book information and add fine if avail
            lib.Left_clear(12, 23);
            lib.Right_clear(12, 23);
        }
        else
        {
            gotoxy(12, 23);
            cout << "Member Does not have any book";
            getch();

            lib.Left_clear(12, 23);
            lib.Right_clear(12, 23);
        }

        gotoxy(12, 23);
        cout << "Do you want to Return any Record <Y/N>: ";
        ch = getche();
        if (ch == '0')
            return;

        lib.Left_clear(12, 23);
        lib.Right_clear(12, 23);

        ch = toupper(ch);
    } while (ch == 'Y');
}

// Function for displaying the report menu
void Library::Report_Menu(void)
{
    char ch;
```

Book Return Form

Date: 10-10-2008

Title: Computer Networks

Membership No. 428

Author(s): Andrew S. Tanenbaum

Name: Shah Rukh Khan

Publisher: Pearsons

Accession No. 11

Address: 112 Jor Bagh

Membership Date: 8-12-2007

Price: 400

Exp. Date: 7-12-2008

Pages: 1000

Membership Fee: 100

Status: Y

Caution Money: 500

Issue Date: 10-10-2008

Retyrb Date: 15-10-208

Do you want to Return any record <Y/N>: Y

```
while (1)
{
    clrscr();
    gotoxy(65, 3);
    cout << "<0>=Exit";

    BOX_CLASS s;
    s.DRAW_BOX(10, 5, 71, 21, 219);
    s.DRAW_BOX(9, 4, 72, 22, 218);
    textcolor(BLACK);
    textbackground(WHITE);
    gotoxy(22, 8);
    cprintf("R E P O R T I N G   C O N S O L E");
    textcolor(LIGHTGRAY);
    textbackground(BLACK);
    gotoxy(25, 12);
    cout << "1: Acquisition Register";
    gotoxy(25, 13);
    cout << "2. Membership Register";
    gotoxy(25, 14);
    cout << "3. Issue Register";
    gotoxy(25, 15);
    cout << "4. List of OverDue Books";
    gotoxy(25, 16);
    cout << "5. Fine Register";
    gotoxy(25, 17);
    cout << "6. List of Expire Members";

    gotoxy(25, 18);
    cout << "0. Return";
    gotoxy(25, 19);
    cout << "Enter your choice : ";
    ch = getche();
    if (ch == 27)
        break;
    else
        if (ch == '1')
        {
```

```
            Acqu_Register();
        }
        else
            if  (ch == '2')
            {
                Member Memb;
                Memb.Memb_Register();
            }
            else
                if  (ch == '3')
                {
                    Issue Iss;
                    Iss.Issue_Register();
                }
                else
                    if  (ch == '4')
                    {
                        Issue Iss;
                        Iss.OverDue_Book();
                    }
                    else
                        if  (ch == '5')
                        {
                         Fine fin;
                         fin.Fine_Register();
                        }
                        else
                         if  (ch == '6')
                         {
                                Member Memb;
                                Memb.Expire_Register();
                         }
                         else
                                if  (ch == '0')
                                        break;
    }
}
```

REPORTING CONSOLE

1. Acquisition Register
2. Membership Register
3. Issue Register
4. List of Overdue Books
5. Fine Register
6. List of Expired Members
0. Return

Enter Your Choice . . .

```
/* The function is used to print the report of acquisition register. The purchase
department of the library
purchases various books. After purchase, these books are inspected and entered
into the library by providing
a library number as accession number to each book.*/
void Library::Acqu_Register(void)
{
```

```
fstream file;
file.open("LIB.dat", ios::in);
file.seekg(0,ios::beg);
clrscr();

int s_acq_no; // Acquisition number
int s_acc_no; // Accession number
char s_title[30];
char s_author1[30], s_author2[30]; // Authors
char s_publisher[30]; // Name of the publisher
float s_price;   // Price of the book
int s_dd, s_mm, s_yy;      // Date of purchase
int s_pages; // Total pages in book
char s_status;   // Present status of book
gotoxy(30, 2);
cout << "ACQUISITION REGISTER";
gotoxy(30, 3);
cout << "--------------------";
int xdd, xmm, xyy;
struct date d;      // For extracting system date
getdate(&d);
xdd = d.da_day;
xmm = d.da_mon;
xyy = d.da_year;
gotoxy(63, 3);
cout << "Date: "<< xdd << "-" << xmm << "-" << xyy;

gotoxy(1, 4);
for (int i = 0; i <= 79; i++)
    cout << "=";
gotoxy(1, 5);
cout << "Sl.";
gotoxy(6, 5);
cout << "Acq.";
gotoxy(12, 5);
cout << "Acc.No.";
// For displaying only 12 characters of each
gotoxy(22, 5);
cout << "Title &";
gotoxy(40, 5);
cout << "Publisher";
gotoxy(54, 5);
cout << "Price &";
gotoxy(63, 5);
cout << "Date(p)";
gotoxy(75, 5);
cout << "Status";

gotoxy(1, 6);
cout << "No";
gotoxy(6, 6);
cout << "No.";

// For displaying only 12 characters of each
gotoxy(22, 6);
cout << "Author(s)";
gotoxy(54, 6);
cout << "Pages";

gotoxy(1, 7);
for (i = 0; i <= 79; i++)
    cout << "=";
```

```
int sln = 0;
int row = 8;
// Displaying the book information
while (file.read((char *)this, sizeof(Library)))
{
    ++sln;
    s_acq_no = acq_no;
    s_acc_no = acc_no;
    strcpy(s_title, title);
    strcpy(s_author1, author1);
    strcpy(s_author2, author2);
    strcpy(s_publisher, publisher);
    s_price = price;
    s_dd = dd;
    s_mm = mm;
    s_yy = yy;
    s_pages = pages;
    s_status = status;

    gotoxy(1, row);
    cout << sln;
    gotoxy(6, row);
    cout << s_acq_no;
    gotoxy(14, row);
    cout << s_acc_no;
    // For displaying only 12 characters of each
    gotoxy(21, row);
    cout << s_title;
    gotoxy(40, row);
    cout << s_publisher;
    gotoxy(55, row);
    cout << s_price;

    gotoxy(63, row);
    cout << s_dd << "-" << s_mm << "-" << s_yy;
    gotoxy(78, row);
    cout << s_status;
    row++;
    gotoxy(21, row);
    cout << s_author1;
    gotoxy(55, row);
    cout << s_pages;

    row++;
    gotoxy(21, row);
    cout << s_author2;


    gotoxy(1, row);
    for (i = 0; i <= 79; i++)
        cout << "-";

    row++;
    if (row > 23)
    {
        row = 8;
        gotoxy(4, 24);
        cout << "Press any key to continue.... ";
        getch();
        clrscr();
    }
```

```
    }
    gotoxy(1, row);
    for (i = 0; i <= 79; i++)
        cout << "=";

    getch();
    file.close();

}
```

ACQUISITION REGISTER

Date: 10-12-2008

Sl. No.	Acq. No.	Title & Author	Publisher	Price & Pages	Date(p)	Status
1	1	Computer Networks Andrew S. Tanenbaum	Pearsons	400.00 1000	10-12-2007	Y
2	11	VB.Net Robert D'Souza	Pearsons	200.00 500	10-12-2007	Y
3	12	ASP.Net James Kelly	Pearsons	200.00 500	8-10-2007	Y
4	14	Computer Hardware Bill Gates	Pearsons	600.00 1200	8-10-2007	Y

```
// Function for Membership register
void Member::Memb_Register(void)
{
    clrscr();
    gotoxy(30, 2);
    cout << "MEMBERSHIP REGISTER";
    gotoxy(30, 3);
    cout << "-------------------";
    int xdd, xmm, xyy;
    struct date d;      // For extracting system date
    getdate(&d);
    xdd = d.da_day;
    xmm = d.da_mon;
    xyy = d.da_year;
    gotoxy(63, 3);
    cout << "Date: "<< xdd << "-" << xmm << "-" << xyy;

    gotoxy(1, 4);
    for (int i = 0; i <= 79; i++)
        cout << "=";
    gotoxy(1, 5);
    cout << "Sl.No";
    gotoxy(7, 5);
    cout << "Memb.No.";
    gotoxy(17, 5);
```

```
cout << "Name &";
gotoxy(40, 5);
cout << "Memb.Date";
gotoxy(51, 5);
cout << "Expir.Date";
gotoxy(63, 5);
cout << "Membership";
gotoxy(74, 5);
cout << "Caution";

gotoxy(17, 6);
cout << "Address";
gotoxy(65, 6);
cout << "Fees";
gotoxy(75, 6);
cout << "Money";

int s_memb_no;   // Membership number
char s_name[30]; // Name of the member
char s_address[30]; // Address of the employee
int s_mdd, s_mmm, s_myy;   // Membership date
int s_edd, s_emm, s_eyy; // Expire date
float s_memb_fee; // Membership fee
float s_caut_fee;   // Caution money


gotoxy(1, 7);
for (i = 0; i <= 79; i++)
    cout << "=";
int sln = 0;
int row = 8;
// Displaying the Members information

fstream file;
file.open("MEMFILE.dat", ios::in);
file.seekg(0, ios::beg);
while (file.read((char *)this, sizeof(Member)))
{
    ++sln;
    s_memb_no = memb_no;
    strcpy(s_name, name);
    strcpy(s_address, address);
    s_mdd = mdd;
    s_mmm = mmm;
    s_myy = myy;
    s_edd = edd;
    s_emm = emm;
    s_eyy = eyy;
    s_memb_fee = memb_fee;
    s_caut_fee = caut_fee;

    gotoxy(2, row);
    cout << sln;
    gotoxy(7, row);
    cout << s_memb_no;
    gotoxy(16, row);
    cout << s_name;
    gotoxy(40, row);
    cout << s_mdd << "-" << s_mmm << "-" << s_myy;
    gotoxy(51, row);
    cout << s_edd << "-" << s_emm << "-" << s_eyy;

    gotoxy(65, row);
```

```
        cout << s_memb_fee << setw(15)
                        << setprecision(2)
                        << setiosflags(ios::left)
                        << setiosflags(ios::showpoint)
                        << setiosflags(ios::fixed);
        gotoxy(75, row);
        cout << s_caut_fee << setw(15)
                        << setprecision(2)
                        << setiosflags(ios::left)
                        << setiosflags(ios::showpoint)
                        << setiosflags(ios::fixed);
        row++;
        gotoxy(16, row);
        cout << s_address;
        row++;
        gotoxy(1, row);
        for (i = 0; i <= 79; i++)
            cout << "-";

        row++;

        if (row > 23)
        {
            row = 8;
            gotoxy(4, 24);
            cout << "Press any key to continue.... ";
            getch();
            clrscr();
        }
    }
    gotoxy(1, row);
    for (i = 0; i <= 79; i++)
        cout << "=";

    getch();
    file.close();
}

// Function for issue register
void Issue::Issue_Register()
```

MEMBERSHIP REGISTER

Date: 10-12-2008

Sl. No.	Memb. No.	Name & Address	Memb. Date	Expir. Date	Memb. Fees	Caution Money
1	10	Shah Rukh Khan 12 Jorbagh	10-11-2006	9-11-2007	500	1100
2	20	Salman Khan 22 Baird Lane	9-08-2007	8-08-2008	100	700
3	30	Aamir Khan N-45 Panchsheel Encl.	8-09-2005	7-09-2006	800	800

```
{
    clrscr();
    gotoxy(35, 2);
    cout << "ISSUE REGISTER";
    gotoxy(35, 3);
    cout << "--------------";
    int xdd, xmm, xyy;
    struct date d;      // For extracting system date
    getdate(&d);
    xdd = d.da_day;
    xmm = d.da_mon;
    xyy = d.da_year;
    gotoxy(63, 3);
    cout << "Date: "<< xdd << "-" << xmm << "-" << xyy;

    gotoxy(1, 4);
    for (int i = 0; i <= 79; i++)
        cout << "=";
    gotoxy(1, 5);
    cout << "Sl.No";
    gotoxy(9, 5);
    cout << "Memb.No.";
    gotoxy(18, 5);
    cout << "Acq.no";
    gotoxy(28, 5);
    cout << "Acc.No";
    gotoxy(49, 5);
    cout << "Books Issued";
    gotoxy(63, 5);
    cout << "Purposed Date";

    gotoxy(55, 6);
    cout << "On";
    gotoxy(65, 6),
    cout << "Of Return";

    int s_acq_no; // Aquisition number
    int s_acc_no; // Accession no
    int s_memb_no;   // Member number
    int s_idd, s_imm, s_iyy;    // Issue date
    int s_rdd, s_rmm, s_ryy;    // Return date


    gotoxy(1, 7);
    for (i = 0; i <= 79; i++)
        cout << "-";
    int sln = 0;
    int row = 8;
    // Displaying the Issued books information

    fstream file;
    file.open("MASTER.dat", ios::in);
    file.seekg(0,ios::beg);
    // Search the record for further modification
    while (file)
    {
        file.read((char *)this, sizeof(Issue));
        if (file.eof())
            break;
        ++sln;
        s_acq_no = acq_no;
        s_acc_no = acc_no;
```

```
        s_memb_no = memb_no;
        s_idd = idd;
        s_imm = imm;
        s_iyy = iyy;
        s_rdd = rdd;
        s_rmm = rmm;
        s_ryy = ryy;

        gotoxy(1, row);
        cout << sln;
        gotoxy(10, row);
        cout << s_memb_no;
        gotoxy(20, row);
        cout << s_acq_no;
        gotoxy(30, row);
        cout << s_acc_no;
        gotoxy(50, row);
        cout << s_idd << "-" << s_imm << "-" << s_iyy;
        gotoxy(63, row);
        cout << s_rdd << "-" << s_rmm << "-" << s_ryy;
        row++;
        if (row > 23)
        {
            row = 8;
            gotoxy(4, 24);
            cout << "Press any key to continue.... ";
            getch();
            clrscr();
        }
    }
    getch();
    file.close();
}
```

ISSUE REGISTER

Date: 10-12-2008

Sl. No.	Memb. No.	Acq. No.	Acc. No.	Book Issued On	Proposed Date of Return
1	100	10	10	10-11-2008	15-11-2008
2	200	10	11	11-11-2008	16-11-2008

```
// Function for overdue books
void Issue::OverDue_Book()
{
    clrscr();
    gotoxy(35, 2);
    cout << "OVERDUE BOOK";
    gotoxy(35, 3);
    cout << "------------";
    int xdd, xmm, xyy;
    struct date d;      // For extracting system date
    getdate(&d);
    xdd = d.da_day;
```

```
xmm = d.da_mon;
xyy = d.da_year;
gotoxy(63, 3);
cout << "Date: "<< xdd << "-" << xmm << "-" << xyy;

gotoxy(1, 4);
for (int i = 0; i <= 79; i++)
    cout << "=";
gotoxy(1, 5);
cout << "Sl.No";
gotoxy(9, 5);
cout << "Memb.No.";
gotoxy(18, 5);
cout << "Acq.no";
gotoxy(28, 5);
cout << "Acc.No";
gotoxy(40, 5);
cout << "Issue Date";
gotoxy(53, 5);
cout << "Return Date";

gotoxy(66, 5);
cout << "Days Overdue";

gotoxy(66, 6);
cout << "As on Sys.Date";

int s_acq_no; // Aquisition number
int s_acc_no; // Accession no
int s_memb_no;  // Member number
int s_idd, s_imm, s_iyy;    // Issue date
int s_rdd, s_rmm, s_ryy;    // Return date
int dmonth, ovrdue = 0;

gotoxy(1, 7);
for (i = 0; i <= 79; i++)
    cout << "-";
int sln = 0;
int row = 8;
// Displaying the Issued books information

fstream file;
file.open("MASTER.dat", ios::in);
file.seekg(0,ios::beg);
// Search the record for further modification
while (file.read((char *)this, sizeof(Issue)))
{
    s_acq_no = acq_no;
    s_acc_no = acc_no;
    s_memb_no = memb_no;
    s_idd = idd;
    s_imm = imm;
    s_iyy = iyy;
    s_rdd = rdd;
    s_rmm = rmm;
    s_ryy = ryy;
    ovrdue = no_of_days(xdd, xmm, xyy, s_rdd, s_rmm, s_ryy);
    if (ovrdue > 0)
    {
        ++sln;
        gotoxy(2, row);
        cout << sln;
        gotoxy(10, row);
```

```
            cout << s_memb_no;
            gotoxy(20, row);
            cout << s_acq_no;
            gotoxy(30, row);
            cout << s_acc_no;
            gotoxy(40, row);
            cout << s_idd << "-" << s_imm << "-" << s_iyy;
            gotoxy(53, row);
            cout << s_rdd << "-" << s_rmm << "-" << s_ryy;
            gotoxy(70, row);
            cout << ovrdue;
            row++;
            gotoxy(1, row);
            for (int i = 0; i <= 79; i++)
                cout << "-";
            row++;
            if (row > 23)
            {
                row = 7;
                gotoxy(4, 24);
                cout << "Press any key to continue.... ";
                getch();
                clrscr();
            }
        }
    }
    getch();
    file.close();
}
```

OVERDUE BOOK

Date: 10-12-2008

Sl. No.	Memb. No.	Acq. No.	Acc. No.	Issue Date	Proposed Date of Return	Days Overdue As on Sys. Date
1	100	10	10	10-11-2008	15-11-2008	26
2	200	10	11	11-11-2008	16-11-2008	25

```
// Function to display the fine register
void Fine::Fine_Register()
{
    clrscr();
    gotoxy(35, 2);
    cout << "FINE REGISTER";
    gotoxy(35, 3);
    cout << "-------------";
    int xdd, xmm, xyy;
    struct date d;      // For extracting system date
    getdate(&d);
    xdd = d.da_day;
    xmm = d.da_mon;
    xyy = d.da_year;
    gotoxy(63, 3);
    cout << "Date: "<< xdd << "-" << xmm << "-" << xyy;
```

```
gotoxy(1, 4);
for (int i = 0; i <= 79; i++)
    cout << "=";
gotoxy(1, 5);
cout << "Sl.No";
gotoxy(9, 5);
cout << "Memb.No.";
gotoxy(18, 5);
cout << "Acq.no";
gotoxy(28, 5);
cout << "Acc.No";
gotoxy(39, 5);
cout << "Issue";
gotoxy(49, 5);
cout << "Returned";
gotoxy(61, 5);
cout << "Returned";
gotoxy(74, 5);
cout << "Fine";

gotoxy(39, 6);
cout << "Date";
gotoxy(51, 6);
cout << "Date";
gotoxy(63, 6);
cout << "On";

int s_memb_no;
int s_acq_no;
int s_acc_no;
int s_idd, s_imm, s_iyy;    // Book issue date

int s_rdd, s_rmm, s_ryy;    // Book purposed return date

int s_cdd, s_cmm, s_cyy;    // Returned date
int s_finfee;

gotoxy(1, 7);
for (i = 0; i <= 79; i++)
    cout << "-";
int sln = 0;
int row = 8;
// Displaying the Issued books information

fstream file;
file.open("Fine.dat", ios::in);
file.seekg(0,ios::beg);
// Search the record for further modification
while (file.read((char *)this, sizeof(Fine)))
{
    ++sln;
    s_memb_no = memb_no;
    s_acq_no = acq_no;
    s_acc_no = acc_no;
    s_idd = idd,
    s_imm = imm,
    s_iyy = iyy;

    s_rdd = rdd,
    s_rmm = rmm,
    s_ryy = ryy;

    s_cdd = cdd,
```

```
        s_cmm = cmm,
        s_cyy = cyy;
        s_finfee = finfee;

        gotoxy(1, row);
        cout << sln;
        gotoxy(9, row);
        cout << s_memb_no;
        gotoxy(18, row);
        cout << s_acq_no;
        gotoxy(28, row);
        cout << s_acc_no;
        gotoxy(37, row);
        cout << s_idd << "-" << s_imm << "-" << s_iyy;
        gotoxy(49, row);
        cout << s_rdd << "-" << s_rmm << "-" << s_ryy;
        gotoxy(61, row);
        cout << s_cdd << "-" << s_cmm << "-" << s_cyy;

        gotoxy(75, row);
        cout << s_finfee << setw(5)
                    << setprecision(2)
                    << setiosflags(ios::left)
                    << setiosflags(ios::showpoint)
                    << setiosflags(ios::fixed);
        row++;
        if (row > 23)
        {
            row = 8;
            gotoxy(4, 24);
            cout << "Press any key to continue.... ";
            getch();
            clrscr();
        }
    }
    getch();
    file.close();
}
```

FINE REGISTER

Date: 10-12-2008

Sl. No.	Memb. No.	Acq. No.	Acc. No.	Issue Date	Return Date	Returned on	Fine
1	100	10	10	10-11-2008	15-11-2008	10-12-2008	52
2	200	10	11	11-11-2008	16-11-2008	10-12-2008	50

```
// Function to list out expiring membership persons
void Member::Expire_Register()
{
    clrscr();
    int tflag = 0;
    gotoxy(20, 2);
    cout << "List of Expiring Membership Person(s)";
    gotoxy(20, 3);
```

```
cout << "-------------------------------------";
int xdd, xmm, xyy;
struct date d;       // For extracting system date
getdate(&d);
xdd = d.da_day;
xmm = d.da_mon;
xyy = d.da_year;
gotoxy(63, 3);
cout << "Date: "<< xdd << "-" << xmm << "-" << xyy;

gotoxy(1, 4);
for (int i = 0; i <= 79; i++)
   cout << "=";
gotoxy(1, 5);
cout << "Sl.No";
gotoxy(7, 5);
cout << "Membership ";
gotoxy(20, 5);
cout << "Name & ";
gotoxy(40, 5);
cout << "Membership";
gotoxy(58, 5);
cout << "Membership";

gotoxy(10, 6);
cout << "No.";
gotoxy(20, 6);
cout << "Address ";
gotoxy(40, 6);
cout << "Beginning Date";
gotoxy(58, 6);
cout << "Expire Date";

int s_memb_no;   // Membership number
char s_name[30]; // Name of the member
char s_address[30]; // Address of the employee
int s_mdd, s_mmm, s_myy;   // Membership date
int s_edd, s_emm, s_eyy; // Expire date
float s_memb_fee; // Membership fee
float s_caut_fee;   // Caution money


gotoxy(1, 7);
for (i = 0; i <= 79; i++)
   cout << "=";
int sln = 0;
int row = 8;
// Displaying the Members information

fstream file;
file.open("MEMFILE.dat", ios::in);
file.seekg(0, ios::beg);
while (file.read((char *)this, sizeof(Member)))
{
   tflag = 0;
   s_memb_no = memb_no;
   strcpy(s_name, name);
   strcpy(s_address, address);
   s_mdd = mdd;
   s_mmm = mmm;
   s_myy = myy;
```

```
s_edd = edd; // Actual expire date
s_emm = emm;
s_eyy = eyy;

// The function returns the value 1 or 0 from date_expire() function
tflag = date_expire(s_edd, s_emm, s_eyy);
if (tflag == 1)
{
    ++sln;
    gotoxy(2, row);
    cout << sln;
    gotoxy(9, row);
    cout << s_memb_no;
    gotoxy(19, row);
    cout << s_name;
    gotoxy(40, row);
    cout << s_mdd << "-" << s_mmm << "-" << s_myy;
    gotoxy(58, row);
    cout << s_edd << "-" << s_emm << "-" << s_eyy;

    row++;
    gotoxy(19, row);
    cout << s_address;
    row++;
    gotoxy(1, row);
    for (i = 0; i <= 79; i++)
        cout << "-";

    row++;

    if (row > 23)
    {
        row = 8;
        gotoxy(4, 24);
        cout << "Press any key to continue.... ";
        getch();
        clrscr();
    }
}
```

List of Expiring Membership Person(s)

Date: 10-12-2008

Sl. No.	Memb. No.	Name & Address	Membership Beginning Date	Membership Expiring Date
1	10	Shah Rukh Khan 12 Jorbagh	10-11-2006	9-11-2007
2	20	Salman Khan 22 Baird Lane	9-08-2007	8-08-2008
3	30	Aamir Khan N-45 Panchsheel Encl.	8-09-2005	7-09-2006

```
    }
    gotoxy(1, row);
    for (i = 0; i <= 79; i++)
        cout << "=";

    getch();
    file.close();
}

// Main Program starts at here
void main(void)
{
    control menu;

    menu.lib_SCREEN();
}
```